Narrative
Remembering

Barbara DeConcini

UNIVERSITY
PRESS OF
AMERICA

Lanham • New York • London

Copyright © 1990 by

University Press of America,® Inc.

4720 Boston Way
Lanham, MD 20706

3 Henrietta Street
London WC2E 8LU England

British Cataloging in Publication Information Available

Library of Congress Cataloging-in-Publication Data

DeConcini, Barbara.
Narrative remembering / Barbara DeConcini.
p.   cm.
Includes bibliographical references.
1. Discourse analysis, Narrative—Psychological aspects.   2. Memory.
3. Fiction—Technique.   4. Hermeneutics.   I. Title.
P302.8.D4   1989   808'.0014—dc20   89–39653 CIP

ISBN 0–8191–7632–X (alk. paper)

To Walt

For "memories gentler, richer, and
more splendid than ever ... which it
is a festival to unfold"

CONTENTS

PREFACE

I began reflecting on how remembering is woven into the very fabric of our human life when I was faced with the need to find a new life-story to tell which would conserve my past while moving away from it. As an intellectual inquiry, this essay is rooted in what was a deeply personal life-work. While I would not now frame the issues in precisely the same way as I did when I wrote this, I continue to believe in their significance.

My deeply felt conviction that the past is not only facticity but also a fund of possibility has been nurtured and supported by several persons. I am pleased to have this opportunity to express my gratitude to some of them. Those who harbor the hope that the study of the humanities can be humanizing could do no better than to seek a home in the Institute of the Liberal Arts at Emory University. I am especially grateful to Robert Detweiler for his sound advice and good cheer; to David Hesla for his unflagging support of me, if not always of my project; and to Don Saliers for his vigorous imagination and gracious sensibility. I wish to thank Edward S. Casey of SUNY Stony Brook for being my "shadow advisor" on the project. As is evident throughout this study, his important work in the phenomenology of remembering has shaped my own thinking. His early encouragement came when I needed it most, and the conversations and correspondence we shared at that time were invaluable.

No project is sustained without the loving support of good friends. I am especially grateful to my parents, my sisters and friends in the Society of the Holy Child Jesus, and my mentors and former colleagues at Rosemont College. Special thanks to Melinda Keane for proofing and myriad other supports. The project was helped immeasurably by Walter J. Lowe. His was always the most sustained support, the best advice, and the most cogent criticism.

In addition I wish to acknowledge the use of previously published materials from the following:

Margaret Atwood, <u>Surfacing,</u> copyright (c) 1972, reprinted by permission of the Canadian publishers, McClelland and Stewart, Toronto; of Andre Deutsch Ltd., London; and of the author.

Saint Augustine, <u>The Confessions</u>, translated by Edward B. Pusey, copyright (c) 1969, reprinted by permission of the publishers and the Loeb Classical Library, Cambridge, Mass.: Harvard University Press.

INTRODUCTION

One of the most common of all literary critical commonplaces in this century is the notion that modern literature is profoundly preoccupied with the problem of time. Critical theorists have always recognized the novel, of course, as a temporally-structured literary art, and a reader need look no further than this century's most significant writers for verification that time is a, perhaps the, major thematic in the modern period. But early in this century Georg Lukacs, with his suggestive notion that "the entire inner action of the novel is nothing but a struggle against the power of time,"[1] drew the connection between time as structure and time as theme which has since figured so prominently in literary criticism of the novel. This critical preoccupation with time is not surprising when we reflect that what we have here is a happy congruence of methodological principle with a concrete body of texts. In this case, the principle is the formalist tenet that form and content are not to be dichotomized in the literary text. Modern fiction then conveniently provides us with a wealth of positive examples in which time functions as both form and content. As practical literary critics, we can examine how the novel's temporal structure and time thematic enhance and support each other in text after text.

On the literary history front, historians of the novel have traced the shift from Victorian to modern fiction in the shift from closed to open forms of experience, from an objective value-laden society in the novel of manners to the self-consciousness of the value-creating individual in existentialist fiction; that is to say, from a largely static spatially-oriented world to life as a temporal process. Indeed, one fruitful way of describing the modern novel is in terms of the personal reconstruction of life in face of the destruction of faith in the paradigms provided by the tradition. In these terms, the modern novel becomes a case study of the pervasive crisis of culture in our time.[2]

From this viewpoint, the time-consciousness of modern fiction drives inexorably toward the story-consciousness of late modern fiction. The preoccupation with the difficulty of finding a story to tell in an age when we are alienated from our tradition and of telling a story when we no longer trust language in its turn, spawns the post-modern movement toward the "characterless" and "actionless" novel. The history of the novel is itself the story of literature's own wrestling with the confines of its temporal forms, forms which have become confining precisely because we have lost confidence in the framework of which they are an expression.

It would be difficult no less than foolhardy to disbelieve the prevailing critical opinion that the whole panoply of modern dilemmas is time-bound and time-related. But to my mind, it is one of the anomalies of literary criticism that, for all the contemporary interest in time in literature and, more particularly, in the modern novel, and for all the interest in the individual self and its shrinking possibilities for a life of meaning and value, there is little literary critical attention paid to the crucial role the human activity of remembering plays in narrative.[3]

It is my contention in this essay that we need a literary criticism alive to the structures and functions of remembering if we are to come closer to the essence of modern fiction. I contend further that such a "remembering hermeneutic" has the virtue of resonance with the contemporary insights of a number of other disciplines in the human studies.

What is entailed by a literary hermeneutic more attuned to remembering than to time? To shift one's focus from time to remembering in the modern novel is not to negotiate a simple Romantic turn from objective concerns to the subjective; nor, concomitantly, is it to exchange critical attention to one set of fictive structures (such as plot, theme, the construction of a fictive world) for another (point of view, narrative voice, characterization). Such a shift would leave us still immured within the Cartesian dichotomy of which the very emphasis on time is a primary symptom. For the preoccupation with the category of time is itself indicative of an objectivizing falsification. To focus on time, with all the substantive quasi-metaphysical weight it implies, is already to abstract from experience--both of fictions and of life. Nor do I want to exchange a critical analysis of memory for one of time in the modern novel. As we shall shortly see in our survey of memory's history in philosophical reflection, such an analysis is still too often a substitution of one objectivized abstraction for another. I am less interested in time than in lived temporality, less interested in the mental (or cerebral) faculty of memory than in the human activity of remembering. My task is not so much to define memory or analyze the way it works as to explore how the human capacities for remembering are ingredient in forms of life and shapes of experience--in human being's temporality. I want to be attentive, not to _mneme_ (substantive/memory), but to _anamnesis_ (gerund/remembering).

The shift I am suggesting is not new philosophically. It takes its lead from Kant's Copernican revolution which recognized that, from the first, even in our temporal/spatial interpretive framework, the mind is always active in cognition.[4] It builds on Husserl's primary insight: that the structure of experience is invariably noetic/noematic. There is no aspect of the object without a corresponding act of consciousness which constitutes it. Anamnesis is constitutive of, no less than constituted by, a world. Exploring remembering as human activity and as constitutive of human being's temporality, then, is meant as a guarantor of this ineluctable noetic/noematic structure. Time is not something which exists "out there" which novelists make use of in constructing their fictive worlds. We are all--novelists and readers alike--creating time by our various specific acts. Among these constituting acts of consciousness, remembering enjoys a certain primacy in relation to our temporality.

This rigorous return to "the things themselves" called for by phenomenology requires practical literary criticism's own wrestling with the confines of its historical forms. If the new criticism rescued us from the throes of subjectivism, it did so at the cost of an objectivizing tendency. The phenomenological return to "the things themselves" must not be confused with the new criticism's attention to "the poem itself." The latter presupposes an objective meaning given in and by the work independent of any and all perspectives on it; the former insists that the thing itself, in its essence, is always already constituted by and constituting consciousness, is always already presented. If we are to correct what now seems a naive new criticism, our concrete interpretations must be grounded in a critical understanding which recognizes the noetic/noematic structure of the reader's being present before the text. A phenomenology of reading will reveal the anamnetic structure of the hermeneutical task itself, for as Ray Hart states, "One cannot stray from memory so long as he is considering anything involving interpretation."[5]

And so, beyond its practical literary criticism, this essay must be theoretical and methodological. It aims to discover a fresh literary hermeneutic. We have isolated at least two meanings of anamnesis in the project: the description of remembering _as a human activity_ in fictions and in life and the description of remembering _as a hermeneutical act._ The two are not unrelated. I am

xi

wagering that there are neglected features of what remembering is in our life that if attended to, will give us hermeneutical tools.

My first task is to nurture into being a richer description of remembering and to elaborate its hermeneutical implications before putting it to the test in the face of concrete literary texts. This means generating a more robust understanding of remembering than is presently available either in the commonsense usage or within the confines of any single discipline. The study of memory cuts across any clearly defined disciplinary boundaries, as even a partial bibliography on the topic indicates. The work on memory within the various disciplines of the human studies alone is itself testimony to the need for an interdisciplinary approach to the problem.

As interdisciplinary, the project unabashedly runs all the risks inherent in trying to build bridges across discontinuous fields; and, to switch metaphors, if it manages not to fall between stools, it is certainly uneasily balanced among them. Moreover, its inter-disciplinariness has a focus weighted toward interpretation. That is to say that, while our approach must be aware of theoretical considerations, we shall proceed hermeneutically. Thus the project does not intend a new theory of memory--not that it purports to be untheoretical, but that it eschews both the possibility and desirability of a single adequate theory. It wishes to be, rather, a theory-laden hermeneutic.

In order to achieve the necessary awareness of theoretical issues, in the first chapter I place my inquiry into remembering within the context of the controlling paradigms for memory in the history of Western philosophical reflection. After noting that contemporary philosophy is unanimous in its rejection of the faculty psychology approach to memory so prevalent in the tradition up to our time, I examine its two major alternatives in the Anglo-American analytical tradition and the continental phenomenological one. While acknowledging the validity of the former's critique and our need to be chastened by it, I choose phenomenology as a more fruitful dialogue partner for reflection's constructive task.

Once having attended to the predominant theories of memory in the philosophical tradition, I establish the hermeneutical grounding for my own reflection on the human activity of remembering in chapter II. To avoid the very tendency I am in polemic against--thought's propensity to

close in upon itself by constructing metatheories--I let
myself be instructed by Paul Ricoeur's second Copernican
revolution, allowing the symbol, in all its surplus of
meaning, to give rise to thought. If the beginning of
philosophy is to be reached, Ricoeur suggests, "it is
first necessary for thought to inhabit the fullness of
language." A philosophy born of meditation on symbols
starts from the fullness of "meaning already there."

> It begins from language which has already taken
> place and in which everything in a certain
> sense has already been said; it wants to be
> thought, not presuppositionless, but in and
> with all its presuppositions. Its first
> problem is not how to get started, but, from
> the midst of speech, <u>to recollect itself</u>.[6]

Thus the task of thinking is itself anamnetic, and
my reflective recollection takes shape in the face of a
concrete symbolic text. In the second chapter, I
juxtapose the quite lamentable treatment of memory in the
predominant philosophical <u>theories</u> with a symbolic text
which can arouse our perplexity about the human <u>activity</u>
of remembering. I choose the Eucharistic anamnesis of
the Christian liturgy not only because it is the symbol
which initiated my own thinking about remembering, but
also because in it we have an exceptionally rich and
multivocal instance upon which to dwell. Eucharistic
anamnesis gives me the concrete impetus for my reflection
by presenting to me in a striking way certain peculiar
features of remembering not addressed by the
philosophical tradition. I am not unaware that it may
seem an eccentric case study indeed, but I am convinced
that it is justified by its fruitfulness. The
remembering proper to liturgical anamnesis is not just
ideologically locatable. Precisely because it is
connected with fundamental human ritual capacities, it
signals a broad-scale human and cultural phenomenon.

The reflection on remembering in part II takes its
lead from the liturgical anamnesis and anticipates the
literary critical task of part III. It unfolds under the
following rubrics: (1) remembering and narrative, (2)
remembering and temporality, (3) remembering and
identity, and (4) remembering and imagining. These
chapters are more in the nature of a generative inquiry
than a seamless web of reflection. That inquiry does not
result either in a definition of memory or in a theory of
acts of remembering. It intends, rather, to contribute
to a hermeneutics of reading. Then, in Part III, I
choose two literary locations to demonstrate such a
"remembering hermeneutic." In my readings of Margaret

xiii

Atwood's _Surfacing_ and Saul Bellow's _Henderson the Rain King_, my aim is to find out how attention to the dense and variegated human activity of remembering offers fresh insights into modern fiction.

[1]Georg Lukacs, The Theory of the Novel, trans. Anna Bostock (Cambridge, Mass.: The MIT Press, 1971; first published, 1920), p. 122. "The greatest discrepancy between idea and reality is time: the process of time as duration. The most profound and most humiliating impotence of subjectivity consists . . . in the fact that it cannot resist the sluggish, yet constant progress of time . . . ; that time--that ungraspable, invisibly moving substance--gradually robs subjectivity of all its possessions and imperceptibly forces alien contents into it. That is why only the novel, the literary form of the transcendent homelessness of the idea, includes real time--Bergson's durée--among its constitutive principles . . . . Only in the novel, whose very matter is seeking and failing to find the essence, is time posited together with the form . . . " (pp. 121-122).

[2]I am indebted to Prof. Angel Medina of the Georgia State University philosophy department for this insight.

[3]See, among others, the fine studies by Georges Poulet, Studies in Human Time (Balt.: Johns Hopkins Press, 1956); Hans Meyerhoff, Time in Literature (Berkeley: U. of California Press, 1955); A. A. Mendilow, Time and the Novel (London: Peter Nevill, 1952); Frank Kermode, The Sense of an Ending (N.Y.: Oxford U. Press, 1967); Sharon Spencer, Space, Time and Structure in the Modern Novel (N.Y.: N.Y.U. Press, 1971); William T. Noon, "Modern Literature and the Sense of Time," Thought 33 (1958).

[4]In Kant's transcendental philosophy, of course, space and time are "mere creations of the imagination."

[5]Ray Hart, Unfinished Man and the Imagination (N.Y.: Herder and Herder, 1968), p. 210.

[6]Paul Ricoeur, "The Hermeneutics of Symbols and Philosophical Reflection," in The Philosophy of Paul Ricoeur: An Anthology of His Work, ed. Charles E. Reagan and David Stewart (Boston: Beacon Press, 1978), pp. 36-37, my italics. For a slightly different formulation, see Ricoeur, The Symbolism of Evil, trans. Emerson Buchanan (Boston: Beacon Press, 1967), pp. 348-349: "[T]he first task is not to begin but, from the midst of speech, to remember; to remember with a view to beginning."

PART I

A CONFLICT OF INTERPRETATIONS

CHAPTER I
PHILOSOPHICAL THEORIES OF MEMORY:

SOME PARADIGMS

How has philosophical reflection addressed itself to the human activity of remembering? Since any full rehearsal of the history of Western philosophy on memory is outside the scope of this essay, we shall content ourselves with a discussion of significant contributions with an eye toward a certain recurrent pattern. We shall discover these contributions in three major "moments" in philosophical reflection: classical, modern, and contemporary. In each case, the pattern is shaped by certain dominant theories of world and mind. Thus our discussion, while organized historically, will seek to elicit the pattern's recurrent themes.

By way of introduction, we can summarize these themes as follows: (1) A philosopher's theory of memory is, to a large extent, shaped by her understanding of time. Undergirding both the classical and the modern alternatives is the acceptance, whether explicit or implicit, of a notion of time taken from the world of physical objects and having nothing as such to do with the human world. Time, conceived of as a linear succession of present moments, is objectified, spatialized, and quantified. (2) Following from this conception of time is the privileged reality status granted to the present. Only the present really exists; the past is no longer; the future is not yet. (3) If the present enjoys a privileged status in the understanding of being, then perception enjoys a primacy in the philosophy of mind, understood as a faculty psychology. Only the faculty of perception can give us what really is, the present. Memory gives us the past; imagination, the future. (4) As a result, imagination and memory tend to be viewed as twin faculties of low epistemic status derivative from perception. (5) The problem of how memory can give us the past is addressed by a theory (called the "representative," "copy," or "image" theory) which posits some sort of mental image, corresponding to the past reality, in the remembering mind. (6) This theory, in its turn, generates the problem of how to distinguish between the images of the imagination and those of memory. The issue is key, for it is the basis for any certainty we have in knowledge.

Twentieth century philosophical alternatives are agreed in their rejection of a spatialized conception of time and a faculty psychology which posits internal mental substances. In their radical critique of these

3

historically dominant theories of world and mind, they open the way for reflection on the neglected issue of the distinctive character of human time. Such reflection, in its turn, topples the traditional understanding of memory. Indeed, once the Aristotelian notion of time and the tradition of faculty psychology have been undermined, philosophical reflection is freed to discover the non-contingent conceptual relation between remembering, conceived as a human activity rather than a mental substance, and personal identity.

It is this development, in its broad outlines, that we shall be tracing in this chapter. There are, of course, exceptions to the generalities. The first and the greatest of these is Plato himself. Any excursis into the history of philosophical reflection on memory must begin with him.

The Classical Tradition

Plato

In the Socratic dialogues, Plato makes a distinction which is quite foreign to our commonsense understanding of memory, i.e., the distinction between anamnesis or recollection on the one hand and memory on the other. Plato's distinction must concern us now, for it has significant consequences for all subsequent philosophical reflection on remembering. For Plato, the problem of memory arises in two essentially separate contexts: (1) in the context of the doctrine of Recollection in the Meno, the Phaedo, and the Phaedrus; and (2) in the epistemological context in the Thaetetus.

(1) Anamnesis is introduced in the Meno as a theory which answers the question, how is one to know, and not merely believe, that a proposition is true? There are really two problems here to which the concept of anamnesis is offered as the solution. First is Meno's argument, following the Sophists, that inquiry is not possible because either one already knows the answer, thus making it unnecessary; or one does not and accordingly will not be able to recognize the truth when he is presented with it, thus making it impossible.[1] Socrates calls this an argument which is both tricky and tiresome![2] Secondly, Socrates is aware--and this is dramatically represented by the questioning of the slave boy--that there are some truths (in this instance, geometrical) which are recognized as true without empirical proof. Indeed, these include not only

geometrical and mathematical truths, but all values as well. Both of these problems are explained by Plato in terms of a remembering. For inquiry to be possible, we must both know and not know that which we are seeking. That is, we must know it but not remember it.

For this solution, Socrates turns to what he has heard from "certain wise men and women who spoke of things divine."[3] These priests, priestesses and inspired poets say that the soul of man is immortal.

> The soul, then, as being immortal, and having been born again many times, and having seen all things that exist, whether in this world or in the world below, has knowledge of them all; and it is no wonder that she should be able to call to remembrance all that she ever knew about virtue, and about everything; for as all nature is akin, and the soul has learned all things, there is no difficulty in her eliciting or as men say learning, out of a single recollection all the rest, if a man is strenuous and does not faint; <u>for all enquiry and all learning is but recollection</u>. And therefore we ought not to listen to this sophistical argument about the impossibility of enquiry. (<u>Meno</u> 81)

It is enlightening to note here the purpose to which Socrates' introduction of the notion of the immortality of the soul is put: to justify the possibility of learning. Even in the <u>Meno</u>, before a full elaboration of the doctrine of the Ideas, Plato's notion of Recollection is bound up with his belief in the soul's reincarnation.

The deductive process is reversed in the <u>Phaedo</u>, where the Socratic understanding of knowledge as Recollection is put forward as <u>evidence</u> of the soul's immortality. In his argument for immortality (far from a disinterested one, as he is faced with his own imminent death), Socrates moves beyond a mere restatement of the doctrine "that knowledge is Recollection" to a fuller elaboration of the doctrine of Ideas.

To do so, he raises the question of how we can compare a present perception to a Recollection and know whether the former matches the latter.[4] We must, he concludes, already have the idea of equality before we even begin to perceive. Such an idea must have been acquired before we were born.

And if we acquired this knowledge before we were born, and were born having the use of it,

then we also knew before we were born and at
the instant of birth not only the equal or the
greater or the less, but all other ideas; for
we are not speaking only of equality, but of
beauty, goodness, justice, holiness, and of all
which we stamp with the name of essence in the
dialectical process, both when we ask and when
we answer questions. (Phaedo 75)

So the process which we call learning is a recovery of
the knowledge which is natural to us: the knowledge of
essences.[5] "May not," Socrates asks rhetorically, "this
be rightly termed recollection?" In the instance he
cites, it is Recollection, the knowledge of equality,
which allows us to form a judgment about the comparison
of a present perception with a memory.

If these ideas existed before we were born as our
inborn possession, argues Socrates, then so did our
souls. Thus the soul is immortal. One further
consequence of this reasoning process must be noted here,
namely, the identification of Recollection as the
knowledge of essences with what is unchanging. For
Plato, the soul and ideas belong to that which is
unchanging; and it follows that Recollection, soul-
knowledge, does too. Sense impressions belong, with the
body, to the changing. Thus Plato makes a clear
distinction between recollection and perception, a
distinction, as we shall soon see, which is obscured in
the subsequent history of philosophical reflection on
memory.

Finally, this primacy and centrality of Recollection
is underscored in the Phaedrus where Socrates addresses
himself to rhetoric, understood not as the art of
persuasion for the sake of any personal or political
advantage, but as the art of speaking the truth and
persuading one's hearers to the truth. Such rhetorical
power depends on the knowledge of the soul, and the
soul's true knowledge is the Recollection of Ideas. For
Socrates, Recollection is not one part of the art of
rhetoric, but the groundwork of the whole.[6]

It is in this context of the indissoluble link he
posits between Recollection and the truth that Socrates
repeats the myth of Theuth, discoverer of letters. In
the ancient legend, Theuth brings his prized invention to
Thamus, King of all Egypt, because he wants to share its
benefits with the Egyptians. But Thamus disallows the
invention, arguing that, far from being an aid to memory,
the capacity of writing will create forgetfulness in the
learners' souls.

Their trust in writing, produced by external characters which are not part of themselves, will discourage the use of their own memory within them. You have invented an elixir not of memory but of reminding; and you offer your pupils the appearance of wisdom, not true wisdom.[7]

Insofar as it weakens a person's capacities for Recollection, which is the soul's way to true knowledge, writing is more a curse than a blessing to humanity.

By means of this Socratic concept of Recollection which links it with the Ideas and the soul's immortality, memory enjoys a centrality in Plato's theory of knowledge which is unmatched in all subsequent philosophical reflection. Because it is the only way to knowledge of the standard subjects of dialectical inquiry, Recollection is of the greatest importance. Dialectical discussion, by which we come to understand such ideas as the equal, the good, the just, and the beautiful, is a process which not only presupposes the participant's capacity to remember relevant data, but actually culminates in Recollection.

This is so because dialectic is especially fitted to elicit a learning derived from the internal rather than the external world. Recollection, then, is the recovery of knowledge which is one's own, from within oneself, and not a knowledge given to one by a teacher (mere information).[8] Socrates' alleged proof of this is the slave boy in the Meno. He insists four times in the course of the dialogue that he is not teaching the boy, but rather the boy is working the ideas out for himself. Beyond this, the concept of Recollection is so significant for Plato because it allows him to argue for the pre-existence of the soul. The capacity to recollect, as we have seen, presupposes prior knowledge-- a knowledge, according to Plato, which must have been acquired before birth.

(2) But Plato discusses memory in a more limited context of epistemology as well, and it is this more limited context which has perdured in the tradition. In the Thaetetus, the question being addressed is, what is knowledge? Here, however, there is no mention of the Ideas or the soul's immortality. After a detailed discussion, the contention that knowledge is merely perception is rejected in favor of the contention that knowledge is true judgment, a process which involves reflection, comparison, and discrimination.[9] This, in

turn, raises the issue of how false judgments are possible. False judgment, it is argued, is the confusion of one real object for another. A typical case is put forward: when someone who knows Socrates sees an indistinct shape from a distance which he mistakes for Socrates. This case of false judgment is one in which a confusion exists between an incoming perception and a memory. Thus the discussion turns to the problem of memory.

In the case at hand, a host of memories is in the mind of the perceiver, including among them the memory of Socrates. The problem is how to match up the incoming perception with one of these stored memories. At this point Plato employs a metaphor by way of illustration.

> I would have you imagine that there exists in the mind of man a block of wax, which is of different sizes in different men; harder, moister, and having more or less of purity in one than another, and in some of an intermediate quality. (Thaetetus 191)

This tablet is the gift of Mnemosyne, mother of the Muses; and when we wish to remember anything we perceive or think, we hold the wax to these perceptions or thoughts in order to receive from them the impression, much as a signet ring does from wax. We remember what is thus impressed as long as the image lasts, but we forget the knowledge when it is effaced. Plato elaborates the metaphor further on, suggesting a correspondence between the varying qualities of the "wax tablets" of different minds and success at matching incoming perceptions with memories.

If this model accounts for the problem of mismatching an incoming perception with a memory, what of a further case: that of a confusion not of perception but of abstract ideas already in the mind? Socrates' example is of a person who adds five and seven and comes up with eleven as the sum. To explain such an error, Socrates distinguishes between "having" and "possessing" knowledge. A person may possess the knowledge that five and seven equals twelve without having it when one needs it in a particular instance. Here the wax tablet model is exchanged for an alternative metaphor.

> Once more then, as in what preceded we made a sort of waxen figment in the mind, so now let us suppose that in the mind of each man there is an aviary of all sorts of birds--some flocking together apart from the rest, others in

small groups, others solitary, flying anywhere and everywhere . . . . We may suppose that the birds are kinds of knowledge and that . . . . when the various numbers and forms of knowledge are flying about in the aviary, and wishing to capture a certain sort of knowledge out of the general store, he takes the wrong one by mistake, that is to say, when he thought eleven to be twelve, he got hold of the ring-dove which he had in his mind, when he wanted the pigeon. (Thaetetus 197, 199)

The wax tablet model accounts for the instance in which the error of judgment is the mis-matching of a perception with a memory; the aviary model, the confusion among memories in the mind. Now it is well worth observing here that both of Plato's metaphors have perdured, either directly or indirectly, in the tradition of philosophical reflection on memory; the wax tablet as the proto-type of copy theories of memory, the aviary as that of storage theories. Indeed, such metaphors appear in a more sophisticated form even in contemporary neuro-physiological memory models.[10] This may reflect philosophy's penchant for understanding memory exclusively in terms of perception--a penchant traceable not to Plato so much as to Aristotle. Before turning to Aristotle's treatment of memory, however, let us pause to reflect on Plato's contribution to our task at hand.

First of all, we must emphasize that, when Plato offers both models, he is clearly speaking metaphorically ("I would have you imagine," "We made a sort of waxen figment in the mind"). Now evidently this is easier to see spontaneously with the aviary model than with the wax tablet. It is not too hard, it seems, to overlook this metaphorical character in the case of the wax tablet model and to begin thinking quite literally in its terms. Once we do so, serious problems arise. Does the mind which tries to match the incoming perception with the image in the wax have to peruse its entire waxen tablet of stored memories to come up with such a match? Surely a long and laborious process which does not concur with our ordinary experience of remembering! Alternatively, does the mind have an approximate notion of where the memory is stored in the waxen tablet? If so, the comparing mind already enjoys a kind of memory not accounted for by the model. If these alternatives strike us as foolhardy, are we not forced to acknowledge that we cannot reify Plato's metaphors for memory without seriously distorting the problems at hand and, in fact, backing ourselves into an infinite regression in our efforts to explain what happens when we remember? The philosophical tendency to do so has, indeed, had just that effect in most subsequent discussions of memory.

In our immediate task, which is to examine the philosophical tradition for the light it sheds on remembering as a human activity, Plato--more than any other pre-contemporary philosopher--is our ally. Not that Plato addresses himself directly to our concrete concerns about remembering,[11] but he has a deep fascination with and appreciation for the role remembering plays in a human being's interior life; and he has, concomitantly, a rich notion of the phenomenon of memory in the life of the mind.

For Plato, Memory, Mnemosyne, is the mother of all the Muses. She gives birth to and nurtures epic and lyric poetry, mime, music, dance, tragedy, comedy, rhetoric, history, and astronomy. His contention that Recollection is fundamental to all other thinking and thus to the good life leads him to grant it a peculiar primacy in his philosophy. Recollection is not relegated to a certain place on the time line (i.e., the past); it is not relegated exclusively to the temporal at all. As the highest faculty of the soul, indispensable in its search for the truth, Recollection enjoys a relation to the eternal not enjoyed by other mental acts. The common criticism of Plato's doctrine of Recollection, of course, is its inseparability from his quasi-mythical dualistic metaphysic.[12] While the metaphysic may be dispensable, his intuitive point about memory's significance and his gesture toward a more synoptic view are not.

Unfortunately, in his efforts to convey this intuition of richness, Plato makes the mistake of separating recollection from memory, thus presaging a dualism which we find in Aristotle's De Memoria et Reminiscentia. This very separation of recollection from memory eventually leads to the wholesale surrendering of recollection from the tradition after Aristotle. (The stunning but qualified exception to this is, of course, Augustine, whose contributions to our understanding of memory will be discussed in chapter V). In this sense, we can see Aristotle as a transitional figure between Plato and the moderns.

Aristotle

While Aristotle devotes most of the second chapter of the De Memoria et Reminiscentia to recollection (presumably because he inherited his interest in it from Plato)[13], he did not accept the metaphysic and epistemology which supported it in Plato. Thus, in

Aristotle, recollection is virtually limited to the recovery through the association of ideas of scientific knowledge and perceptions which one had before, a deliberate effort to find one's way among memory contents.[14] As such, it is little more than a specialized case of recalling. Thus it need not concern us here, for Aristotle gives his primary attention to what he considers to be memory proper. Let us turn, then, to Aristotle's philosophy of memory. To understand it, we must look first, not to the De Memoria itself, but to two earlier treatises whose thought undergirds it. From the Physics we need to glean some sense of his notion of time and from the De Anima, his theory of knowledge. All that he says about memory presupposes these ideas.

In the Physics, Aristotle's treatise on time is part of the inquiry into the essence of Nature. His prior discussion of place, space, and motion provides him with the lexicon he needs for his definition of time. Time, he asserts, is "the number of movement in respect to before and after."[15] The time at issue is something to be calculated and measured; it belongs, that is, to the world of physical objects and has nothing as such to do with the human world. One salient feature of this notion of time is the role assigned to the now. Time is construed as a succession of nows. Thus, time is objectified, spatialized, and quantified. The most persistent version of this in the Western philosophical tradition is the conceptualization of time as linear succession.[16]

We see in the De Anima how Aristotle's theory of knowledge is a logical companion of this scientific understanding of time as linear succession, with its preoccupation with the present. If the present enjoys a privileged status in the understanding of being, then perception, and sensory perception in particular, enjoys a primacy among mental acts.[17]

For Aristotle, all knowledge comes through the senses. "No one could ever learn or understand anything, if he had not the faculty of perception."[18] What exactly, asks Aristotle, is the nature of this faculty of perception? When we say that we see an object that is in the world, we certainly do not mean to suggest that the physical object itself enters our eyes but rather some representation of it. What is the relationship between the physical object and that which enters our eyes? How can we know there is a resemblance between the two, and in what sense does the representation resemble the original? In response to these problems, he writes,

11

By a "sense" is meant what has the power of receiving into itself the sensible forms of things without the matter. This must be conceived of as taking place in the way in which a piece of wax takes on the impress of a signet ring without the iron or gold.[19]

What strikes us immediately, of course, is that Aristotle borrows Plato's memory metaphor to explain perception! The sensible forms of objects, brought in by the five senses, are initially worked upon by the imaginative faculty, and it is the images so formed which become the material of the intellectual faculty. Imagination is the essential intermediary between perception and thought. Aristotle is remarkably explicit about this: "Even when he thinks speculatively, he must have some mental picture with which to think"; "the soul never thinks without a mental picture."[20]

Now in this Aristotle departs from Plato, who believes that dialectical thinking (which culminates in recollection) rises above the need for images. Richard Sorabji suggests the reason for Aristotle's departure.

Objects of thought must be housed somewhere. Plato had supposed that the objects of dialectical thought were ideal Forms, which exist separately from the sensible world. But Aristotle believes that very few things can exist separately from the sensible world. So the objects of thought need a sensible vehicle. And a convenient vehicle is the sensible form, which exists in external physical objects, and which during perception is transferred to one's sense-organs.[21]

Aristotle pushes his inquiry somewhat further in the De Memoria (which is an appendix to the De Anima), using his supposition that thinking requires an image to argue for the idea that memory requires an image. The second treatise opens with a quotation from the earlier work. "As has been said before in my treatise On the Soul about imagination, it is impossible even to think without a mental picture."[22] "Memory," he continues, "even the memory of objects of thought, is not without an image. So memory will belong to thought in virtue of an incidental association, but in its own right to the primary perceptive part."[23] Any connection between memory and the intellect is merely incidental. In memory, thought works on the stored images from sense perception. He goes on to observe that "it is apparent, then, to which part of the soul memory belongs, namely the same

12

part as that to which imagination belongs" (450^a 22). Thus is launched the whole tradition of faculty psychology which considers perception to be the "more primordial act," "the act of acts from which all other acts of mind are seen to stem,"[24] and thus considers imagination and memory as twin faculties which are mere offshoots of perception.

We already know that the object of perception, that most primordial of acts, is the present, the privileged temporal mode. What, then, asks Aristotle, is the object of memory?

> [M]emory is not perception or conception, but a state or affection connected with one of these, when time has elapsed. There is no memory of the present as the present, as has been said. But perception is of the present, prediction of the future, and memory of the past. And this is why all memory involves time (449^{b}24).

But here a puzzlement arises. How can what is past be present? For for while the object of memory is the past, memory happens in the present. Following his theory of thinking as elaborated in the De Anima, Aristotle thinks that some kind of image is necessary to remembering. In the earlier work, the problem was a spatial one: how the objects of perception can be said to be in the mind. Here the problem is analogous, but the issue is temporal rather than spatial. If the problem is analogous, so too is the solution. It is clear, he writes, that one must think of the affection (i.e., the present memory) "as being like a sort of picture, the having of which we say is memory. For the change that occurs marks in a sort of imprint, as it were, of the sense-image, as people do who seal things with signet-rings" (450^{a}25).

It is worth emphasizing here the explicit parallelism in Aristotle's thinking between the problem of the memory image and the problem of the sense image. There the question was how that which enters the sense organ (in our case, the eye) resembles and refers to the original object. Here it is the question, how can an event which is taking place in the present (the memory event) resemble and refer to an event which took place in the past (the original perception or thought now remembered)? How, that is, can it be experienced as transcendent or transtemporal rather than immanent or immediately present? Aristotle's answer is that just as one can regard a picture or drawing either as something in its own right or as a picture or drawing of something else, so one can understand an image as something in its own right or as being a copy of something. The forming of the mental image, at the moment of perception or thought, is like making a seal with a signet ring (a reiteration of the De Anima metaphor); the mental picture from the sense impression is like a "figure drawn on a panel" or "a sort of picture" (450^b20, 450^a25). The latter, that is, is a copy or representation of the former, an image of an image.

Aristotle's picture functions as a model of explanation much the same way as Plato's wax and aviary did. The problem, however, is somewhat different and somewhat more sophisticated. Plato's problem was how images are stored in the mind and retrieved when needed. Aristotle's is one of temporality: how can a present mental act be taken as referring to the past? Just as with Plato, however, the picture model does not really solve the problem. Pictures are regarded as of something else only because the observer can remember the something else so depicted. To hold that the mental pictures are connected with past perceptions and not simply experienced as something in the present is already to presume that the mind has memory.[25] We are left with the same infinite regression. Earlier in the treatise, Aristotle offers a somewhat similar link when he says that "when someone is actively engaged in memory, he perceives in addition that he saw this, or heard it, or learned it earlier" (450^a 15). But what, precisely, is this perception of "earlier"?

Even if we find his answers unconvincing, we must grant that Aristotle's questions have maintained their vitality throughout philosophical reflection on memory. And the answers he gives--that memory is a mere outpost of its parent act, perception; that memory is essentially imagistic, a passively reproductive function of low epistemic status; and that the memory image is a copy of the original perception--have been the major currents in modern philosophical thinking about remembering.[26] Indeed, we find in Aristotle's De Memoria a philosophical discussion of memory similar to, but fuller and more detailed than, that found in the best known British empiricists. It is to this modern tradition, and especially to the thought of Hobbes, Locke, and Hume, that we must now turn in our tracing of the pattern of memory's treatment.

The Modern Empiricist Tradition

In terms of our interest in the philosophy of memory, we can view these modern philosophies as variations on certain Aristotelian themes which we have been tracing in our exposition. Undergirding them all is, first of all, the implicit acceptance of the understanding of the physical time of objects as applying willy-nilly to human time. Time is a succession of presents. Following from this is the privileged reality status granted to the now in the succession, with a concomitant primacy granted to perception in the philosophy of mind conceived of as a faculty psychology. Finally, imagination and memory continue to be seen as twin faculties derived from perception.

In modern philosophical discussions of memory, representative theories are the predominant current of thought. Eventually, the focus of debate becomes the question of how to distinguish memory images from other kinds of mental images, how, that is, we are to know that the present memory experience does in fact reproduce or represent what was previously experienced. This problem becomes particularly acute if we are to ground all our knowledge of the past in memory. Thus, eventually, begins the search for some "memory indicator,"[27] some feature of the remembering itself which differentiates it from other image productions. Let us turn now to the thought peculiar to each of our three representatives of the modern treatment of memory.

Thomas Hobbes

Thomas Hobbes' proto-empiricist view is that all mental acts are derivatives from sensation, "the Originall of them all."[28] To comprehend the nadir to which memory declines in his psychology, we must first look at some length at the Hobbesian notion of sensation itself. Following after Galileo and Descartes, Hobbes propounds a most diminished doctrine of sensory experience. In his natural philosophy, Galileo had held that sensations were secondary qualities, mere appearances of bodies, whose real properties were extension, figure, and motion. As such, sensations are phantasms in the head, caused by the primary properties of external objects interacting with sense organs. Descartes had decried the senses as deceptive, chimeric, and confused. In reacting against the Cartesian dichotomy of world and mind, and deeply influenced by Galileo, Hobbes replaced Descartes' two substances with two levels of reality: the really real is the material world of body and motion; experience has the status of mere fancy. He constructed a psychology in

conformity with the Galilean principle of motion. In the
De Corpore, he proclaimed that "we have discovered the
nature of sense, namely, that it is some internal motion
of the sentiment."[29] In the opening chapter of the
Leviathan, entitled "Of Sense," he explains that the
external body or object presses on the organ of sense,

> which pressure, by the mediation of Nerves, and
> other strings, and membranes of the body,
> continued inwards to the Brain, and Heart,
> causeth there a resistance, or counterpressure,
> or endeavor of the Heart, to deliver itself:
> which endeavor because outward, seemeth to be
> some matter without. And this _seeming_, or
> _fancy_, is that which men call _Sense_.[30]

Sensations are nothing but physical motions. They have
an external character merely because of the "outward
endeavor" of the heart, "so that Sense in all cases is
nothing else but originall fancy" caused by the pressure
of external things upon our sense organs.[31]

Hobbes' doctrine of imagination and memory, which
follows immediately in the _Leviathan_, is an explicit
deduction from this newly discovered principle of
inertia, applied now to human psychology. It
demonstrates all too clearly how a philosopher's theory
of sensory experience predetermines his possible theories
of the two supposedly derivative twin acts. Imagination,
according to Hobbes, is nothing but decaying sense (i.e.,
the image is retained but now grown obscure); memory
differs only in that the fading image is accompanied by
a feeling of familiarity, "for he that perceives that he
hath perceived remembers."[32]

> This _decaying sense_, when wee would express the
> thing it self . . . wee call _Imagination_. . .
> . But when wee would express the _decay_ and
> signifie that the Sense is fading, old, and
> past, it is called _Memory_. So that _Imagination_
> and _Memory_ are but one thing, which for divers
> considerations hath divers names.[33]

As R. S. Peters comments, Hobbes' fundamental
mistake was "to attempt to distinguish performances, such
as perceiving and remembering, by reference to subjective
hallmarks vaguely consistent with his mechanized theory,
rather than by reference to the epistemological criteria
written into them."[34] He neglects the status of the claims
made by these various acts of mind; in the case of

memory, the thetic commitment to past reality that is inseparable from acts of remembering.[35] He seems, for example, to equate what is past with what is familiar, and it is difficult to see how he can distinguish remembering from perceiving again in a case where the second perception lacks vivacity. Moreover, as Erwin Straus wryly comments, if all sense is seeming, all memory decaying sense, and all intellect derived from sense, it is hard to understand how the phantasmagoric character of sense could have ever been discovered or known as such!

As a writer, however, Hobbes preserved throughout the familiar attitude of the life-world where hearts and brains are not apprehended as fancies but seen as real things, described in detail by anatomists and physicians and well known in general by hunters, butchers, and cooks.[36]

Straus may be being a bit unfair to Hobbes, since he presumably was not denying the existence of the biological organs but rather offering a peculiarly naturalistic and mechanistic doctrine of their relationship to experience. Thus we find in Hobbes' faculty psychology an example par excellence of that peculiar propensity of some philosophers to absent their theorizing from the data of their own ordinary experience. Reading Hobbes, one is continually questioning whether he could possibly have believed what he was saying.

Hobbes' position that imagination and memory are in fact one and the same act, simply viewed from different perspectives, is the extreme version of the philosophical tendency to see imagination and memory as twin faculties. A less extreme claim would have it not that they are identical but that they differ only in degree. The locus classicus of this latter claim is David Hume's Treatise of Human Nature.[37] We shall examine Hume's notion of memory's relation to imagination and perception presently, but first we must turn to his famous predecessor in the British empiricist tradition. Hume largely constructs his own philosophy on John Locke's argument against the Christian platonists' theory of innate ideas.

John Locke

In Book I of his Essay Concerning Human Understanding, entitled "Neither Principles Nor Ideas Are Innate," Locke sets out to refute what he took to be the

17

commonly accepted theory of the time "that there are in
the understanding certain innate principles; . . . as it
were stamped upon the mind of man; which the soul
receives in its very first being, and brings into the
world with it.[38] Such "ideas" were, as we have seen,
central to Plato's philosophy in which they are the only
objects of the soul's true knowledge, available to us in
this life exclusively through the process of dialectical
thinking which culminates in recollection. Christian
platonists, denying Plato's belief in the pre-existence
of the soul, substituted for the inborn image-free Recollection of the Ideas, inborn representations of them,
which they call "innate ideas." In their thinking, it is
by reflection on such innate ideas that we come to the
knowledge of the truths of mathematics, metaphysics, and
morality.

Locke considers the appeal to such principles the
root of dogmatism and the chief obstacle to the progress
of knowledge.[39] But in denying the existence of innate
ideas, Locke still accepted the way of picturing the
mind's relationship to the world which accompanied the
doctrine. According to this picture, the mind is an
immaterial entity with the power to receive representations of things in the external world, to reason about
these representations, and somehow to translate them into
bodily actions in the world. In his Introduction, Locke
defines the term idea as "whatsoever is the object   of
the understanding when a man thinks."[40] Since they are
not innate, however, ideas must come from experience,
which he defines as "sensation and reflection" (p. 248).

Ideas of sensation are conveyed into the mind
through our senses; ideas of reflection, by the mind's
observation of its own processes. While the former are
representations of what is external to us (in the world),
the latter are entirely subjective. From this notion of
understanding, Locke develops his theory of memory.

What we remember is always mental in nature. Locke
supposes that the objects of perception, and thus of
memory, are solely ideas. Memory is,

> as it were, the storehouse of our ideas. For
> the narrow mind of man, not being capable of
> having many ideas under view and consideration
> at once, it is necessary to have a repository
> to lay up those ideas, which at another time it
> might have use of (p. 276, my italics).

Memory somehow manages to store these representations of
sense and reflection, or copies of them, and has them

handy when they are needed for thinking. From this, it is an obvious step to treat ideas, which supposedly provide the means of thinking, as mental images. While Locke sometimes seems to take this step, Hume clearly did so.[41]

Interestingly enough, Locke must have become dissatisfied with his storehouse model for memory, however, for in the second edition of the Essay, he attaches to it this qualifying comment:

> But our ideas being nothing but actual perceptions in the mind, which cease to be anything when there is no perception of them, this laying up of our ideas in the repository of the memory signifies no more but this--that the mind has a power, in many cases, to revive perceptions which it has once had, with this additional perception annexed to them, that it has had them before. And in this sense it is that our ideas are said to be in our memories, when indeed they are actually nowhere, but only there is an ability in the mind when it will revive them again, and, as it were, paint them anew on itself (p. 276, my italics).

Here we can see Locke struggling against his own suppositions about memory, suppositions which are themselves inherited in a long tradition. It is no wonder, judging from this one case, that Copleston comments, "he gives throughout the impression of being an honest thinker."[42] It seems that while he at first took the notion of a memory storehouse quite literally, later he decided that the storehouse model was to be understood simply as a metaphor for an ability. Not since Plato have we seen this willingness to treat one's own metaphors for memory with a certain lighthandedness. Locke has not departed from the empiricist understanding of memory's function in faculty psychology, but the picture he offers is somewhat less materialistic than that which we find in Hobbes and Hume.

Within the confines of his epistemology, which still considers perception as the primordial act of mind, Locke grants to memory a certain privilege of place. It is "in the next degree to perception," being, indeed, "secondary perception." But "it is of so great moment," he asserts, "that, where it is wanting, all the rest of our faculties are in a great measure useless. And we in our thoughts, reasonings, and knowledge, could not proceed beyond present objects, were it not for the assistance of our memories" (pp. 278-279).

Thus while we must credit Locke for moving toward a somewhat less materialistic notion of memory with his concept of memory as an ability, still the basic metaphor of memory as a storehouse of previous perceptions continues to operate in the second edition. He neither overcomes the materialism of the empiricist tradition, nor does he question the common supposition of memory's derivation from perception.

David Hume

Hume's departure from Locke's position may at first seem purely terminological. For Locke's "ideas of sensation" he substitutes "impressions," reserving the term "idea" for Locke's "ideas of reflection," i.e., representations of thought, imagination, and memory. But Hume soon saw that such a conception of how we know excludes any chance of certainty in our knowledge, and this eventually led him to a skepticism not shared by Locke.

According to Hume, "all perceptions of the human mind resolve themselves into two distinct kinds, which I shall call impressions and ideas."[43] Those perceptions which enter the mind "with most force and violence," i.e., sensations, passions, and emotions, are impressions. Ideas are "the faint images" of impressions which occur in such acts as thinking, remembering, and imagining. Hume is less concerned than was Hobbes to offer any analysis of the processes by which representations of the material world enter the mind. Impressions, he rather dismissively notes, "arise in the soul from unknown causes."[44] His real concern, however, is the relation between impressions and ideas. "Every simple idea is derived from a corresponding impression."[45] All thinking, then, involves mental imagery, and the constituents of these images are, of necessity, representations of sense impressions. Both imagination and memory "borrow their simple ideas from impressions, and can never go beyond these original perceptions."[46] All imagining (and consequently all remembering) for Hume "amounts to no more than the faculty of compounding, transposing, augmenting, or diminishing the materials afforded us by the senses and experience."[47] The ideas of memory, presumably because they are more closely tied to the original impressions, are less faint, however, than other ideas. For when an earlier impression reappears and "retains a considerable degree of its first vivacity and is somewhat intermediate betwixt an impression and an idea," this is a memory.[48]

20

This, then, becomes the first criterion Hume offers to distinguish memory from imagination: (1) "The ideas of the memory are much more lively and strong than those of the imagination" (p. 7). Later on in the _Treatise_, however, he questions the very criterion he has established.

And as an idea of the memory, by losing its force and vivacity, may degenerate to such a degree, as to be taken for an idea of the imagination; so on the other hand an idea of the imagination may acquire such force and vivacity, as to pass for an idea of the memory (p. 96).

He makes a comparable volte-face regarding his second criterion, namely that (2) "The order and form of the original impressions is retained in memory alone" (pp. 8-9) for he later concedes that it is "impossible to recall past impressions, in order to compare them with our present ideas, and see whether their arrangement be exactly similar" (p. 85). Hume's third criterion for the differentiation of memory from imagination sets memory on the side of perception over against imagination and seems to be a corollary of the first. (3) "The belief or assent, which always attends the memory and senses . . . alone distinguishes them from the imagination" (p. 86). What is this belief other than what Hume earlier calls the vivacity of perceptions? He does not address this question.

In subsequent likeminded searches for memory indicators, Bertrand Russell will later conclude that we trust memory images because of their characteristic "feeling of familiarity" and "feelings of pastness";[49] and William James will hold that "the object of memory is only an object imagined in the past . . . to which the emotion of belief adheres."[50] For James, this emotion of belief seems to be comprised of "a feeling of the past direction in time: and a consequent "feeling of warmth and intimacy."[51]

Before leaving our discussion of Hume's faculty psychology, it is worth noting here two of its limiting consequences for his understanding of memory.

(1) His view implies a severe limitation on the possible objects memory can take. He writes,

Now since nothing is ever present to the mind but perceptions, and since all ideas are deriv'd from something antecedently present to

21

the mind; it follows, that 'tis impossible for us so much as to conceive or form an idea of anything specifically different from ideas and impressions.[52]

Such a limiting of the objects of memory to ideas and impressions is, of course, simply a consequence of what he understood to be the limits of human understanding and perception generally.[53]

(2) If our primary information is simply representations, and our thought simply copies of these representations, then we cannot assess the accuracy of these sense representations or form any ideas of the real world apart from our impressions of it. The result of this line of reasoning in Hume's thought is what he calls "consequent skepticism" (to distinguish it from the "antecedent skepticism" of Descartes' method of radical doubt). Hume's consequent skepticism about the certainty and extent of our knowledge of the real world is based on his examination of our mental faculties. Any belief we entertain in our reason or our memory, then, is nothing more than a natural instinct.

But since "nature by an absolute and uncontrollable necessity has determined us to judge as well as to breathe and feel,"[54] Hume decided that he could maintain his skepticism and still continue to perceive, remember, and theorize about such processes! According to Hume, however, all such philosophical theorizing is reduced to natural instinct, and philosophical judgment itself can never escape the confines of the philosopher's own subjectivity.

In hindsight, Hume's skepticism seems the virtually inevitable end-result of a way of thinking about the relationship between world and mind which we have been examining in Hobbes and Locke as well. Whatever the specific terminology they employ or the structures they posit, each is responding to an abiding philosophical problem: the search for certainty in knowledge. Such certainty is intended, of course, as a reply to philosophical skepticism. But a cardinal point of Hume's philosophy of mind is the denial of anything behind impressions and the contention that every simple idea is a copy of a corresponding impression. Thus understanding must de facto be limited to these mental contents. His conclusions can produce only skepticism, for "no justification can be given for belief in the existence of the self and an external world."[55] Our having such beliefs can be accounted for only by psychological explanations. Reason cannot justify them, since we have nothing but impressions and ideas.

The very problem of the verifiability of knowledge is a consequence of the philosophy of mind generally attributed to Descartes and evident as well in Galileo's natural philosophy, which divorces mind from body, mental experience from the external world. In his attempt to refute Descartes' rationalism, Hobbes anticipates Locke and Hume by substituting for the Cartesian dichotomous substances, two realities: the material world of body and motion and the fanciful realm of "experience." In Locke's view, all the materials for knowledge are provided by sense perception, but the extent and certainty of sensible knowledge is limited. Eventually, in Hume, the British empiricist tradition reduces all knowledge to copies of impressions. We have lost any certainty that our mental processes have the capacity to lead us to a true knowledge about the world outside the self.

The consistent version of the empiricist question regarding memory is: how can we _know_ that our memory truly refers to something in the past? And since our knowledge of the past comes to us through the faculty of memory, how can we know anything about the past? The problem of memory becomes the critical version of the problem of the possibility of certainty of any kind. The true significance of Hume's skepticism for our purposes is its acknowledgement of the failure of the empiricist tradition, and of faculty psychology generally, to resolve this question.

At this point in our discussion, it may be useful to recapitulate what faculty psychology has meant in the history of philosophy on memory. In practice, to posit memory as a single faculty of mind, with emphasis on its status as an internal mental substance, is to attend, as we have seen, to such questions as: (1) What is the nature of the faculty of memory? (2) What mental processes or entities does it involve? (3) What are its proper objects? (4) What exactly happens in the mind when I remember? The expectation, that is, is that the concept of memory has a unity disclosable by analysis. The result of such practice in the history of philosophy on memory has been the positing of a whole range of mental mechanisms to solve theoretical problems about memory. We have already seen several examples of this. In response to the problem of how it is possible that what has happened in the past can be present in memory, for example, Aristotle argues that there must be some sort of mental image, corresponding to the past reality,

23

in the remembering mind--thereby launching a centuries-long tradition of representative theories of memory. In response to the problem of how then we are to distinguish memory images from other mental images, Hume and a host of others argue for certain memory-indicators: feelings of pastness and familiarity, emotions of belief, feelings of warmth and intimacy, the saying to myself that I have experienced this before.

Among such philosophers, it seems to count for nought that our ordinary experience of remembering often-times gives the lie to such entities and processes. Presumably this is so because insofar as philosophical doctrines of memory are developed in line with general ontological and/or epistemological principles in the philosophy of mind, they tend to push beyond popular usage and ignore commonsense understandings. For this reason, it was necessary for us to sketch in something of these philosophers' epistemologies if we were to do any justice to their memory theories.

Now it has become a commonplace of contemporary philosophy to acknowledge the falsity of the notion that memory is to be understood as a single power or faculty of mind, in symbiotic relation to imagination and deri-vative from perception. Contemporary philosophy's two major alternatives to such a faculty psychology emerge from linguistic analysis and phenomenology.

Contemporary Alternatives

Linguistic Analysis

The project of linguistic analysis is to tackle and destroy the problems historically troubling philosophy by analyzing the ordinary concepts of everyday language and mundane communicative experience. This project springs from the premise that language is itself our primary reality, and there is no way beyond or behind it to the realm of pure idea (the rationalist alternative) or pure experience (the empiricist alternative). For the linguistic analyst, the nature of human being in situ is linguistic. The locus classicus of this kind of "ordinary language philosophy" is the later work of Ludwig Wittgenstein, most notably The Blue and Brown Books and Philosophical Investigations.

As regards memory, language analysis attacks faculty psychology by demonstrating that there is no unity to the concept of memory and that the search for such a unity, such a metaphysical nature, is futile. Thus its task vis-à-vis the tradition we have been examining is fundamentally analytic, systematic, and destructive. The most thorough-going of such analyses of memory to date has been done by Norman Malcolm, one of the foremost American Wittgensteinian philosophers. In Knowledge and Certainty, Malcolm offered "Three Lectures on Memory" which analyze the problem of how memory can be said to provide certainty about the past. In the more recent Memory and Mind, he offers a critical study in the philosophy of mind on memory in which he shows that the philosophical tradition has been plagued by the wrong questions about the phenomenon of memory. My own exposition of language analysis' critique of memory's treatment in the history of philosophy owes much to Malcolm's critique. In the spirit of ordinary language philosophy, however, I shall be using examples drawn from my own linguistic experience.

In his examination of the history of philosophical reflection on memory, Malcolm uncovers a certain logic in the progression of problems raised about memory; it is the logic we have already referred to in our foregoing discussion. Once we assert, as does Aristotle, that memory's proper object is the past, then we must discover how what is past can be present. Hence follows the representative or copy theory of memory. This, in its turn, raises the need to discern how memory images differ from other mental images, and the search for some infallible memory-indicator begins in earnest. An analysis of our actual use of language attacks each of these premises in turn.

(1) The object of memory. "No one would say," writes Aristotle, "that he remembers the present, when it is present." In other words, the proper objects of memory are limited to what is past. But I do indeed speak of remembering the present when it is present. On a visit to Philadelphia, I may exclaim nostalgically, "I remember this corner grocery store"; at a summer concert in the park, I may think to myself as I peruse the crowd, "I remember that couple"; when I come across an old skirt in the back of my closet, I may say, "I remember this skirt." In each of these instances, it is the present object that I am remembering.

Nor is it accurate to say that it is impossible to remember the future. I can, for example, in response to my husband's query, reassure him that I remember my next week's dental appointment. All of these examples are correct ways of speaking about memory which communicate the meaning I intend. Contrary to Aristotle, then, it is

25

incorrect to say that the object of memory is in the past. I am not, in the final example, remembering the act of having made the dental appointment, but rather that I will be going to the dentist next week. In these instances of remembering, the objects of my memory are no more in the past than they are in the future or the present; they simply cannot be assigned any temporal location.

(2) The memory image. Let us take another example which illustrates that, while memory may be accompanied by a mental image, it need not be. In response to the question, "Do you remember where you put the car keys?", I may say, "Yes, they're in the top desk drawer"; I may simply go to the study, open the drawer, and remove the keys without any comment, all the while thinking about what I am going to make for dinner; I may re-trace my steps on entering the house (either actually or imaginatively), saying as I go, "First I dropped the groceries in the kitchen, then I went to the closet to hang up my coat . . . ", and eventually open the drawer with the keys in it. I may say I cannot remember where the keys are, chastising myself all the while for my carelessness; but in my search through such likely places as the car ignition, my purse, coat pocket, various counters and drawers, eventually discover them. Some of these activities may be accompanied by images, others may not. It seems clear from this example that there is no activity per se which is proper to the remembering. The remembering does not necessarily consist in any specifiable activity, whether mental or physical.

Indeed, we may speak of remembering when no activity at all is involved. I remember Hopkins' "Felix Randal" and could, if called upon, recite it by heart. Such a reciting of the poem would not be the remembering of it, though it may prove my remembering to incredulous friends. I may remember several specific details of my religious novitiate which never arise in conversation and which I may never indicate in any way. Or I may remember one or other of them at a specific moment and simply smile to myself ruefully or sigh or tell someone about it. Often enough, memory takes the form of story telling. We may say of someone, "She has vivid memories of her childhood in Jackson, Mississippi" simply because she has so frequently told us stories about growing up there.

Imagine one further case. I cringe when I see a doberman pinscher. Perhaps I do so because of stories I have heard about them; perhaps when I was a small child a similar dog jumped on me and frightened me; perhaps I am simply not a lover of large dogs. In the first two instances, some sort of "remembering" is involved in my present reaction. But when asked why I react so negatively to dobermans, I may simply respond that they are nasty dogs and I am afraid of them.

Often we speak of remembering to indicate processes of trying to remember or of dwelling on some episode or of reliving it. Many occurrences which we call remembering, however, involve no such processes at all. I, for example, have a great memory for poetic verses and song lyrics. Given half a chance, I will sing, say, all the songs from My Fair Lady without a moment's hesitation. Such performances are not necessarily accompanied by mental images. Surely this is at least partially explained by the fact that I am not blessed with a strong visual imagination. Often for me to remember someone is not to call up a mental image of that person so much as to experience an emotion I associate with the person or with my relationship to her. We employ the word "remember" to refer to a widely diverse range of uses in our ordinary language, but this does not mean that we have only a vague or generalized understanding of what we mean by our speaking about remembering.

Part of the confusion on this question of memory images results from our having in our ordinary language various ways of picturing the process or mental state indicated by the words "memory" and "remembering." These range from what we might call the popular and metaphorical to the technical and scientific. Such usages need not purport, however, to be philosophical or physiological descriptions of actual processes.

We take memory trips, for example, and stroll down memory lane. Such spatial metaphors imply setting out from where we are toward another, previously visited place. "Memory lane" suggests, perhaps, a path lined with distinct mnemic shrubbery or a corridor of the mind where memories hang like framed pictures on walls. We speak of preserving our memories as if they were perishable fruits in tightly sealed jars or flowers pressed between the pages of old yearbooks. Notice, for example, Rainer Maria Rilke's stunning way of picturing memory in this excerpt from a letter:

When winter comes, I shall have memories, gentler, richer, and more splendid than ever. I feel that. As if I had costly fabrics in chests that I cannot open because days not yet in order stand like heavy vessels on their

lids. Sometime there will be order, and I
shall raise the lid and reach through heavy
scent for the materials which it is a festival
to unfold.[56]

Many more commonplace memory metaphors trade on this
same analogy. Our memory is like a container or
receptacle, the contents of which are memories. The
activity of remembering is like opening the container.
Thus we speak, as did Locke, of the storehouse and the
treasure chest of memory, or of the tablets of the mind
on which memories are impressed, or of memory as a camera
lens, or of memory banks, tapes, traces, and computers.
These latter images are simply the technological
equivalents of the former ones. Memory is seen as a
machine. There is no substantive difference between
memory viewed as an impression stamped on wax (the
philosophers' favorite metaphor) or as data coded into a
computer (preferred by scientists). It is simply a
matter of updated technology. We browse through picture
albums at photographs but employ sophisticated methods
for data-retrieval from computers. The more
technological our memory metaphors become, the more
emphasis we seem to place upon methods of storage and
processes of retrieval. Memory gets conceptualized
simply as access to information.

Implicit in all these metaphors is a static, substantive, and discrete notion of memory. The mnemic
contents remain unchanged from the original; what varies
is simply the mode of access to them. The trouble begins
when we make such popular metaphors into general
theories. It may be that the metaphors are influenced by
traditional philosophical understandings or vice versa;
the point at issue is that it is foolhardy to confuse
popular metaphorical speech for philosophical or physiological description of actual processes and entities.[57]

(3) The search for memory-indicators. In our previous discussion of the empiricist tradition, we
enumerated several celebrated attempts to distinguish the
image which supposedly always accompanies remembering
from other mental images.[58] Hume proposed that memory
images are livelier and stronger and are tied to the same
order and form as original impressions. Our ordinary
experience gives the lie to this proposal on both counts.
In the first case, who among us has not often found
(sometimes to our peril!) that our imaginations and
fantasies are more vivid than our memories. In the
second case, memories frequently arise by associations of
ideas, emotions, and sensations (witness Marcel's
celebrated experience with the madeleine in Proust),

quite out of their original sequence. Hume himself, of course, came to admit both points. It frequently takes a deliberate effort, such as my description above of the search for the car keys or checking one's appointment calendar, to place past events in our minds in proper sequence.

Bertrand Russell suggested that genuine memory images are accompanied by "feelings of familiarity" which lead us to trust the images and "feelings of pastness" which lead us to refer them to some time in the past. Russell offers little insight into the nature of these feelings, however. Since we often think we are remembering when we are imagining (Freud's hysterics weren't alone in this problem), feelings of familiarity and pastness cannot provide sufficiently reliable touchstones. Furthermore, if we question why it is that such feelings grant me the belief that my image is of something that occurred and the confidence that it is accurate, we can find no answer. Supposedly then, this belief is simply a natural human power. If so, why must we posit these feelings at all in our efforts to understand memory?

In his critique of these theories in the history of philosophy's concern with the nature of memory, Malcolm suggests that their fundamental error is the initial assumption that there must be an act, experience, or event of remembering which has a specifiable content. Thus we generate the picture of the memory act or memory event as a container and suggest as its contents an image of a past event. But our ordinary experience disputes this picture. Take our example of losing my keys. Suppose I ask my husband if he remembers where I left them, and, in response, he goes to the desk drawer and removes them. In this case, the most relevant thing that occurred is my husband's going into the study and getting the keys out of the top drawer. This, however, cannot be the memory act or memory event that the philosophers are looking for, because this same action can have multiple meanings. Suppose, for instance, he responds, "No, I don't have any idea where you put them," but then opens the drawer to find a pencil and discovers the keys.

Our efforts to know exactly what the phenomenon of remembering is lead us to posit either an outer or inner occurrence in which the remembering consists, but the endeavors of the memory theorists are futile precisely because there is no such decipherable inner or outer occurrence. The memory act or memory event is not something which exists, according to the linguistic analyst. As Malcolm comments,

People remember things, but nothing that
occurs, either inner or outer, is the
remembering. The question, "In what does
remembering consist?" should be answered in
this way: It doesn't consist in anything![59]

In his extensive analyses in Memory and Mind,
Malcolm is, in fact, simply being a faithful and
painstaking Wittgensteinian. Wittgenstein writes in the
Philosophische Grammatik:

If someone asked me, for example, "Have you
ever before seen the table at which you are now
sitting?", I would answer: "Yes, I have seen
it countless times." And if further questioned
I would say that I have sat at it every day for
months. . . . What act or acts of remembering
take place there? I do not see myself in my
mind "sitting every day at this table for
months." But yet I say that I remember having
done this, and I can later prove it in various
ways. Last summer too, for example, I lived in
this room. But how do I know that? Do I see
it in my mind? No. Then of what does the
remembering consist in this case? If I inquire
as it were into the ground of the remembering,
there float up in my mind separate pictures of
my earlier residence, but certainly not with
their dates. And before they have floated up,
and before I have called up in my mind various
proofs, I say correctly that I remember having
lived here for months and to have seen this
table. Remembering, therefore, is certainly
not the mental process which, at first sight,
one would imagine. If I say, rightly, "I
remember it," the most different things can
occur, and even merely this: that I say it.
And when I say here "rightly," of course I am
not laying down what the right and the wrong
use of the expression is; on the contrary, I am
just characterizing the actual use.[60]

Malcolm's project is simply an extended reflection on the
implications of Wittgenstein's comment. It implies a
radical critique of inherited theories in the history of
philosophy.

The contention of language analysis is that the
assumption of an intrinsic "memory event" is not
intelligible on close examination of our linguistic
experience. Its critique is aimed not only at the

philosophers but at contemporary scientific theories of memory as well, since these theories are deeply influenced by the philosophical tradition we have been examining. Paradoxically enough, whereas contemporary philosophy has discarded the philosophical tradition's notions of how memory works, that tradition has been preserved--albeit in a somewhat transformed manner--in contemporary scientific thinking about memory.

Contemporary psychologists and neuro-physiologists would find our discussion thus far little more than the recounting of historical curiosities. They assume that remembering requires a memory process, but that this process occurs in the brain rather than in the mind. Both viewpoints want to account for what happens when we remember, but their aims differ. In general, the history of philosophy posits mental mechanisms in an effort to explain how memory is a source of knowledge or justified beliefs. Physiological psychologists posit physical mechanisms to explain how memory responses are caused. Thus the philosophical mental mechanisms tend to be images or feelings, whereas the physical mechanisms are comprised of unconscious neural states and processes. However, these theories evidence, in Malcolm's phraseology, "a striking continuity of thought."[61] As an example, let us consider the correlation between the philosophers' memory image and the psychologists' memory trace.

The principal properties of the memory image--that it is a representation of the past experience and is identical in structure with it--are repeated in the memory trace. In The Place of Value in a World of Facts, published in 1938, Wolfgang Kohler makes this argument for such a memory trace.

What has happened in our past life could hardly co-determine our present activities unless to some extent the past were preserved far beyond the time of its occurrence. We clearly mean this when we say that events of the past become conditions of the present mental processes. Much time may pass between an original experience and the moment in which there is unmistakable evidence of its delayed effect. Some authors seem to think that we need not assume an entity which survives during the interval as a representative of that previous experience, and which becomes effective when present circumstances are favorable. They ought to realize what this view implies: a first event would influence a second, even though between the two there is an empty period, no connection and no continuity, sometimes for hours and days, occasionally for years. I should hesitate to adopt this notion which is so strikingly at odds with all our fundamental ideas of functional interdependence or <u>causation</u>.[62]

According to the principle of psycho-physical isomorphism, an experience's structural properties match the structural properties of its biological correlates. Thus, when an experience occurs, there is a simultaneous structurally identical neural state or process which establishes a trace of the experience, isomorphic both with its neural cause (the original event) and with the experience isomorphic with that cause (the remembering). So argues John Hunter in a 1971 essay published in <u>Mind</u>.

It seems reasonable to suppose that there is some correlate in our nervous system of every experience we have, that this correlate is <u>causally responsible</u> for our experiences and that the mechanism by which we remember an experience is not one of somehow storing the experience itself, but of somehow storing the neurological correlate of it.[63]

We are reminded of Hobbes' pressures and counter-pressures of nerves, strings, other membranes and heart. The physiological psychologists themselves offer analogies for this memory trace which are peculiarly familiar to anyone acquainted with philosophical reflection on memory. The trace is like "a print of a coin in wax" where the structure of the imprint matches the structure of the coin, or like "a groove in a phonograph record" which has a structural correlation with the music it records.[64] It is important to emphasize that this memory trace, about which the psychologists speak so definitively, is a theoretical construct as much as Hobbes' pressures on strings were, and not an entity or process which has been surgically discovered and identified in the brain.

Malcolm's critique of the memory trace intends to demonstrate that such a postulate springs from confused notions of causality, specifically the muddling of the notions of retention and storage. What do we mean when we say that we retain something? In ordinary language usage, we mean that we previously had it and still do. Malcolm's example is that of a woman who has retained her good looks. This usage suggests that she was previously good-looking and still is, though surely it does not imply that she has kept her good looks in storage.

Now this is not to deny, of course, that sometimes what is retained _is_ stored. But dispositions and abilities are examples of things which are retained without being stored. By their very nature, knowledge and beliefs are retained. But does memory knowledge, which is retained knowledge, **necessarily** imply storage? Although we speak metaphorically of storing something in our memory, we are not justified in taking these natural storage metaphors as proof of literal storage in memory traces.

In other words, linguistic analysis accuses the physiological theorists of simply transferring a philosophical mental mechanism to a neural one in their notion of the memory trace. Philosophical thinking, with its propositions about the constitution of memory, controls the thinking in what purports to be an empirical science. Thus scientific thinking about memory is subject to the same over-intellectualizing which characterizes the history of philosophy's treatment of memory. The result is a "mythology of traces"[65] in a field devoted to empirical research.

Linguistic analysis recognizes its relationship to the philosophical tradition as predominantly critical and destructive. On its own terms, then, we can hardly fault it for its noticeable lack of a constructive philosophical theory of memory. Its contribution to the ongoing discussion of the topic, however, must not be overlooked. To appreciate that contribution, we must see it against the backdrop of the effort to understand memory in the history of philosophical reflection which we have been tracing. Linguistic analysis comes at the end of a long and discouraging search for such under- standing. The language philosophers suggest that the heart of the trouble springs from faculty psychology itself with its presupposition that there must be a metaphysical unity to the concept of memory. By shifting the questions, by addressing itself to our ordinary experience and our ways of speaking about memory and remembering, linguistic analysis brings a _bona fide_ liberation to our reflections on remembering. Anyone who wishes to reflect philosophically on the question of memory must be attentive to and educated by its critique and take fair warning from it. We must look elsewhere, however, for a positive constructive basis for our own reflection.

Our reflection on certain neglected features of remembering arises from different, though not contradictory, interests. Contra the history of philosophy's concern with faculty psychology it is, as well, outside the linguistic philosophers' concern with the diverse uses of the terms "memory" and "remembering" in everyday life. But since my project is a description of the human activity of remembering--presupposing that human being is a self which has a world--it necessarily implies a concern with language which mediates the self-world relation.

Such a reflection on remembering must be part of a hermeneutic of human being, showing how memory is engaged in the constitution and cognition of human being. Without being either an ontology or an epistemology proper, it must be, nonetheless, properly ontological and epistemological.[66] That is, it must look at personal being as under way and as she grasps herself, in the world, cognitively, on the way. What I mean to suggest by this way of putting the issue is that memory is not simply a mode of knowing but also a way of being human; and that, therefore, the truth of memory is not merely a cognitive truth but a participation in personal being-from and being-toward.

Such language is foreign to the tradition we have been examining. It presupposes a richer sense of human time than the linear succession model which, as we have seen, dominates the history of philosophical reflection on memory. Before leaving the history, therefore, it remains to uncover the sources of this new understanding of human time and the effects it has had on our understanding of memory. For this, we must turn to the other contemporary alternative to faculty psychology, phenomenology, and to its originator, Edmond Husserl. Before doing so, however, we must examine the thought of phenomenology's great twentieth century predecessor in the philosophy of time and memory, Henri Bergson.

Henri Bergson

Bergson recommends himself to our consideration in the history of philosophy on memory not only because of his influence on Husserl's thought, but in his own right.[67] His Matter and Memory is one of the few major philosophic works on memory. In it, he deals with a central problem of modern philosophy, one which we have already had occasion to refer to in our treatment of the British empiricists, namely, what has come to be called the mind/body problem. Although this issue is implicit in much classical and medieval philosophy, it comes into

34

its own as a clearly distinguishable and pressing problem with Descartes.

For Descartes, the "Cogito, ergo sum," the self-consciousness that I exist as a thinking being, is the foundation of all knowledge, since it alone is a conviction which allows no doubt. Such spontaneous certainty is not available, however, about the material world whose existence requires proof. Even if such proof can be mustered--and Descartes goes about doing so--we cannot enjoy the kind of certainty about the material world that we have about our own thinking being. The picture which emerges from Descartes' philosophy is of a universe composed of two kinds of substances: matter and consciousness. Matter is characterized by extension in space; consciousness is non-extended and directly given in thinking. Mind and matter meet in an uneasy alliance in persons. As we have already noted in our previous discussion of British empiricism, Descartes' polarization soon gives way in one branch of philosophical reflection to a priority on matter and a reduction of mind and ideas to little more than the fanciful effect of matter in motion. The idealist alternative, which has not entered into our consideration of memory, reverses this priority.[68]

Bergson accepts neither alternative. "We maintain, as against materialism," he writes, "that perception overflows infinitely the cerebral state; but we have endeavored to establish, as against idealism, that matter goes in every direction beyond our representation of it.[69] Bergson's project in Matter and Memory is to narrow the ever-widening gulf between these two positions by uncovering aspects of each substance in the other: thought-like qualities in matter and matter-like qualities in thought. It is in this context of rapprochement that he raises the problem of memory. Ironically enough, in his effort to overcome the matter/mind split, he proposes yet another dichotomy, this time within memory itself.

For Bergson, there are two kinds of memory: habit memory, a current motor response of the body which does not represent the past but merely repeats it in response to present stimuli; and pure memory, which actually brings the past into consciousness. Habit memory is more the memory of the body, designed to ensure living organisms' adaptations to present situations. Action-oriented, it does not record the past for its own sake but rather is a purely mechanistic response to an appropriate stimulus.

The bodily memory, made up of the sum of the sensorimotor systems organized by habit, is then a quasi-instantaneous memory to which true memory of the past serves as base.[70]

It is this "true memory of the past" or "pure memory" which captivates Bergson's attention. Only human beings possess pure memory, since it is the province of the mind rather than the body. "When we pass from pure perception to memory (i.e., pure memory), we definitely abandon matter for spirit."[71] This memory, according to Bergson, records in the form of mental images all the events of daily life as they occur, providing the contents of occasions of recalling. Thus Bergson continues to understand pure memory to be representational and image-bound, and even asserts that pure memory retains our past conscious states "in the order in which they occur."[72] He goes far beyond Locke's realization of our thought's need for "the assistance of memory," however, when he asserts that "consciousness signifies, before everything, memory."[73]

In defense of his concept of pure memory as wholly spiritual, Bergson argues against any correlation of memory images with the then newly touted hypothetical memory traces in the brain. The details of his "proof" need not concern us here, but it is Bergson's contention that memory retains the whole of our past; the brain simply acts as a memory-filter, an action-oriented mechanism designed to promote forgetting rather than remembering! This seems to imply a challenge to the tradition's degradation of memory. Bergson affirms memory as a continuing presence, a superfluity of meaning.

Unfortunately, despite his self-acknowledged aim, we do not find much in Matter and Memory, however, to help us overcome the mind/body problem. His own dualism clearly emerges, though it differs from the materialists'. Whereas materialism conceptualizes in spatial terms, either identifying mind with brain activity (Hobbes) or considering it existentially dependent on that activity (Locke and Hume), Bergson conceives the relation between mind and body as temporal. To make this clear and to appreciate his real significance for our project, we must now turn to his doctrine of time and duration.

The problem of memory is closely tied to the problem of time. Since Aristotle, the notion of time undergirding discussions of memory has been the scientific, mathematical, and spatialized conception of time as linear succession. In this view, let us reiterate, the present encompasses the real, to which being attaches in a preeminent way. Past and future have no real being: the past no longer is; the future is not yet. Thus the past inhabits a "metaphysical shadow-land"[74] into which consciousness penetrates by means of memory. Time is composed of an infinite series of presents, and it is only in this instantaneous present that we really <u>are</u>.

Central to Bergson's outlook is his distinction between this kind of time and the time we actually experience. While most of our practical life is dominated by such mathematical units of time (hours, days, years), when we turn to our direct experience we find little or nothing which corresponds to this. Rather, we experience time as a flowing succession of states which blend one into the other in an indivisible process. Corresponding to his category of pure memory, Bergson calls this distinctively human time "pure time" or "real duration." It is active, concrete, and ongoing. The great mistake of Western philosophy has been to consider the spatialized mathematical time to be reality. Bergson attacks the identification of the present with being which is integral to such a spatializing of time.

> Nothing is less than the present moment, if you understand by that the indivisible limit which divides the past from the future. When we think this present as going to be, it exists not yet; and when we think it as existing, it is already past.[75]

If the present is merely that instant which divides the past from the future, it has no being of its own. But such a notion of the present, insists Bergson, is denied by our own temporal experience.

> If what you are considering is the concrete present <u>such as it is actually lived by consciousness</u>, we may say that this present consists, in large measure, in the immediate past.[76]

The <u>human present</u> (as opposed to the mathematical present) is a durational segment of dynamic time which includes within itself both past and future dimensions. It is plainly mistaken, according to Bergson, to conceive it as an instant which excludes the past and into which the past intrudes only by the faculty of memory. To abstract time in such a mechanistic way is to do violence to our actual lived experience; it is to dismember the temporal flow of our lives into static, mutually exclusive moments without duration. On the contrary, Bergson understands that the most essential aspect of lived temporality is its dynamic and durational character.

Such an understanding of time must have revolutionary consequences for our consequent theories of memory. Instead of being reduced to a mere mental or physiological faculty which transports an image of the past into present consciousness, memory becomes a constituent dimension of temporal consciousness itself, without which consciousness would not be possible. "Consciousness," asserts Bergson, "signifies, before everything, memory."

It is this intuition of the inherent connection between consciousness and memory which makes Bergson so crucial a thinker in our survey of certain prevailing paradigms for memory in the history of philosophy. What we have seen underlying that history is the tendency, evident in Aristotle and those who followed him, to reduce the present to an instantaneous point. In his insistence on human temporality's durational flow, Bergson reverses this trend.[77] Bergson, however, does not answer the question of how such a prolongation of the present is effected in and by consciousness. Our search for an answer to this question leads us to the thought of Edmund Husserl.

Edmund Husserl

Although Husserl did not devote any single work to the subject, some of his most challenging--as well as neglected--analyses are given over to the phenomenon of memory. Contemporary phenomenologists, most notably Edward S. Casey and John Brough, have begun to redress that neglect. My own discussion of Husserl's understanding of memory is heavily indebted to their work.[78]

While the phenomenological project undergirds much of my own reflection in this essay, here I shall limit myself to explicating Husserl's analysis of memory as it relates to the themes we have been tracing in memory's history in philosophical reflection. By now we can expect, for example, that what he says about memory will be built upon his understanding of time; and we shall have to see where he stands on the issue of memory's relation to perception and on the image theory of memory which is so predominant in the Western tradition.

Following Bergson, Husserl asserts that "it belongs to the essence of lived experiences to have to be spread out in such a way that there is never an isolated punctual phase."[79] He grounds this assertion in his analysis of internal time-consciousness.

Phenomenology of Internal Time-Consciousness

Husserl argues that every experience or act of consciousness is intentional, i.e., directed toward an object. All consciousness is consciousness of something. But experience is itself experienced and thus also known; i.e., consciousness is always implicitly self-consciousness as well. Memory, the consciousness of what is past, is no exception to this rule. This is not to say that in our ordinary non-reflective experience we are conscious of the act and of its object in the same way. While the object of consciousness is fully intended or thematized, our awareness of the act of consciousness is most often simply implicit or marginal. If, however, we attend reflectively and explicitly to these acts of consciousness, what we discover, according to Husserl, is the absolute flow of consciousness itself.

To distinguish such acts of consciousness from empirical objects in the world, Husserl calls them "immanent objects" or "immanent temporal unities." They are temporal in that they possess duration and run off in a succession of phases. "Every experience," he writes, "is given as something enduring, flowing, changing in various ways."[80] While time is the irreducible form of both immanent and transcendent realities, the time of the experience of the act of consciousness (as distinguished from the object of consciousness) is immanent or inner time. While the object of, for example, a memory is an event in objective time, the memory of it is a unity in the immanent time of consciousness. The two times are, however, intentionally related, since events in objective time are present to consciousness through the intentional experiences which unfold in inner time.

According to Husserl's analysis, such acts of conscious life (memories, perceptions, sensations, wishes, etc.) belong to "the layer of immanent 'contents,' whose constitution is the achievement of the absolute flow of consciousness" (p. 44). He views this time-constituting flow of consciousness as a succession of interrelated phases, one of which is actual while others have elapsed or not yet arrived. Each momentary phase has a threefold intentional structure; consciousness experiences its acts as a continuum of these phases with the "fundamental temporal distinctions:

39

Now past (future)" (p. 44). While one phase is experienced as actually now, others are experienced as just past, and still others as yet to be. Correlated with the Now phase of the act of consciousness is an actual phase of the absolute consciousness through which the Now of the act is constituted. Husserl calls this Now phase "primal impression" or "primal sensation." But this Now phase possesses a second intentional moment, which Husserl calls "primary memory" or "retention," through which the elapsed phase of the act is experienced as just past with respect to the new actual Now. What is more, the original actual phase of the ultimate flow possesses a third intentional moment, "protention," which is the consciousness of the future phases of the act. "In each primal phase, which originally constitutes the immanent content, we have retentions of preceding and protentions of coming phases of precisely this content" (p. 45). Finally, since acts of consciousness run off in immanent time, the whole process repeats itself moment after moment. A new phase will be experienced as Now (that which, the moment before, was protentional); the prior Now phase will be experienced as just past; the prior retentional phase as just past, and so on. Each act of consciousness (and remembering is no exception) is "a unity constituted in inner time through the phases of the absolute time-constituting flow with their impressional, retentional, and protentional moments."[81]

Husserl's reason, then, for claiming that "there is never an isolated punctual phase" in lived experience is supplied by his analysis of the structure of internal time-consciousness. According to this analysis, the present as an instantaneous point is overcome in one direction by "a continuous streaming backwards of every new experience" in retentional phases and overcome in the other direction by a drawing forward in protentional phases.[82] The contents of an act of consciousness sink back or down in consciousness through successive retentions until they reach imperceptibility. Consciousness' retentional and protentional phases stretch the initial moment of the act of consciousness, thus granting it duration. As we have noted above, Husserl calls the retentional structure of consciousness "primary memory": primary, in that its object is the immediate past; memory, in that it is the consciousness of something as having already happened. Because its objects are the just elapsed phases of an act presently running off for consciousness, the past of primary memory is, in Casey's words, "a past that, paradoxically, is still part of the present: it is the present-as-just-past, the present in the very process of becoming past."[83] Through primary memory, the present moment lingers in consciousness as just-having-been.

It is this three-fold intentional structure of consciousness' acts (primary impression/retention/protention) which generates what Husserl calls "the living present," a temporality rich with the sedimentations of the immediate past and intimations of the immediate future.[84] Husserl even calls retentions and protentions "the primitive, the first and fundamental, forms of the past and future,"[85] through he does not claim that they constitute past and future proper, which are temporal domains in their own right. It is this past proper which is the object of memory in the usual sense, which Husserl sometimes calls "secondary memory." Memory is a present act of consciousness; and, as such, it has the same three-fold intentional structure as other acts of consciousness. But its object is the past. "In memory we stand in the Now, in the object of memory we stand in the past Now," writes Husserl (p. 40). Our next task, then, must be to consider the relationship of retention and memory in Husserl's thought.

Retention and Memory

According to Husserl, primary and secondary memory are absolutely distinct, though inseparable, modes of consciousness. Following him, we may elaborate their distinctiveness under three headings.

(1) The first and most obvious difference between retention and memory has to do with temporal position. Whereas retention is the consciousness of the immediate past or of "the present-as-just-past," memory intends "something further past" (p. 45) which is no longer retained in consciousness, i.e., which has become so thoroughly dissociated from the present that it can only be recollected or called back to consciousness. But Husserl does admit that there are cases in which what is retained can be remembered, in which case both would have the same position vis-à-vis the Now. Since in such a case, what is retained and what is remembered coincide, difference in temporal position cannot be a sufficient criterion for distinguishing retention from memory in every case.

(2) In his painstaking analysis of "Husserl on Memory," John Brough holds that the essential distinction between retention and memory for Husserl lies in their belonging to "different dimensions of consciousness."[86] Whereas retention is a moment of the absolute time-constituting flow of consciousness, memory is a unitary

41

act of consciousness constituted by the flow. "Retention differs from memory as what is constituting differs from what is constituted."[87] As an enduring act in immanent time, remembering has the status of a relatively independent unit, while retention is simply one dimension in the threefold intentional structure of the ultimate flow of consciousness.

(3) What is more, retention and memory give their objects differently. In the retentional phase of consciousness, we "see" what is past, or better, we see the present not as Now but as elapsing. The past constitutes itself presentatively in retention which is, in Husserlian language, "ordinary consciousness of the past. . . Its being past is a Now, is something present itself" (p. 46). Memory, on the other hand, re-presents rather than presents the past. It intends the whole elapsed object of consciousness as if it were running off again for consciousness. Even if we could retain everything in our consciousness, memory would still be vital to consciousness. Retention has only a passive capacity: it "watches" our experiences recede; but memory enables us to relive our experiences representationally. It is this reliving capacity of memory which grounds our reflective capacities, since it is through memory that we can attentively run through our experiences again. The phenomenological project itself is constructed on our remembering capacities.

But if the two modes of consciousness are distinct, they are, as well, inseparable. Retention is a necessary condition of remembering in at least three ways. (1) As we have seen above, it is through retention (as well as primary impression and protention) that the objects of consciousness are originally constituted. Without such originary constituting of objects of consciousness, no memory of them would be possible. (2) In addition, without retention, the act of remembering could not be experienced, since retention is an intentional moment of the ultimate flow of consciousness through which all acts of consciousness, including remembering, are constituted. (3) Thirdly, we have noted that Husserl holds that retention, as the primary form of the past, constitutes our original sense of the past.

How then does memory elaborate the sense of the past which it inherits from retention? As an intentional experience, memory, like all other acts of consciousness, is constituted in inner time-consciousness. But, Husserl notes, "memory as such has its own intentionality, namely that of representation" (p. 46). Memory's distinctive characteristic is that it represents what is past. In this, Husserl follows Aristotle who understands memory primarily in terms of its relationship to the past. As a present act which intends the past as its object, memory contains within itself a difference in time determination.

Now the first and most obvious thing we could say about what is past is that it is <u>not</u> Now. But the past which the present act of remembering takes as its object is not only the not-Now but the no-longer-present and the having-been-present. For such an act to be possible, according to Husserl, it must be that what is remembered was once present in the same unity of time in which the memory is now actual. Put in egological terms, "what is remembered is an elapsed position of my own life, recaptured through its actually present portion."[88]

Husserl frequently refers to memory proper as "secondary memory" in order to distinguish it from retention or "primary memory." Memory is "secondary" not in importance but in the sense that it is posterior to and discontinuous with the experience we are recalling. For an act of remembering, the past must have a certain compression and closure; all its open protentions must have become fixed retentions. The past, that is, must have acquired sufficient determination and unity ("the unity of the remembered," in Husserl's phrase) to be remembered precisely as past, as "once-having-been."[89]

How is such a representation of the stably situated past accomplished in acts of remembering? As we have seen thus far in our discussion, the philosophical tradition's predominant answer to this question is the representative theory, which holds that memory's object can be known only by indirection, through the mediation of an image which is a copy of the original experience. John Brough brings forward convincing evidence to suggest that the early Husserl held such a theory, but in his later writings explicitly rejects it. Let us examine the terms on which Husserl rejects the image theory of memory and the alternative he espouses.

Rejection of the Representative Theory

Husserl rejects the traditional representative theory of memory on descriptive and logical grounds; i.e., (1) it does not account for memory as we experience it, and (2) it cuts us off from any access to the past.

(1) Suppose as I sit at my desk this morning, I remember the tennis match I saw recently. The expert

volleying between Navratilova and Graf which I immediately experience in my memory "does not pretend to be a more or less analogous image" of what I experienced last night; what is intended in my memory "is not something similar to what appears there, intended is what appears itself . . . " (p. 50). And what appears, precisely because it is not a present image of the past event, but the past event itself, is "not now present . . . it is represented" (p. 50). Only this understanding of memory and its object avoids the suppression of the temporal distance which we have seen to be one of the presuppositions of memory.

According to the image theory, memory can not be anything more than an indirect consciousness of the past, through the mediation of a present image, but reflection on our ordinary experience confirms that the consciousness achieved in remembering is a representing of the past through identity and not through mere pictorial similarity. The object of my memory (in this case, the tennis match) and what appears in my act of remembering are identical. "Memory," Husserl insists, "is not pictorial consciousness but something totally different" (p. 49).

The problem Husserl finds with the image theory is that it cannot explain memory as a direct consciousness of the past. According to the image theorists, something is perceived as present which also serves as an image of what is not present. But pictorial consciousness does not give consciousness of the object itself; it gives only the image of the past object. Memory's very sense precludes such an identification of the remembered object and the present image, for the remembered object is "by all means not given as Now" (p. 50). What we apprehend as past in memory must be really past. Thus Husserl asserts that "the past in memory's case does not mean that in the present act of remembering we make ourselves an image of what existed earlier."[90]

(2) From a logical standpoint, in excluding direct access to the past, the image theory precludes our having any idea of the past at all. If the direct and immediate object of memory is always and only present as an image, then only the present is directly experienced in consciousness. But if consciousness cannot possess the past directly, how can it possess it at all? How can we know that the present image conforms to what is past? Traditional image theorists, as we have seen, were led by this dilemma on futile searches for some "memory indicator." If it is not possible to compare the present image with the past to verify that the present image is

indeed of the past, then no access to the past is possible. If consciousness does have access to the past directly, then the image theory is an unnecessary postulate.

Husserl thinks that the image theory is a misinterpretation of memory. No image stands between the past and the present in consciousness. He is not claiming that memories never contain images, but rather that the intuition of the past itself cannot be a pictorialization. Memory must be the direct consciousness of what is past.

As we have seen, image theorists posit the image because they assume that only what is present can be directly known. If this is the case, then every form of consciousness must be or be built upon perception, for only perception gives us the present as present. All getting beyond the present is mere derivation and indirection. In denying the image theory of memory, Husserl is, mutatis mutandi, denying this assumption of memory's derivativeness from perception.

Perception and Memory

"Reproduction," Husserl writes, "is not, as Hume and the sensualistic psychologists since Hume think, something on the order of a poor imitation of perception or a weaker echo of it, but precisely a fundamentally new mode of consciousness."[91] Husserl, of course, does not deny that perception is indeed a direct consciousness of its object. His claim is that "in memory the object also appears itself" (p. 52). Whereas perception's object is present, however, memory's is past. In providing direct access to what is past, memory is a mode of consciousness sui generis and irreducible to any other mode of consciousness. Husserl thus rejects the identification of memory with perception which has been so prevalent in the tradition. How, then, are they to be distinguished one from the other, and how are they related?

In both perception and memory, objects are given directly, but they are given differently. Perception gives its object as present itself; memory gives its object as represented. According to Husserl, reproductions have "the character of itself-representation" and "memory is itself-representation in the sense of the past."[92]

While their modes of givenness differ and memory cannot be reduced to a merely pictorial or a perceptual mode, Hesserl does not deny the two acts' intimate

45

relatedness. For in memorial representation, the same object or event given perceptually in an earlier Now runs off again for consciousness, but now as past. Memory's objects are no longer there to be seen, touched, heard; they lack the "bodily presence" of the objects of perception. What is remembered is given in a "unique modification" (p. 53), the sense of which Husserl tries to convey under the category of the as if. Thus, in my memory of the recent tennis match, the volleying "comes to givenness 'as if now'" (p. 59). The difference between perception and memory is the difference between a presentational and a representational mode of givenness. Memory thus has a double intentionality. Whereas perception intends only the present object, memory intends a past act and the object of that act. Past act and past object are not intended in the same way in memory. The past act (of perception) is known only implicitly: "The perception is not meant and posited in the memory, rather its object is meant and posited" (p. 55). Presumably, however, phenomenological reflection can attend to the act itself, thus thematizing and explicitating it.

It seems clear that for Husserl memory is always memory of an earlier perception: "It belongs primarily to the nature of memory that it is consciousness of having-been-perceived" (p. 54). In Husserl's understanding, this is the case because what is remembered appears as having-been-present, and perception is the act of consciousness which constitutes the present. Thus he describes memory as "a part of present experience in which a concrete part from the st·eam of past experience of the same subject is represented."[93]

Now since an act of consciousness, once past, can never again be given originally, memory is the capacity which frees us from entrapment in the immediate present. Without memory, past experiences and their objects would be irrevocably lost to consciousness. It is through memory that I can reach back to the I which experienced the tennis match, the I which learned "Felix Randal" by heart, the I which lived a religious novitiate, the I which was frightened by a large dog. This I, writes Husserl, "is continuously identical throughout all these reproductions, identically my I, and in its past reality known to me in the present memory with a steady certainty."[94]

Our sense of personal identity, of "persistence over time as continuously the same person,"[95] requires memory. Steeped in time, consciousness' flowing phases can never be stopped, can never be preserved in living actuality.

46

Without our capacities for remembering, we would be denied access to the length and breadth of our lives.[96] Immured in the present, we would be without a self-consciousness; indeed, without a self.

Husserl's great achievement, to my mind, is to have grounded this intuition of the fundamental role remembering plays in conscious life in rigorous philosophical reflection. In his thought, remembering as a capacity and an activity of consciousness in the phenomenology of mind has at last come into its own. Far from being a mere offshoot of some more primordial act, remembering is a distinct mode of consciousness itself. As an indispensable part of time-consciousness, remembering reveals itself to be a pervasive feature of human experience. Indeed, it is part of what we *mean* by "personal identity," part of the grammar of the concept. It is not just that being a person requires rememberings; but that in describing *actual* personal life, we are describing patterns of consistency in the exercised capacities of remembering.

There is, as we have seen, little in the philosophical tradition before this century to suggest such a logic of relation between remembering and personal identity.[97] There is, however, a tradition of the *experience* of such a relation whose history parallels that of Western philosophical reflection. In our next chapter, as an antidote to the philosophical tradition's impoverishing view of memory, we shall reflect on this parallel tradition as it is articulated in a symbolic "text": the Eucharistic anamnesis of the Christian community. The practice of liturgical anamnesis has remained fundamentally unchanged by philosophical thinking about memory through the centuries precisely because it is connected with fundamental human ritual capacities.

While our reflection on the liturgical anamnesis will draw us into the internal understanding of the Christian community, we do not mean to suggest that the remembering articulated there is simply ideologically locatable and thus of limited significance. Rather, we are wagering that, precisely because of its ritual embeddedness, the liturgical anamnesis can reveal certain neglected features of remembering which, if attended to, can enrich our understanding of remembering's role in our actual personal lives notwithstanding our relationship to the Christian or any other religious tradition. Such remembering is a pervasive cultural and human phenomenon, instanced here in a peculiarly rich and suggestive case.

[1]Michael Wyschogrod, "Memory in the History of Philosophy," in Phenomenology of Memory, ed. Erwin Straus (Pittsburgh: Duquesne U. Press, 1970), p. 6.

[2]For the purposes of my discussion, I am not distinguishing between Socrates and Plato on memory.

[3]Plato Meno 81. Unless noted, all other references to the Platonic dialogues are noted in the text and are to the translation of B. Jowett, The Dialogues of Plato, (New York: Random House, 1937).

[4]As we shall see in our subsequent discussion, this is the philosophical question about memory which has daunted memory theorists for thousands of years.

[5]As John E. Thomas notes in "Anamnesis in New Dress," The New Scholasticism 51 (Summer 1977), Socrates' notion of Recollection still does not account for how we got the ideas in the first place.

[6]Frances Yates, The Art of Memory (Chicago: U. of Chicago Press, 1966), p. 37.

[7]Plato Phaedrus 275 (trans. Yates).

[8]Richard Sorabji, Aristotle on Memory (Providence: Brown U. Press, 1972), p. 37.

[9]A. E. Taylor, Plato: The Man and His Work (London, 1892), p. 339.

[10]I discuss this influence of the philosophical tradition on contemporary scientific theories of memory in the section below on linguistic analysis.

[11]While Plato does not address himself to our features of remembering explicitly, his theory of Recollection is suggestive in several ways: 1) In Recollection, we see memory as a disclosure, a way of bringing forth out of the self. This recovery of the self achieved through Recollection is provocative for our category of memory in the construction of personal identity. Indeed, psychoanalysis has borrowed the Platonic term, anamnesis, for precisely this process in therapy. 2) By not restricting memory to time, Plato opens the way to conceiving of memory in terms of a dense temporality, unrestricted to the present moment. 3) Socrates calls upon Mnemosyne, Mother of the Muses, when

he wants to tell a story in the *Euthydemus* 275: "How can I rightly narrate? . . . Like the poets, I ought to commence my relation with an invocation to Memory."

[12]There have been several attempts to reinterpret Platonic anamnesis in contemporary philosophical reflection. Among them, I have found the most thought provoking to be John E. Thomas' in "Anamnesis in New Dress," Gregory Vlastos' in "Anamnesis in the Meno," Norman Gulley's in "Plato's Theory of Recollection," I. M. Crombie's in *An Examination of Plato's Doctrines*, and F. M. Cornford's in *Principium Sapientiae*.

[13]Sorabji, p. 35.

[14]Yates, pp. 33-34.

[15]Aristotle *Physics* 219b 1-2, cited by Michael Murray, *Modern Critical Theory: A Phenomenological Introduction* (The Hague: Martinus Nijhoff, 1975), p. 165.

[16]Murray, pp. 165-166.

[17]Edward S. Casey, "Imagining and Remembering," *Review of Metaphysics* 31 (Dec. 1977):188. Thi is the basis of Heidegger's critique of Western philosophy in *Being and Time*. In the Introduction, he states: "In our process of destruction we find ourselves faced with the task of Interpreting the basis of the ancient ontology in the light of the problematic of Temporality. When this is done, it will be manifest that the ancient way of interpreting the Being of entities is oriented towards the 'world' or 'Nature' in the widest sense, and that it is indeed in terms of 'time' that its understanding of Being is obtained . . . Entities are grasped in their Being as 'presence'; this means that they are understood with regard to a definite mode of time--the 'Present'." *Being and Time*, trans. John Macquarrie and Edward Robinson (New York: Harper & Bros., 1962), p. 47.

[18]*De Anima* 432^9 9, cited by Yates, p. 32. All other references to the *De Anima* are to Yates' translation, unless otherwise noted.

[19]*De Anima* 424a, cited by Wyschogrod, p. 8.

[20]Yates, p. 32.

[21]Sorabji, p. 6.

[22]Aristotle *De Memoria et Reminiscentia* 449^b 30, trans. Yates, p. 33.

[22]Aristotle _De Memoria et Reminiscentia_ 449[b] 30, trans. Yates, p. 33.

[23]Aristotle _De Memoria et Reminiscentia_ 449[b] 30, trans. Sorabji, p. 49. Page references in text are to this translation.

[24]Casey, "Imagining and Remembering," p. 188.

[25]Wyschogrod makes this point in "Memory in the History of Philosophy," p. 10.

[26]In "Imagining and Remembering," Casey argues these points convincingly. I am greatly indebted, not only to this essay, but to all his work on the subject of remembering.

[27]I have borrowed this phrase from Norman Malcolm, _Memory and Mind_ (Ithaca: Cornell University Press, 1977).

[28]Thomas Hobbes, _Leviathan_, p. 85, cited by Casey, "Comparative Phenomenology of Mental Activity: Memory, Hallucination, and Fantasy Contrasted with Imagination," _Research in Phenomenology 6_ (1976), ed. John Sallis, p. 2. Page references in text are to this source.

[29]Hobbes, _De Corpore_, cited by R.S. Peters, _The Encyclopedia of Philosophy_, 1972 ed., s.v. "Thomas Hobbes."

[30]Hobbes, _Leviathan_, cited by Erwin W. Straus, "Phenomenology of Memory" in _Phenomenology of Memory_, p. 58.

[31]Ibid.

[32]Cited by Peters, p. 37.

[33]Hobbes, _Leviathan_, cited by Casey, "Imagining and Remembering," p. 189.

[34]Peters, p. 38.

[35]The notion of thetic commitment is Casey's in _Imagining_ (Bloomington: Indiana U. Press, 1976), p. 189.

[36]Straus, p. 59.

[37]Casey makes this point in "Comparative Phenomenology," p. 3.

[38]John Locke, _An Essay Concerning Human Understanding_, in _The English Philosophers from Bacon to Mill_, ed. Edwin Burtt (New York: Random House, 1939), p. 247.

[39]Burtt, p. 247.

[40]Locke, _An Essay Concerning Human Understanding_, in _English Philosophers_, p. 247. Citations within text are to this edition.

[41]D. G. C. MacNabb, _The Encyclopedia of Philosophy_, s.v. "David Hume," p. 76.

[42]Frederick Copleston, _A History of Philosophy_ 5 (Westminster, Md.: The Newman Press, 1964), p. 70.

[43]Hume, _A Treatise of Human Nature_, cited by MacNabb, p. 76.

[44]Ibid., p. 77.

[45]Ibid.

[46]Hume, _A Treatise_, ed. Selby-Bigge (Oxford: Oxford U. Press, 1955), p. 85. Unless noted, references in the text are to this edition.

[47]Hume, _An Inquiry Concerning Human Understanding_, ed. C. W. Hendel (Indianapolis: Bobbs-Merrill, 1955), p. 27.

[48]Hume, _A Treatise_, I, 1, 1, cited by Malcolm, p. 18.

[49]Bertrand Russell, _Analysis of Mind_ (London: Allen & Unwin, 1921), p. 161.

[50]William James, _Principles of Psychology_ (New York: Diver, 1950), p. 652.

[51]James, pp. 650-651.

[52]Hume, _Treatise_, cited by Malcolm, p. 19.

[53]This is Malcolm's point in _Memory and Mind_, p. 19.

[54]Cited by MacNabb, p. 83.

[55]_The Encyclopedia of Philosophy_, 1972 ed., s.v. "Empiricism," by D. W. Hamlyn, p. 502.

[56]Rainer Maria Rilke, _Letters, 1892-1910._

[57]This thesis is implicit in all that Malcolm says in Part II of Memory and Mind. Cf. discussion below of memory traces.

[58]Recently, image theories of memory have been attacked, most notably by Husserl (see discussion below). In the history of philosophy on memory, such "realist" or "direct awareness" theories have been rare, indeed; and they have not been accompanied by any thorough-going constructive analyses. Recent proponents of direct awareness theories of memory include Thomas Reid in Essays on the Intellectual Powers of Man, Samuel Alexander in Space, Time and Deity, and William Earle in "Memory," Review of Metaphysics 10 (Sept. 1956).

[59]Malcolm, Memory and Mind, p. 53.

[60]Ludwig Wittgenstein, Philosophische Grammatik, cited by Malcolm, p. 12.

[61]Malcolm, p. 168.

[62]Wolfgang Kohler, The Place of Value in a World of Facts (New York: Liveright, 1938), pp. 234-235.

[63]John Hunter, "Some Questions about Dreaming," Mind 80 (1979), p. 71.

[64]Malcolm, p. 179.

[65]Malcolm, p. 199.

[66]I have borrowed this way of putting things from Ray Hart, Unfinished Man and the Imagination (New York: Herder and Herder, 1968), p. 182.

[67]Husserl was not familiar with Bergson's philosophy of time when he prepared his own lectures on time in 1905 and 1910, published by Heidegger a quarter of a century later as Vorslesungen zur Phanomenologie des inneren Zeitbewusstseins. But in 1911, when Alexander Koyre brought word of Bergson's philosophy to the Gottingen Circle, Husserl is said to have exclaimed: "We are the true Bergsonians." Indeed, Max Scheler was the one who persuaded a German publisher to start publishing Bergson's work in German (Cf. H. Spiegelberg, The Phenomenological Movement: A Historical Introduction. Vols. I & II. The Hague: Martinus Nijhoff, 1960, pp. 119, 236, and 399).

[68]For a discussion of Kant, see chap. 6 of this essay.

[68] For a discussion of Kant, see chap. 6 of this essay.

[69] Henri Bergson, Matter and Memory (New York, 1911), p. 235.

[70] Ibid., p. 197.

[71] Ibid., p. 313.

[72] Ibid., cited by T. A. Goudge, The Encyclopedia of Philosophy, s.v. "Henri Bergson," p. 289.

[73] Ibid., cited by Goudge, p. 288.

[74] Wyschogrod, p. 18.

[75] Bergson, Matter and Memory, p. 193.

[76] Ibid., p. 194.

[77] The other significant thinker for this reversal is the American William James, who had a direct influence on Husserl's phenomenology of internal timeconsciousness (cf. Spiegelberg, pp. 111-116). In the interests of economy and the pattern of development I have been following in this survey, I have excluded James from my discussion. See William James, Principles of Psychology.

[78] See particularly John Brough's essays on "The Emergence of an Absolute Consciousness in Husserl's Early Writings on Time-Consciousness," in Man and World 5 (Aug. 1972), pp. 298-326, and "Husserl on Memory," The Monist 59 (1975-1976), pp. 40-62; and Edward S. Casey's Imagining: A Phenomenological Study, "Comparative and Phenomenology of Mental Activity," "Imagining and Remembering," "Imagining and Remembering: In Time and Beyond Time" (an unpublished paper).

[79] Husserl, The Phenomenology of Internal Time-Consciousness, trans. James S. Churchill (Bloomington: Indiana U. Press, 1964), p. 70, modified by Casey, "Imagining and Remembering," p. 200.

[80] Husserl, Zur Phanomenologie des Inneren Zeitbewusstseins (1893-1917), ed. Rudolf Boehm, Husserliana, Band X (The Hague: Martinus Nijhoff, 1966), p. 127, cited by Brough, "Husserl on Memory," p. 43. Unless noted, references in text are to Brough's citation of this edition.

[81] Brough, p. 45.

[82] Casey, "Imagining and Remembering," pp. 200-201.

[83] Ibid.

[84] Ibid., p. 201.

[85] Husserl, _Analysen zur Passiven Synthesis_ (The Hague: Martinus Nijhoff, 1966), p. 326, cited by Casey, "Imagining and Remembering," p. 201.

[86] Brough, p. 45.

[87] Ibid.

[88] Brough, p. 42.

[89] Casey, "Imagining and Remembering," p. 203. Husserl's phrase is from _The Phenomenology of Internal Time-Consciousness_, p. 80.

[90] _The Phenomenology of Internal Time-Consciousness_, p. 84.

[91] Husserl, _Passiven Synthesis_, p. 325.

[92] Brough, p. 52.

[93] Husserl, _Passiven Synthesis_, p. 353.

[94] Husserl, _Passiven Synthesis_, p. 310, as cited by Brough, p. 56.

[95] Casey, "Imagining and Remembering," p. 194.

[96] Brough, p. 61.

[97] For a brief discussion of the empiricist tradition's interest in the connection between memory and personal identity, see chap. 5 of this essay.

CHAPTER II

EUCHARISTIC ANAMNESIS: REMEMBERING

AS A FORM OF LIFE

I have selected an early text, the Great Eucharistic Prayer from the Roman liturgy of Hippolytus (written down circa A.D. 215) to initiate my reflection on remembering. Following the presentation of the text of the prayer, I shall comment about my selection.

1.   We render thanks to you, O God, through your beloved child Jesus Christ, whom in the last times you sent to us as saviour and redeemer and angel of your will;

2.   who is your inseparable Word, through whom you made all things, and in whom you were well pleased.

3.   You sent him from heaven into the Virgin's womb; and conceived in the womb, he was made flesh and was manifested as your Son, being born of the Holy Spirit and the Virgin.

4.   Fulfilling your will and gaining for you a holy people, he stretched out his hands when he should suffer, that he might release from suffering those who have believed in you.

5.   And when he was betrayed to voluntary suffering that he might destroy death, and break the bonds of the devil, and tread down hell, and shine upon the righteous, and fix the limit, and manifest the resurrection,

6.   he took bread and gave thanks to you, saying, "Take, eat; this is my body, which shall be broken for you." Likewise also the cup, saying, "This is my blood, which is shed for you;

7.   when you do this, you make my remembrance."

8.   Remembering therefore his death and resurrection, we offer to you the bread and the cup, giving you thanks because you have held us worthy to stand before you and minister to you.

9.   And we ask that you would send your Holy Spirit upon the offering of your holy Church; that, gathering them into one, you would grant to all who partake of the holy things (to partake) for the fullness of the Holy Spirit for the confirmation of faith in truth;

10. that we may praise and glorify you through
your child Jesus Christ, through whom be glory
and honour to you, to the Father and the Son
with the Holy Spirit, in your holy Church, both
now and to the ages of ages. (Amen.)[1]

This _Apostolic Tradition of Hippolytus_ is the single
most important source of information we possess on the
liturgy of the Church before the fifth century, for it
contains the earliest surviving text of a Eucharistic
Prayer which has not been extensively revised. Dom
Gregory Dix even suggests that the general structure of
the first part was an inheritance from the days of the
Jewish apostles in Rome.[2] The prayer represents the local
tradition of Rome at the time of Hippolytus and is
regarded by liturgical historians as an individual
specimen rather than an invariable form, though even as
such it has been influential in our own period's
liturgical renewal. Among the reasons for this are that,
according to Dix, the prayer is "tidier" in arrangement,
more logical in its sequence, less confused by later
inessentials, and more theological and precise in its
language about the Eucharistic action than any other
early texts still extant.[3] Thus it has become a "model"
prayer, for it shows the structure of praying
eucharistically.

I have selected it not only because of its early
dates and these qualities, but because the very spareness
of its expression makes it a more manageable text for our
discussion. Other liturgies (the St. James and the
Clementine, for example) offer much lengthier
elaborations of the anamnesis, but focusing on the com-
paratively spare Hippolytan text will allow us to make
the case more cogently for the features of Eucharistic
anamnesis adumbrated below.

Before turning to the discussion of these features,
I must make one other caveat. Even though we shall be
working with the prayer-language of the Eucharist, we
must never lose sight of the fact that the Eucharist is
not only or even primarily language. Since the Eucharist
is liturgical worship, the "text" comprises both words
and actions. As ritual activity, the Eucharistic words
and actions are ingredient in each other's logic and must
always be taken together. From the start, then, we must
have in mind that the Eucharistic "text" includes this
larger reference.

In theological discourse about liturgy, the word
anamnesis used in a technical way refers to the prayer
within the Eucharist which follows the consecration of

58

the bread and wine and in which specific attention is called to remembering. In our text, this begins at #8 above: "Remembering therefore his death and resurrection, we offer to you the bread and cup, giving thanks to you. . ." But historians of liturgy and liturgical theologians agree that this self-consciously anamnetic utterance in the Eucharistic discourse expresses the meaning of the entire action. In it the significance of the liturgical action is gathered or re-collected into a focus. The whole Eucharistic action is anamnetic; the Great Eucharistic Prayer is its privileged essential and enacted expression. It is the anamnesis which makes explicit the meaning of the Eucharist in all the various liturgies, for it is here that the Church declares what it is doing when it celebrates. Thus as Jungmann notes, "It is precisely the anamnesis . . . which is the fundamental form of the actual liturgy of the Mass."[4] In his study of The Eucharistic Memorial, Max Thurian reiterates this understanding:

> The anamnesis has its special place in the eucharistic prayer after the words of institution, but the memorial must not be restricted to this alone. Indeed the whole eucharistic prayer is a memorial.[5]

Dom Gregory Dix shows in his classic historical study of the Eucharist how the understanding of Eucharist as anamnesis is clearly brought out in all the traditions of the liturgy since the patristic period, even in those liturgies which do not include a specific anamnetic prayer.[6] To focus our attention on the anamnesis, then, is to attend to the very heart of the liturgical action. We can best comprehend the Eucharist as a single, continuous, whole action performed in response to Christ's command to "Do this as my anamnesis." It is, fundamentally, the anamnesis of his redeeming action.

Before going any further in our discussion, we must give our attention to this word "anamnesis." Our English translation of anamnesis, by way of the Latin noun memoria, as remembrance, commemoration, or memorial, does not adequately embrace the Greek participial term. Already we find ourselves hampered by a fallacious substantizing tendency, for memorial connotes something which is past and absent now brought to mind, whereas in the Greek anamnesis conveys the re-calling or re-presenting of something not as absent but as presently operative by its effects.

The Hebrew root ZKR (of which anamnesis is the translation) appears in both Old and New Testaments with this public quality, this sense of activity and of presence. As C. Spicq says, "Anamnesis is not any sort of remembrance, either subjective or entirely inward, but a recalling: a manifestation--by word or deed--which compels the recalling of the past."[7] As it is used in the Scriptures, anamnesis means recalling or representing before God a past event so that it becomes alive and active in the here and now.[8] The Hebrew ZKR is connected with the name of God (Pro. 10:17, Jb. 18:17, Ps. 134 (135):13), and is inseparably linked with activity (Nm. 15:40, Ps. 102(103):18). It occurs as well in discourse about memorial sacrifice (Lv. 24:7, Nm. 10:10), the covenant (I Chr. 16:17-18, Ex. 6:5-6), and the Pasch (Ex. 12:14, Dt. 16:1-3). In Biblical usage anamnesis involves a real presence--of God to God's people or of the people to God. The believer prays and offers sacrifice so that God may remember her, i.e., see her with a view which encompasses her whole identity. And God requires that the people remember by re-enacting earlier Divine manifestations so as to experience them anew in their power, presence, and effects.

This placing before God in prayer is never a merely subjective or private recollection. Nor is Biblical prayer a simple grateful apprehension of God's blessings. Rather, it is precisely an anamnesis of the Lord's wonderful works. To do the anamnesis of the Lord's actions in the lives of the people is at once to praise God and to ask that God's blessings be renewed. In the Scriptures, then, to pray means to do anamnesis, to remember in the hope that God too will remember to have mercy. If we are to understand Eucharistic anamnesis, we must first of all see it within this framework of liturgical piety and prayer both in the Hebrew Scriptures and in Judaism.

We must relate it as well to the larger context of ritual activity. The Greek term "anamnesis" is part of the mystery cult lexicon in Hellenist and Roman religious life.[9] Indeed, we can trace anamnesis in the history of ritual activity throughout widely divergent times and cultures. Taking our lead from comparative religionists, we find that the word "anamnesis" has a history of embeddedness in ritual discourse long before it is used in Christian liturgy. In these varied contexts, anamnesis invariably carries with it the sense of an activity of remembering--performatory and public--which belies the apparent pastness of the past, and which provides the past access to the lived present. Eucharistic anamnesis, like all ritual remembering, represents, presents, and makes present. We shall examine below this mode of temporality peculiar to anamnesis; here we must elaborate somewhat further its logic as ritual _activity_.

To focus on the logic of anamnesis as ritual is to suspend the more familiar ontogenetic version of the question of the relationship of myth and ritual, a version which is, fundamentally, the question of the origins of language. We are not interested here in how we _got_ to the concept of anamnesis, but in what it _is_ to "remember" in the full sense of anamnesis. We start where we already find ourselves: within language. We discover ritual activity to be languaged. To understand the logic of ritual anamnesis, therefore, is to understand how it is already hooked up with certain ways of perceiving and speaking about our experiences--with certain narratives and certain emotions, for example. It is to understand how this activity is connected with a whole way of being in the world. The grammar of liturgical anamnesis is already embedded in experiences and practices. Since anamnesis' meaning is dependent on its use--that is to say, its uniform relation to certain circumstances--understanding it means understanding a whole "form of life." Liturgical anamnesis needs to be explored in a context of specific life-use. We will discover how it means only by discovering this logic. Even, and perhaps particularly, in a ritual context, remembering is first of all a human activity, intimately and inextricably bound up with the shape of our human lives. In order to elaborate this logic of the Eucharistic anamnesis, let us consider its most salient features: (1) its narrativity, (2) its imaginal matrix, (3) its constituting character for the worshipping community, and (4) its temporality. This list is particularly striking when it is compared with the dominant themes in the history of philosophical reflection on memory.

Narrativity

How is it that the Eucharistic anamnesis re-presents the past? Notice in our Hippolytan text that the anamnesis is spoken in the context of a _narrative_. The first aspect of anamnesis which strikes me is precisely this: that Eucharistic remembering is not simply an interior state of mind but is enacted by a community, and that this activity involves, among other things, telling stories. Indeed, narrative is the only way Eucharist takes place. This giving thanks cannot be done without narrative forms of remembering. What one remembers in the activity of anamnesis is already story-shaped. Let us linger in reflection on these two dimensions of anamnesis' narrativity: its active quality and its narrative density.

Discovering a close connection between the activities of remembering and narrating initially comes as a surprise. Our commonsense understanding of each activity hardly suggests a relationship between them. To make the further claim that, at least in the case of the Eucharist, such a connection is inherent in the activities' logic must seem startling indeed. But here the Latin roots are instructive. I suggest that they offer some sound etymological ground for drawing out this interconnection. The etymologies for our English words for narrate and remember are the Latin _narrare_ and _memorare_. In Latin, these infinitives are synonymous. Both translate "to narrate, to tell a story." _Narrare_ means "to make known; hence, to relate, to tell, to narrate"; _memorare_, "to mention, call to mind, recount, relate (a story)."[10] Etymologically, then, _memorare_, far from referring to some totally inner mental process or state, involves a telling--and a peculiar kind of telling at that. The Latin term suggests that to remember actually implies telling a story. This aspect of anamnesis is implicit in the name traditionally applied to the words of institution in the Great Eucharistic Prayer, the "institution narrative." The term "institution narrative" well serves to gather under one rubric several aspects of liturgical anamnesis, even though liturgical theologians tend to refer to the "institution narrative" without attending to its narrativity at all.

Granted that the Eucharistic anamnesis re-presents the past as a narrative, then we may ask, what story does the anamnesis tell? We notice that Eucharistic anamnesis is, indeed, directed toward a specific story, the Last Supper event. The Last Supper narrative stands at the core of the entire Eucharistic action (6-7). But keeping in mind that our "text" is composed of actions as well as words, we notice that the activity of the Last Supper narrative is not simply in the telling--the words are accompanied by a series of mimetic gestures as well. Indeed, the most clearly mimetic gestures in the entire rite are these representations of the Last Supper event. While telling the story of Christ's actions at the Last Supper, the celebrant performs such actions as blessing and breaking the bread, blessing the cup, and sharing the bread and cup with the community gathered around a table, consciously imitating the very actions described in the narrative and elaborated in the scriptural accounts of the Last Supper and the post-resurrection meals.

While it is certainly true, as Dix assumes throughout his study, that the Last Supper is the source rather than the exact model for the liturgical performance, the rite does have nonetheless this distinctive mimetic quality. The change from the Apostolic practice of eucharistizing within the context of a supper to the sparer rite with which we are still familiar, rather than excluding the mimetic dimension, actually serves to heighten it by restricting it to the heart of the liturgical action. It also serves to correct a common misapprehension about mimesis. Far from being a mere slavish repetition of the past, mimesis is a creative presenting again.

In its commingling of narrative and enactment, the Eucharistic liturgy reveals once again its nature as ritual activity. Because myth and rite are ingredient in each other's logic, the story is embodied. Nor is the rite mute; rather, there are always narratives which convey its meaning and consecrate its efficacy. It is not that the ritualized remembering is one way of connecting the story with the rite but that anamnesis is the logic of this interdependence. Ritualizing means recalling the past in its narrative shapeliness; we name this mimetic enactment anamnesis. Conversely, we may question whether there could be anamnesis without this mimetic dimension, gestures to embody the storied action which is the ground and source of the making present. Liturgical anamnesis is re-membering, a word in the lexicon of ritualization to which I want to grant more latitude than mere mental process. Part of Eucharistic anamnesis' peculiar richness for our purposes is just this challenge it presents to our Western philosophical predilection for mind/body bifurcations with its concomitant reduction of memory to an exclusively mental act.

To affirm the mimetic quality of Eucharistic anamnesis is not necessarily to grant it priority over the narrative dimension. In the history of the Eucharist, mimesis is subordinated to the anamnetic narrative. When the mimetic dimension of the liturgy grows disproportionately strong, it has consistently been pruned for the sake of anamnesis.

Let me summarize my first conclusion about anamnesis' narrativity, its active quality. The Eucharistic anamnesis is constituted by the very act of narrating with its attendant gestures, and not merely by the prayers which articulate its meaning. It is by reproducing the actions of Jesus and the receptive response of his apostles at the Last Supper, within the context of the narrative, that the Church accomplishes the anamnesis. This is not to suggest, however, that the Eucharist simply mimes the Last Supper event. The mimesis includes within itself the Church's conception of who Jesus is after the resurrection.

We miss the point of the Eucharistic liturgy if we limit the anamnetic narrative to the Last Supper event. Attending to the Great Eucharistic Prayer's narrative thickness and scope, we discover a condensation of story layers. Among these narrative strata, let us briefly reflect upon the following four.

(1) The narrative is not restricted to telling the Last Supper event, for that event self-consciously recollects and represents the Jewish liturgical traditions of Pasch and Atonement, liturgical events which themselves have a narrative configuration. Jesus' words and actions at the Last Supper have a liturgical character as _recapitulations_ of the history of God's saving action in the lives of the chosen people. In Judaism, God is present both in originary historical events and in the rituals which commemorate them.

The Last Supper event stands in peculiar relationship with this liturgical tradition. In the Christian understanding, it neither abolishes nor merely repeats the Jewish Pasch; it brings it to fulfillment. The activity of bringing to fulfillment, however, presupposes that what is fulfilled is contained within the fulfillment. Liturgical discourse, we might say, discovers itself already embedded in a tradition which furnishes its key paradigms in the form of stories (as well as images, symbols, metaphors, etc.). To follow the Last Supper story is, first of all, to follow the story which that event was remembering.

The Last Supper event was itself grounded in a way of hearing and speaking (and thus of understanding, feeling, imagining, and remembering) for which Scripture provided an orientation in its key narratives. Those narratives, together with the Last Supper narrative, form warp and woof of our liturgical remembering. We cannot know the meaning of the Last Supper event without knowing the meaning of the events which precede it. Following that story requires following the stories within which it finds its shape.

(2) What is more, as the Hippolytan text makes clear, the narrative of the Last Supper event fans out to embrace a more comprehensive narrative of Christ's own Pasch, his dying and rising action which is symbolically represented in the Last Supper action (8). In this

sense, the Last Supper is a peculiar kind of "remembrance forward": Jesus symbolically enacts a story which he is about to enact in his passion and death.

(3) But to do the anamnesis of Christ's death and resurrection is to do the anamnesis of the entire redemptive action of Christ. In the phrase "my anamnesis" the possessive must be understood as an objective genitive, i.e., "the anamnesis of me." Those gathered do the anamnesis of the person of Christ, the fullness of his offered self always being accepted by the Father. The Son's historicity, his proclamation of the Good News in his historical circumstances, his acceptance of its consequences for his own being to the point of offering himself as sacrifice--these are all his anamnesis, his life story.[11]

(4) If the narratives in which the anamnesis finds itself embedded are radically historical, they are not exclusively so. Notice in our text how the historical events find their place within a yet more comprehensive narrative framework which stretches beyond time itself in its remembering (1-3). Indeed, it is the whole history of salvation, of God's saving will for humanity, which comprises the story. That story has such paradigmatic power that all other stories (including the believer's own, as we shall discuss below) mean from it. It is less a story which believers tell than a story by and in which they are told.

If we move from our Hippolytan text to a comparison of various liturgical texts, we find verification of this significance of the narrative dimension of anamnesis. In some Eucharistic prayers, only the Last Supper, death, and resurrection of Christ are told; others include various other mysteries in the history of salvation. Some, like our own, gather into their narrative sweep a remembering before and beyond time. In the Addai and Mari Anaphora and in the liturgy of St. Mark, for example, the story of God's creation of all the orders of being is elaborated; the liturgy of St. James places emphasis on the creation of human beings from the earth in God's image and on life before the fall. The Anaphora of Basil makes explicit mention of the serpent and the fall. Both James and Mark include the giving of the Law and the age of the prophets in their narratives. Like our Hippolytan text, the liturgy of St. James gives an account of the virgin birth; and, while Hippolytus mentions only the death and resurrection of Christ, Basil and others include the ascension, his being seated at the right hand of the Father, and the second coming. It is noteworthy that, in the Eucharistic liturgy, anamnesis is

directed not merely toward events which happened in the
past, not even toward events which are beyond the world's
history. Paradoxically, it embraces within itself, as
well, future events.

The choice of events included within the Eucharistic
narrative is not unrelated to the particularized meaning
of a given Eucharistic celebration. A Eucharistic Prayer
which includes Jesus' nativity as part of its story
engenders different theological meanings and religious
dispositions, for example, from one which emphasizes such
transcendent events as the transfiguration and the
ascension. Such particular emphases often form the basis
of the proper prayers for specific liturgical feasts.
This is a point, once again, about the logic of the
rite's narrative matrix. On the other hand, what this
narrative variation reveals is that, whatever separate
events in the life of Christ and the history of God's
relationship with humanity are told, the anamnesis
remembers the whole mystery of Christ. To do anamnesis
is to be plunged into this mystery of salvation made
present and active here and now in the Eucharist.

In summary, shall we say then that what is re-presented in the Eucharistic anamnesis is a narrative? But
this way of putting it does not comprise all we have been
claiming for anamnesis' narrativity. Should we not
rather say, in the light of our discussion, that the very
re-presenting has a narrative shape, indeed, that to do
anamnesis is to narratize? The activity of narrating
constitutes Eucharistic anamnesis. To speak of
Eucharistic anamnesis as narratizing, however, is to be
drawn into a second feature of this remembering: its
imaginal matrix. To understand the liturgical anamnesis
we must keep in mind the distinction between an event
which merely occurs and an event which is told.
Narratizing is a poetic act.

Imaginative Qualities

At the outset we must confront an objection. Isn't
the claim that narratizing is a poetic act an extravagant
overstatement of the case? Our commonsense
understanding, while granting that certain kinds of
narratives are poetic or imaginative (most notably
fiction), would hold that others patently are not (most
notably history). Fictional narratives are invented,
whereas historical narratives report what actually
happened. But, according to this disclaimer, isn't the

narrative in which Eucharistic anamnesis is grounded purportedly the report of an actual historical event or series of events, of which we have written documentation in the Scriptures? Following this reasoning, our claim for the imaginal matrix of the Eucharistic anamnesis seems unjustified.

I want to bracket this question of where to locate Scripture's truth claims on a continuum which runs the gamut from history to fiction and focus on two other claims already implicit in the above paragraph. The first is that history is a species of narrative; the second, that all narratizing (including history) is a process of imagination. If these two claims are justified, then whatever our position on the nature of Scripture's truth claims, we will have made the case of Eucharistic anamnesis as an imaginative activity. To clarify this role of imagining in the Eucharistic anamnesis, I shall reflect upon two features which reveal themselves in a phenomenology of narrative discourse and which we have already discovered to be ingredient in our liturgical text, one at the level of sense (plot), the other at the level of reference (mimesis).

Mythos or Plotting

Let us return to the distinction mentioned above between an event which merely occurs and that event as told.[12] The formal character which fiction and history share lives in that gap; they both have a narrative structure. The historian works in that great gulf between what happened in the past and what is historically known. She does not merely tell a story, but by imaginative reconstruction makes a set of events into a story. Historical explanation proceeds not by formal argument but by emplotment. To be historical an event must be more than a single occurrence; it must contribute to the development of a plot.[13] The singular event receives its definition from its interpolation into a discourse already displaying narrative form in its sequentiality and its particular directedness. This is a feature of narrativity which history shares with all other forms of narrative. In the institution narrative of Hippolytus, for example, Jesus' actions at the Last Supper are woven into a narrative texture. Emplotted, they achieve their narrative thickness and scope at least partly because of their placement within a sequence of events and experiences which, for all their apparent contingency, reveal a teleological movement. In historical narratives, events are made into a story through a process and yet claim to be representative of reality.

This implies a further sense in which an event which is told differs from an event which simply occurs. Telling a story involves a series of choices. We do not need a day in which to recount a day's events; rather, story-telling includes activities of selecting, shaping, and structuring. Many different stories can be shaped from the same set of events. The episodes in Christ's life are highly selected in our Hippolytan text. While some actions are elaborated (5-7), others are telescoped (4, 8). Still others which do not even appear in this liturgy are included, as we have seen, and even highlighted in other texts. Indeed, we can make a theological point on the basis of this dimension of plotting. A comparison of liturgical texts reveals, on the one hand, that selectivity enhances particular aspects of the mystery of Christ, thus shaping the dispositional life of the believer in specific ways; and on the other, that no matter which episodes are included in the Great Eucharistic Prayer, what the narrative intends is the whole mystery of Christ. If this is true in even the spare narrative of the Hippolytan liturgy, how much more so of the four gospel narratives. In both cases, not only is there selectivity of episodes, but events are at the service of a larger shaping. Explanations are included in the story-telling as legitimations of the movements the narrative makes--they help us to follow the story to its conclusion. Explanations, that is, function within a narrative discourse, and not, for example, within a scientific or philosophical one. These kinds of choices, evident in the liturgical text and common to historian and fiction-writer alike, are activities of the imagination.

By virtue of the plot, all narratives combine in various proportions chronological and non-chronological dimensions.[14] Plotting is, first of all, bound to a chronological order. Our Hippolytan text is episodic and sequential. It draws upon our competence in following stories, satisfying our expectations that certain contingencies will affect the development of certain outcomes. Far from a random act, plotting follows a logic of procedure which is grounded in our historical condition. Christ's passion is narrated in a sequence which carries us from beginnings to endings. Events of conception, birth, suffering, and death occur in ordered succession. Both the specific episodes of the Last Supper and the more comprehensive events in the narrative are bound to this chronological sequence.

But the activity of telling a story does not consist in the mere piling up of selected episodes in chronological sequence. To tell a story is to establish a relationship among the episodes, to grasp them together, to lift up some significance out of the plurality. To follow a story is to elicit a configuration from the succession, to relate episodic parts to meaningful wholes. Indeed, narrative structure discovers its essence in this paradoxical competition between sequence and pattern. Our capacities to tell and follow stories are rooted in our capacities to reflect upon events and to perceive their teleological structure. In Wittgensteinian terms, it is this imaginative activity of emplotting which grounds the family resemblance in the language games of historical and fictional narration.

By pulling together two modes of narrative discourse (history and fiction) which are commonly contrasted and by showing their underlying consistency in the notion of emplotment, we have answered the voice of objection raised at the outset of this discussion. At the level of sense, liturgical anamnesis reveals itself to be an imagining activity by virtue of its narrative structure. But we have not yet addressed the further question of what is distinctive about liturgical anamnesis within the range of narratizing genres. Into which sub-category of narrative does liturgical anamnesis fit? Let us return to this question, bracketed above, by inquiring into the kind of remembering activity which goes on in the Eucharistic narrative. I have claimed that in Eucharistic anamnesis to remember is to narratize and that narratizing involves imagining. What, precisely, is the character of the remembering which happens in the liturgical anamnesis? What is the believing community doing when it says "we remember"?

If we turn to the standard typologies of memory offered by philosophy and experimental psychology alike, we find meager clarification of our case. They ordinarily distinguish two major types of memory: factual (remembering how or remembering that) and personal (remembering from my own historical past). Neither category comprises the activity of liturgical anamnesis. The believing community is certainly doing something other than merely calling to mind that or how Christ suffered and died; and it is not simply remembering an event from its own historically experienced biography. For a third option, and one more attuned to the role of imagining in anamnesis, we must look beyond these traditional distinctions toward the work of myth/ritual theorists and depth psychologists of the Jungian persuasion. Perhaps Eucharistic anamnesis'

69

peculiar character is more akin to other ritual anamneses which remember a time before and beyond time, an immemorial past that is not restricted to one's own personal experiences. As in Plato's anamnesis, this past is beyond collective as well as personal history; it is pre-historical. Such remembering is mythic in status; its content impersonal or pre-personal. In mythic anamnesis we recollect the archaic immemorial past from the imagining of archetypal presences.[15] A narratizing and a remembering which is mythic in status offers us a third option on our history/fiction continuum, an option which presses beyond our historicity toward our archaeological and teleological directedness.

Indeed, there is something of this in our Hippolytan text, for we are invited explicitly to remember a time before the beginning and after the end, a first and last time, the time of God. On the other hand, any such purely ahistorical archetypal anamnesis is precluded by the very historical character of Christianity. In liturgical anamnesis, remembering intends actual historical events. Whether we inquire into the kind of remembering which happens in Eucharistic anamnesis or into the kind of narrative discourse which the Eucharistic anamnesis is, the available typologies prove inadequate for our inquiry. We have, indeed, surrendered the whole scope of personal memory to the scientists who narrowly define the personal as an event witnessed by me. In the Eucharistic anamnesis we discover a peculiar mix which transcends the easily adumbrated sub-species of remembering and narrative discourse ordinarily open to us.

Liturgical anamnesis makes special claims, for while its narratized remembering takes an historical object, it is not related in an objective way. Its purpose is not simply the re-enactment of historical knowledge. Nor does it simply move away from the empirical toward the fictional or mythic. The event for believers is not simply constituted, that is, by the set of historical events in Christ's life which are narrated, for these events are the founding events of the community so comprised. The event, as a communal speech-event, is inseparable from its telling. The Eucharist tells the story of a community which makes sense of its existence as a community by telling and doing the story. The narrative's life-use presupposes a training in imaginative discourse. It is by sharing the tradition which was created by this narrative telling and doing that believers re-member the story.

The events are not emplotted, if you will, either by an historian who imaginatively reconstructs the past or by a novelist who constructs a metaphorical world as an image of the real one. To do anamnesis is to tell the story in which the believer discovers herself. Thus the activity is neither simply a story-telling or story-following. Rather, by placing herself within the mystery (itself an imaginative task), she becomes implicated in the story. It is less the case that one interprets the story than that one is interpreted by it. Without its having been a moment in one's own historically lived experience, the story one remembers in the Eucharist is the most deeply personal of rememberings, for it shapes and interprets all the other stories which the believer's biography comprises. It is the story by and in which the "I" as an individual and the "we" as a community are told.

The Eucharist anamnesis is a narrative which contains the historical, fictional, and mythic while transcending them, a remembering which is limited neither to the biographically experienced nor to the impersonal. It is the most radically personal of rememberings because it is by doing the anamnesis that the community re-members who it is. To do anamnesis requires of them not a denial of the critical perspective out of which our history/fiction distinctions arise, but a recollecting beyond critical thinking, an imaginative and faithful remembering which opens up to a second naiveté.

To speak about the believing community as "remembering itself" in the anamnesis brings me to the second basis for my claim that in the Eucharist we discover an extensive collaboration between remembering and imagining. We are ready to move beyond the world of the text (the level of sense) to the world in which the text lives and to which it points (the level of reference). Eucharistic anamnesis both tells a story and is representative of reality. Our next task is to reflect upon which reality is pointed to and how the pointing is accomplished.

Mimesis or Metaphoricity

In our discussion of anamnesis as narratizing, we discovered the coinherence of mythos and mimesis to be characteristic of the narrativity of the Eucharistic anamnesis. Now we have shown how, at the level of sense, mythos or plotting is an imagining activity. It remains for us to verify our claim that anamnesis embraces imagining even at the referential level. To do so, let

71

us return to the mimetic dimension of anamnesis. In taking this route, I am, with Paul Ricolur, following Aristotle's analysis of poesis. If, for Aristotle, the essence of poesis is mythos or plotting, its scope is mimesis. In an Aristotelian theory of tragedy, it is the conjunction of mythos as plot and mimesis as creative imitation which is the paradigm of the referential claim of poesis.[16]

We are ready to see the force of the assertion that mimesis is creative imitation rather than mere repetition; for by virtue of its mimesis, the Eucharistic anamnesis reenacts the reality of Christ's actions at the Last Supper in its essential traits. Indeed, as we have seen, the spareness of the imitative words and gestures has a magnifying effect rather than the reductive one we might suppose. We can see in this an analogy to Aristotle's claim that poetry is truer than history because it intends the universal rather than the particular. This shaping and selecting in mimesis is the counterpart to the first claim: that the image which mimesis offers is more than a replica of a previously given reality. Mimesis' character as creative imitation (and not mere repetition) is grounded in its offering a metaphor of reality. A metaphor refers to reality not to replicate it but to prescribe new meanings; metaphors both make and re-make reality. Displaying an intentionality of their own, they are models for perceiving in a new way. By virtue of its mimesis, Eucharistic anamnesis does not simply repeat the past. In remembering the past as it does, anamnesis re-members (i.e., re-makes) reality. Anamnesis carries cognitive import at the referential level through its very metaphoricity.

To focus on this metaphoricity of mimesis (and thus on the imaginal matrix of anamnesis' referential claims), let us take as the object of our reflection the words and gestures of consecration which form the very heart of the Eucharistic liturgy. If we can make the case of imagining at the very nexus of the anamnesis' truth claims, we will have succeeded in showing the profound symbiosis of remembering and imagining evidenced in the Eucharistic liturgy. While one can make the case that the whole liturgy is metaphorically textured, such selective focusing is not arbitrary, for this is the key moment in the Eucharistic action, and as such, has been the privileged object of the intensest reflection, debate, and disagreement in the history of Christian theologizing on the Eucharist among the various denominations. A certain predilection of abstraction, however, has served theological reflection poorly, obscuring the theological implications of the richness of liturgical action. Recent theology is discovering that the metaphoricity of its first order discourse may provide a more fecund soil for its assertions than certain impoverished philosophical categories have been able to do.

Just as our description of anamnesis' narrativity led us to elaborate several layers of narrative thickness in the Eucharistic Prayer, so too here our reflection uncovers a multivalent density in the words, "This is my body." What is more, far from functioning merely as a decorative or didactic device, this metaphorical richness in the bread/body identification is our only access to the liturgy's meaning. But it is, indeed, an access and not a barrier; for we discover ritual activity to be languaged, and we come to it ourselves already formed in certain ways of perceiving and speaking, already steeped in certain narratives, already trained in certain dispositions. The bread/body metaphor, for all its radicality, is embedded in a matrix of specific life-use which embraces our ordinary human experience as well as our particular experience within the Christian community.

In the context of this study, I can do no more than offer some examples of this embeddedness. Let us, then, focus on the vehicle of the metaphor, the bread, and look at (1) our ordinary experience of bread, (2) certain experiences and practices of the Hebrew tradition which are organized around the image of bread, and (3) the New Testament context for the Eucharist in order to elaborate something of the multivalency of reference subsumed into the Eucharistic claim that "This is my body."

(1) Perhaps the most obvious thing to note about bread at the start is its familiarity and pervasiveness in our ordinary human experience. All our common associations with bread are ingredient in our encounter with it in the Eucharist, and one way of exploring the metaphor's meaning is to contemplate its range and depth by means of these associational radiations. The liturgy trades on this embeddedness of bread in our life-use with its symbolic evocations. Bread carries with it, for example, associations of nourishment, nurture, health, hearth, and home; the productivity of human work; meal, fellowship, and communion; ordinariness, nature, the natural, the earth's fruitfulness, life itself. This very pervasiveness and power to evoke a whole network of significances leads one to suspect it to be an archetypal image which appears in various religious traditions as what Eliade calls a "symbolic paradigm."[17] Indeed, it seems to haunt all human discourse.

(2) As we move from these broad associations to consider another level of the metaphor's organization, we can describe it as a typical symbol in the particular linguistic community which eucharistizes. We notice, first of all, how the Hebrew tradition draws upon these ready-to-hand symbolic reverberations while at the same time it particularizes and complicates them in new ways. Here our focus will be a single example and its exfoliations, the one most germane to our Eucharistic context: the Feast of the Pasch. The Pasch is itself the anamnesis of the decisive event in Israel's election as Yahweh's chosen people: the deliverance out of Egypt.

This historical occurrence fused and gave an entirely new religious significance to what were, at an earlier date in Hebrew history, two distinct seasonal festivals. Both were Springtime celebrations of first fruits: the Passover, a pastoral feast which dedicated the first flocks; and the Unleavened Bread, an agricultural feast which dedicated the first fruits of the barley harvest. These celebrations of nature and of thanksgiving for the earth's fruitfulness were transformed into the communal recollection of how Yahweh saved the people by an intervention in history.[18] In the book of Exodus we find the expression of this new meaning:

> Moses said to the people, "Keep this day in remembrance, the day you came out of Egypt, from the house of slavery, for it was by sheer power that Yahweh brought you out of it; no leavened bread must be eaten. On this day, in the month of Abib, you are leaving Egypt. And so, in this month, when Yahweh brings you to the land . . . he swore to your fathers he would give you, a land where milk and honey flow, you are to hold this service. For seven days you will eat unleavened bread, and on the seventh day there is to be a feast in honor of Yahweh. And on that day you will explain to your son, "This is because of what Yahweh did for me when I came out of Egypt" (Ex. 13:3-9).

According to the Yahwist tradition, Yahweh directed the Hebrews to take unleavened bread for nourishment on their journey because there was no time to prepare food when they left Egypt.[19] Thus eating unleavened bread becomes the reminder or memento of God's saving intervention in the lives of the people.

We can already begin to see how our ordinary associations with bread are complicated under the pressure of the specific narratives and practices of the Hebrew community, and how Scripture provides the paradigms for the interpretation of a symbol in its key stories and images. Added to the notions of natural fruitfulness, nurture, security, and stability which cluster around bread are notions of insecurity, persecution, and leaving home. For the Hebrews, celebrating the Pasch by eating unleavened bread is a formation in remembering to find their home and security, not in the good things of this world, but in Yahweh's decisive choice of them. What is more, the image acts like a two-edged sword, for to eat leavened bread brings expulsion from the community. During the liturgical celebration of the Pasch, one eats unleavened bread under peril of being cut off from Israel precisely because eating it has become bound up with remembering one's Hebrew identity and its foundation in a special relationship with Yahweh.

This organization of meaning around the bread metaphor is continued and developed in the Scriptural narrative of the Israelites' desert experience. The forty years' wandering is an elaboration of the story of how Yahweh shows care for the people by feeding them and how Yahweh in return requires that they seek their security and nurture in Yahweh alone. The manna from heaven is a way both of revealing that care and of testing their fidelity. God satisfies their physical hunger with bread so that they will "learn that I, Yahweh, am your God." When the Israelites reveal once again their paucity of trust by greedily gathering more than they can use, the very bread breeds maggots and smells foul. So here too bread becomes the sign of contradiction, driving the wedge between the ways of this world and the ways of the Lord.

Drawing on this symbolic quality of bread, Deuteronomy links the provisional character of the desert experience with the promised land to which Yahweh is leading the people; the former is a formation of heart for the latter, a formation in right remembering. The promised land is characterized as the land where "they will eat bread without stint." When the Israelites cross the Jordan into Canaan, they keep the Pasch by eating unleavened bread made from the land's harvest.

From that time, from their first eating of the produce of that country, the manna stopped falling. And having manna no longer, the Israelites fed from that year onwards on what the land of Canaan yielded (Jos. 5:12).

The Pasch recovers its character as both an agricultural festival and a remembrance of the deliverance from Egypt. The ceasing of the manna marks the end of the desert period and the entry into the land of the promise. Bread has been the motif which runs through the core narrative from the earliest understandings of the Pasch through its historical transformation, from the promise through the period of testing to the fulfillment.

Such examples, selected from the key narratives which shape Israel's self-understanding, reveal to us something of the bread metaphor's insistence within the Hebrew tradition. The key concepts in Israel's self-understanding--chosen people, covenant, promised land, law, fidelity and infidelity, the security and insecurity of a life of faith--all have metaphorical roots in the image of bread. As a dominant metaphor in the discourse, the notion of bread assumes the power to bring together other metaphors in the text which are also borrowed from our ordinary human experiences to form a tightly interwoven metaphorical complex which, in its turn, engenders a conceptual diversity. It is in the conjunction of these two distinct metaphorical capacities (that it both gathers subordinate images and scatters meanings at a higher level) that the metaphor's capacity to create new meanings resides.[20]

These new meanings push beyond the linguistic boundaries which ordinarily delimit our notions of hunger and satiety. In feeding the Israelites, Yahweh is training them to remember that God's self is their food, the very source not only of their origins but of their ongoing life and prosperity, a prosperity not to be measured in materialist terms:

> Remember how Yahweh your God led you for forty years in the wilderness, to humble you, to test you, and know your inmost heart--whether you would keep his commandments or not. He humbled you, he made you feel hunger, he fed you with manna which neither you nor your fathers had known, to make you understand that man does not live on bread alone but that man lives on everything that comes from the mouth of Yahweh (Deut. 8:1-3).

Thus the meaning of the image has been completely transformed by the narrative. Bread has come to signify the creative and preserving word of God. That the community is indeed radicalized by the metaphor-complex and its consciousness shaped by its narratized significances is evidenced over and over again in the discourse. The image of Yahweh as the one who not only feeds the people but whose word is their very food, appears as a motif in the Scripture's most self-involving mode of speech, the vocative expressions of the praying community.

(3) This web of intersignifications which we have been tracing through the key narratives and practices of the Hebrew community is gathered into Jesus' words and actions at the Last Supper and thus into the Christian community's liturgical anamnesis of that event. It is because bread functions as a root metaphor for this particular linguistic community that the speakings and doings involving bread are ruled usages which carry with them a form of life. To appreciate this more fully, we must look at a third level of the metaphor's organization, its usage within the New Testament; for it is the New Testament context which is most immediately ingredient in the Eucharistic meaning of bread.

In a variety of episodes and utterances, the gospel narratives and the epistles continue to enlarge and complicate the metaphorical significance of bread, interweaving it with other key metaphors into a cluster which includes bread/wine/water/food/meals/feasting/ fasting/home. But since my purpose is not to offer an exhaustive analysis of this metaphorical cluster in the New Testament, I shall take a single example as the focus of my discussion, allowing several of these metaphorical strands to exfoliate from its matrix.

It seems to me hardly disputable that the sixth chapter of John's gospel is one of the crucial texts for articulating the Eucharist's metaphoricity. Alone among the evangelists, John does not include the institution of the Eucharist within his account of the Last Supper, but places Jesus' eucharistic discourse in bold relief, in a separate chapter much earlier in the narrative. Such placement, along with the language used, serves to highlight the symbolic quality of Jesus' action and to emphasize the relationship of the Eucharist both to the Old Testament context we have been exploring and to a whole range of actions and sayings in the gospel which are bound to the bread metaphor. John's placement of this chapter also emphasizes the relationship between the Eucharist, the "bread of life," and Christ's passion and death, which is key to the Church's liturgical under-standing when it eucharistizes. The bread of life discourse offers a hermeneutic for the Paschal mystery. What is achieved through event at the narrative's climax in John's gospel is achieved through language-event in chapter VI.

Episodically, the discourse follows Jesus' miraculous feeding of a crowd of thousands with five loaves and two fishes. Although all four evangelists include the miracle of the loaves in their narratives, it is only John who, in his placement of the discourse on the Eucharist, invites so explicit a comparison between the two events. As a sign of his identity and mission, Jesus' feeding of the crowds trades on the metaphoricity of bread as it appears in the Old Testament. For just as Yahweh's covenantal care for the Israelites is symbolized over and over again in the Old Testament as God's feeding them, so Jesus, who is sent from God, gives bread to the hungry. But, again following the pattern of the Old Testament metaphor, the miracle of the loaves becomes a sign of contradiction and a two-edged sword. In both instances, giving bread is both a sign of God's care and the occasion for bringing judgment against the people.

In the Old Testament, the Israelites greedily gather more bread than they need and all too often prefer material well-being and physical satiety over the covenant. In John's account, Jesus accuses his followers of comparable bad faith. They do not follow him because of the signs he works, but because he provides all the bread they want to eat. In his berating them, Jesus plays on this multivalency which bread enjoys in the Hebrew tradition:

> Do not work for food that cannot last, but work for food that endures to eternal life (John 6:27).

Refusing to attend to this metaphoricity, the people retort that "Our fathers had manna to eat in the desert; what work will you do?"; and there follows the lengthy and passionate discourse on the bread of life. I quote from it here at some length:

> I am the bread of life.
> Your fathers ate the manna in the desert and they are dead;
> but this is the bread that comes down from heaven,
> so that a man may eat it and not die.
> I am the living bread that comes down from heaven.
> Anyone who eats this bread will live forever;
> and the bread that I shall give is my flesh, for the life of the world.
> . . . .
> I tell you most solemnly,

if you do not eat the flesh of the Son of Man and
drink his blood,
you will not have life in you.
Anyone who does eat my flesh and drink my blood has
eternal life,
And I shall raise him up on the last day.
For my flesh is real food and my blood is real
drink.
He who eats my flesh and drinks my blood lives in me
and I live in him.
As I, who am sent by the living Father
myself draw life from the Father,
so whoever eats me will draw life from me.
This is the bread come down from heaven;
not like the bread our ancestors ate: they are
dead, but anyone who eats this bread will live
forever (John 6:48-51, 53-58).

The progression of thought in chapter VI, then,
follows this pattern: Jesus miraculously feeds the
hungry crowds with bread; they follow him to make him
their king; he accuses them of bad faith in
misinterpreting the sign of his power; they in turn ask
for another sign comparable to the manna in the desert;
Jesus responds by offering them the bread of life which
is his flesh. Now there is something quite striking
about this progression. It seems on the part of Jesus'
followers a peculiar hardness of heart, indeed, which
would require yet another sign after the miraculous
feeding and would compare the miracle of the loaves
unfavorably with the manna in the desert. Yet, in John's
account, Jesus confronts their incredulity not by
pointing up the extraordinary character of what he has
just done, but by pushing his claims further still. Far
from offering his followers reassurances for believing in
him by reminding them of what has happened, he challenges
them beyond the limits of both experience and memory. He
does this by a way of speaking which breaks open all
their ordinary assumptions, even their religious
assumptions, by using a language they find intolerable.

In the discourse on the bread of life, there are no
fewer than four references to the manna in the desert.
Just as that bread "came down from heaven," symbolic of
Yahweh's providence, and was no ordinary nourishment, so
too the bread which Jesus will give has come down from
heaven sent by the same living God. In his references to
the manna, however, it is the contrast rather than the
comparison between the two signs which Jesus stresses.
The manna was provisional, temporal, and finite, the
appropriate metaphorical vehicle for a people fresh from
the fleshpots of Egypt and not yet ready for the promised

land, whereas the bread which is his very flesh contains eternal life. The bread which Jesus gives is to be the new Pasch, the new and everlasting covenant of God with God's people. The paradoxical character of the claims Jesus is making here can find no other language appropriate to its expression than that of metaphor. Both by this explicit comparison and contrast of the Eucharist with manna and by his placement of the event "shortly before the Jewish feast of Passover," John is trading on the rich metaphoricity and religious symbolism which bread enjoys in the liturgical memory of the Jewish community, at the same time as he uses that metaphorized remembering to break open both the all-too-human and the religious preconceptions of Jesus' followers. One's capacities to receive such breaking apart--which include linguistic and imaginative capacities--become the litmus for accepting the word with its claims to a truth which re-members all one's ordinary assumptions. What Jesus requires of his followers is a remembering capable of imagining new possibilities, a remembering whose grounding in the past is an opening toward the future.[21]

It is difficult to conceive of a more audacious expression of the God/human relationship than this discourse on the bread of life--or a more threatening one. "If you do not eat the flesh of the Son of Man and drink his blood, you will not have life in you." It is no wonder John includes within his account that, after this, many of his disciples left him. These words demanded a decisive choice on the part of his hearers. The personal decision for the New Covenant is as definitive as that for the Old Covenant, expressed in Deuteronomy as the choice between life and death (Deut. 30:15). The terms of its expression are even more demanding, for here to choose life is to eat Jesus' flesh and to drink his blood.

Throughout the discourse Jesus insists on the truth claim of his metaphorical speech. It is a truth claim of such centrality that, once granted, it calls into question all other claims to the truth. The metaphorical language topples one's ordinary conceptions, turns reality upside down, if you will--not, it is claimed, for the sake of turning sense into nonsense but in the service of a radically new sense-making, a deeper and freer truth. In so doing, it deals the death blow to a whole conception of personhood. It proposes to the believer that her self, rather than being constituted by a direct presence to itself, is allowed her from outside herself, that she is the recipient and not the source of her identity. In terms of the bread metaphor, the one who dwells within this word must allow her notion of what ordinary bread is to be shaped by the realization that "My flesh is real food." She must shape her conception of every aspect of human life according to the Word made flesh. Here is the ultimate metaphorical usage of bread. In its visceralness and its requirement for a radically transformed mode of perceiving and acting, it sounds the depth of language's imaginative powers in the service of revealing religious truth.

In my effort to demonstrate the imaginal matrix of the Eucharistic discourse at the level of reference, I have focused on these Scriptural metaphors precisely because the languaged activity of the Eucharist is embedded in the ruled usages whose paradigms are provided by the Scriptures. The form of life to which the Eucharist refers is shaped by these key metaphors, narratives, and sayings. If the Scriptures are the texts from which the Eucharistic anamnesis means, the Eucharist is the activity which both gives and continues the life of the Scriptures. The Christian community's self-understanding is born of this interplay in the grammar of anamnesis, for it is in the Eucharist that the community's communal memories are told and enacted.

Can we not claim that in the Eucharistic anamnesis we have a clear and striking case in which remembering and imagining are acts indispensable in collaboration with one another, both at the level of the discourse's sense and also at the level of its reference? To do anamnesis is, at the least, to exercise one's imaginative capacities. Moreover, it is not simply that the anamnesis qualifies as an imagining activity, but that its imaginativity is peculiarly rich and dense, just as we have seen its narrativity to be. The words, "This is my body" trade on a staggering range and depth of symbolic condensation.[22] The early Church, with its familiarity with the rich concept of anamnesis and its concomitant emphasis on the Eucharist as an activity, was spared the later scholastic confusions between substance and accidents and its aftermath up to our own time in transubstantiation/transsignification debates among the Christian churches.

I have been focusing on the vehicle in the meta-phorical assertion "This [bread] is my body" in my description of anamnesis' imaginal matrix at the level of reference. If we shift our attention to the tenor of the metaphor, to "my body," we can explore an entirely different range of considerations which I alluded to above in my mention of the Eucharist's implications for a new conception of personhood. With such a shift, we elicit a third feature of the Eucharistic anamnesis, its constituting character for the worshipping community.

Constituting Character

I shall begin my reflection on this third feature of the Eucharistic anamnesis by attending more closely than we have up to this point to the Eucharist's mode of utterance. Since the word "anamnesis" is contextual, its meaning dependent on its use, we must be attentive to the discourse in which it is uttered if we are to comprehend that meaning. To understand Eucharistic anamnesis, we must see it within the context of personal and liturgical prayer both in the Hebrew Scriptures and in Judaism.

To eucharistize means to give thanks, and we have already seen how the story being remembered in the Eucharistic anamnesis conditions the mode of the activities performed. Eucharistic anamnesis is a prayer form uttered in the vocative, addressed to God and enacted in God's presence. Note how the Hippolytan liturgy's institution narrative takes this form: "We render thanks to you, O God, through your beloved child Jesus Christ, whom in the last times you sent to us as saviour and redeemer. . . . " (1). It is a recalling in the fullest sense, i.e., both a remembering and an address. It is thus ineluctably confessional. Eucharistic anamnesis is not simply ritual activity but ritual worship. Its intentionality is directed toward a specific hearer whose name the believer knows, whose presence she trusts, in whose story she dwells.

Now this mode of utterance has significant implications for those who speak in this way. The vocative mode of speech in prayer and worship is peculiarly personal because the knowings and feelings it expresses are necessarily self-involving.[23] Prayer, as a vocative mode of speech addressed to God, is assertive as well as expressive, for it shows the connection between the one who prays and the words she uses about God.[24] Once again, let me cite an example from our Hippolytan text: "We offer to you the bread and cup, giving thanks because you have held us worthy to stand before you and minister to you" (8).

As the on-going communal prayer of the Christian community, liturgical worship is a rule-keeping activity of the language of religious belief. By keeping alive the stories, metaphors, and concepts in which belief is grounded, it keeps in place the paradigmatic descriptions of God, the self, the community, and the world. The understandings and dispositions expressed in prayer are given in that very way of speaking about God. Because prayer is a sense-making activity (and not simply a subjectively expressive one), those who pray make sense of themselves in performing the very activity.

This logic of connection between what we say and do when we pray and our identity and self-understanding is nowhere clearer than in the case of the relationship between the worshipping community and the Eucharist it celebrates. To examine this point more concretely, let us return to the words of consecration, "This is my body." If we ask the question, to what does the word "body" refer, our first response is, of course, that it refers to Christ himself. But if we return to Jesus' eucharistic discourse, i.e., to the metaphors and concepts which ground our anamnesis, we find we must extend the reference of "body" in the light of the claims made there about the effects of the liturgical action we are performing when we say and do "Take, eat: this is my body." Once again, we must begin to trace something of the multivalency of the Scriptural language about the Eucharist if we are to understand what the worshipping community means when it says "This is my body."

He who eats my flesh and drinks my blood
lives in me
and I live in him.
As I, who am sent by the living Father,
myself draw life from the Father,
so whoever eats me will draw life from me.

To eat Christ's body is to be let in on the relationship between Parent and Child, a relationship of such intimacy that it needs to be expressed by the word "in." This language of indwelling is central to the claim Jesus makes that whoever eats his body will live forever. It is because eating Christ's flesh means living in him that we will live forever. Indeed, the promise of an indwelling relationship such as the Son enjoys with the Father is at the heart of Jesus' promises, and as such is reiterated not only in the eucharistic discourse, but in John's account of the Last Supper discourse, thus serving as a motif which draws the two together:

If anyone loves me he will keep my word
and my Father will love him
and we shall come to him
and make our home with him.
. . . .
I am in my Father and you in me and I in you
(Jn. 14:23,20).

83

Notice, first of all, how this promise reveals something about God's self. One obvious implication of Jesus' language of indwelling is that to be God must mean to be in intimate relation. Secondly, in the <u>ordo cognescendi</u>, to understand who God is seems to imply understanding who God is for us, for the God revealed to us here is one who is for us to the extent of desiring to be in us and to bring us into God's self. The paradox is that the God who is Everything and is in Everything is the word made flesh. The language of indwelling suggests that the mystery of God, being a mystery of relation, is a mystery of self-emptying. To become enfleshed and to give us one's flesh to eat become the most fitting expressions of the mystery of God.

The knowing contained in the Eucharistic anamnesis is, then, first of all, a knowing about God and secondly, as a consequence of this, a knowing about ourselves. What does this promise reveal about those who hear the word and eat the body of Christ? How does this language keep the self-conception of the believer in place? How is her identity shaped by the activity she performs as she opens herself to its meaning? A radical shift of perspective on the part of the worshippers becomes the condition and enabler of any entrance into its meaning if one is to approach it on its own terms. If indwelling precludes a self-enclosed identity for Jesus, it precludes it as well for those who shape their lives by his word. It is no longer possible for such a believer to be alone, no longer possible to consider oneself as self-constituting or self-grounded. To eat the body of Christ so qualifies the Christian's identity that, we could say, the metaphor pushes toward an ontological claim. There where one is most oneself is precisely where one most opens out onto God who is source, possibility, and promise. The identity of the Christian is indirect, in that she knows that she is mediated to herself from outside.

In the Pauline epistles we find the earliest Scriptural reflection and commentary on the Eucharistic activity which has characterized the Christian community from its inception. The words spoken by the Lord at Paul's conversion, "I am Jesus, whom you are persecuting," imply that Christians are identified with the risen Christ. It is no wonder then that for Paul, who lived his life out of the memory of that paradigmatic event, human beings are reconciled to God by becoming parts of Christ's body.

Just as each of our bodies has several parts
and each part has a separate function, so all
of us, in union with Christ, form one body, and
as parts of it we belong to each other (Rom.
12:4-5).

This becomes the description of the Church: "Now the
Church is his body, he is its head" (Col. 1:18).
Elsewhere Paul writes:

He [God] has put all things under his
[Christ's] feet, and made him, as the ruler of
everything, the head of the Church; which is
his body, the fullness of him who fills the
whole creation (Eph. 1:22-23).

Paul sees this reconciliation as already achieved in the
Eucharist, as the representative act of the Christian
life which performs the anamnesis of Christ's own
redemptive act:

The bread that we break is a communion with the
body of Christ. The fact that there is only
one loaf means that, though there are many of
us, we form a single body because we all have
a share in this one loaf (I Cor. 10:17).

Both the Church and the Eucharist are the body of
Christ and must be so, if we can predicate of the
Eucharist what is predicated of Christ's own act and
offering. Thus, as anamnesis, the Eucharist becomes the
distinguishing and constitutive action of the believing
community. This multivalency of reference in "my body"
is crucial to an understanding of Eucharistic anamnesis.
In offering Christ, the Church offers herself. Anamnesis
is at one and the same time a recalling of Christ's
saving action, a recalling to the Father, a recalling of
the Son to the Father, and a proclamation by the Church.[25]
To "do my anamnesis" ranges, we can now see, beyond the
story of Christ's death and resurrection to the whole
Christ, the community of believers already redeemed by
that saving action. Their story is taken up into and
manifested in his. The community both becomes and
discovers who it is by remembering liturgically who he
is. They become members of his body by re-membering
themselves, i.e., re-constituting themselves, putting
themselves together in him. The offering is the same
offering which Jesus made once for all and yet it is
constantly renewed, thus building up the body of Christ.
In and through the anamnesis, the community becomes who
it already is by actualizing the redemption already
achieved historically and forever by Christ. Anamnesis

thus reveals the mode of temporality peculiar to the Christian experience: the already-but-not-yet of eschatology.

As the Hippolytan liturgy shows, the effect of such anamnetic action is unity: "We ask that you would send your Holy Spirit upon the offering of your holy church; that, gathering them into one, you would grant to all who partake of the holy things (to partake) for the fullness of the Holy Spirit. . . . "(9). It is in the unity of believers, as the body of Christ, that the saving action of Christ is re-presented. In his epistles, Paul stresses over and over again this unity of the body of Christ which brings all Christians together in one Spirit: "May the peace of Christ reign in your hearts, because it is for this that you were called together as parts of one body" (Col. 3:15).

> The saints together make a unity in the work of service, building up the body of Christ. In this way we are all to come to unity in our faith and in our knowledge of the Son of God, until we become the perfect Man, fully mature with the fullness of Christ himself (Eph. 4:13).

This effect of unity is a favorite theme of the Church Fathers as well. According to Augustine, "The virtus which is there [in the Eucharist] understood is unity, that being joined to his body and made his members we may be what we receive." And again, "If you have received well, you are that which you received."[26]

It becomes clear how we can talk about the Eucharistic anamnesis' capacity to shape the affective life. Such "remembering in Christ" opens up new ways of being in the world which would not otherwise be available, which are only now possible because the believer lives in Christ. It delineates a range of experiences, emotions, dispositions, and understandings. What are the contours of the affective and passional life of one who performs this remembering? In the second citation from Augustine above, we can see how this action begins to shape certain attitudes and expectations. In re-actualizing the covenant of salvation between God and human beings, making covenant with the Father in Christ, the community, we might say, "texts itself" in the anamnetic act. It does so in the context of thanksgiving. As Jungmann notes,

> Thanksgiving and remembering are closely connected. If we look at the content of

thanksgiving, it is seen to be nothing else but "thinking of." To think of that which has been received, to express it, and to show it; to recognize and acknowledge it, to show by acknowledgement at least in words and perhaps with more than words.[27]

In the Eucharist, remembering and thanksgiving are ingredient in each other's logic. Jungmann, however, does not go far enough in his analysis. I want to challenge his "perhaps with more than words," for to perform this thankful remembrance with the fullness of symbolic truth carries with it the shaping of the lives of the members of the community.

By engaging in so searching and radical a remembering, the community, as Paul reminds us, runs the risk of eating and drinking its own condemnation (I Cor. 11:28). Texting oneself anamnetically carries with it certain clearly specified life requirements and excludes a whole gamut of ways of being in the world. And there is a definitive quality about the choice. The Pauline epistles begin to fill in the morphology of this remembering in which the worshipping community is engaged.

Christ, our passover, has been sacrificed; let us celebrate the feast, then, by getting rid of all the old yeast of evil and wickedness, having only the unleavened bread of sincerity and truth (I Cor. 5:8).

Bear with one another charitably, in complete selflessness, gentleness, and patience. Do all you can to preserve the unity of the Spirit by the peace that binds you together. There is one Body, one Spirit, just as you were called into one and the same hope when you were called (Eph. 4:3-4).

Unity, concord, gratitude, gentleness, patience, rejoicing, fidelity, contrition, ministry to all the members of the one body--such live actualities are ruled in by anamnesis. Obversely, ruled out are discord, resentment, spitefulness, alienation, all forms of licentious behavior, and the like. Paul makes very clear, moreover, that this ruling in and ruling out is not the result of some ethical commitment to the good life but of the Christian's living "in Christ." This living in Christ, actualized in the Eucharist, becomes the mode of discerning what the Christian life looks like and how it differs, not only from a life of evil, but from the ethical and Judaic law-governed life as well (Co. 2:20-3:4).

In the Christian life, one's self-identity is inextricably bound up with the person of Christ. This is the full reach of the multivalency of the Eucharistic body metaphor. "I live, now not I, but Christ in me," Paul writes, and "When a man is in Christ, he is a new creature altogether." For the Christian community, to do anamnesis is to enact its reason for being and to constitute itself. For such a re-membering, the peculiarly constitutive language of the vocative in prayer is appropriate--and may even be required.

We have been reflecting on how it is that in the Eucharist remembering is a self-constituting activity. Eucharistic anamnesis reveals the interdependence between a person's capacities for remembering and the morphology of her dispositional life. But if Eucharistic anamnesis is a formation in Christian dispositions, this is so because, in actualizing the redemption already achieved by Christ, it actualizes a new mode of being for those who live in him as members of his body. Now this actualizing capacity, this capacity to make present what is past, is a feature of anamnesis which has undergirded our discussion not only of its self-constituting character but of its narrativity and imaginative qualities as well. In our description of each of anamnesis' most salient features, we have been led to note that Eucharistic anamnesis signals a peculiar relationship to temporality. Indeed, we posited this at the outset as integral to the very definition of the term. It remains for us to focus more directly upon this relationship between remembering and temporality in the Eucharistic anamnesis.

Mode of Temporality

Let us begin our reflection by returning to what we posited at the outset about the mode of temporality in the Eucharistic anamnesis in order to draw out its implications more directly. I have said that if we are to appreciate how anamnesis functions in the Christian liturgy, we must see it against the backdrop of the practices of prayer which we find in the Hebrew Scriptures and in Judaism. We are now in a position to develop this relationship more specifically.

In these contexts, prayer is understood as an anamnesis which has, if you will, two movements. Its first movement is a recalling before God by us of the past events of God's saving lovingkindness; its second, a recalling of these events to God so that God may make their saving power present and actual for us here and now.

Liturgical historians generally agree that the Christian Eucharist took as its formal model the Jewish prayer form known as the berakhah (benediction). The berakhah has a tripartite literary form. It begins with the benediction proper (from which the whole prayer takes its name), a short, often stereotyped call to divine praise. This is followed by the central element, the anamnesis of the mirabilia Dei, which develops at greater length the motive for the praise of part one. As such, the anamnesis' object is less a particular circumstance as perceived by a single individual than the on-going blessing of Yahweh as both perceived and remembered by the community. These blessings are of two kinds: (1) the wonders of the Lord which are displayed in the whole natural creation, and (2) the wonders which Yahweh has performed in the history of the chosen people (cf., for examples, Psalms 8 and 136, the latter of which, called the "Great Hallel," is recited at the Passover meal). The third part of the prayer is a repetition of the initial benediction, now often more specifically colored by the rememberings of part two.

We can follow this pattern very clearly in the prayer of thanksgiving after a meal as it is used in the Passover celebration. This particular benediction, the Berakhah Hammazon, is for the most part contemporary with the lifetime of Jesus and may well be an ultimate source of the Christian eucharistic thanksgiving.[28] It begins with a triple blessing. After a blessing the one who nourishes ("Blessed are you, Lord our God, King of the Universe, for you nourish us and the whole world. . . . ."), comes a blessing for the earth ("We will give thanks to you, Lord our God, because you have given us for our inheritance a desirable land, good and wide, the covenant and the law, life and food"), and a blessing for Jerusalem. On the feast of Passover, there follows this anamnesis:

> Our God and God of our fathers, may there arise in your sight, and come, and be present, and be regarded, and be pleasing, and be heard, and be visited, and be remembered our remembrance and our visitation, and the remembrance of our fathers, and the remembrance of the Messiah, the son of your servant David, and the remembrance of Jerusalem, the city of your

holiness, and the remembrance of all your
people, the house of Israel: for escape, for
prosperity, for grace, and for lovingkindness
and mercy, for life and for peace, on this day
of the Feast of Unleavened Bread. Remember us
on this day, Lord our God, for prosperity, and
visit us on it for blessing, and save us on it
for life. And by the word of salvation and
mercy spare us, and grant us grace, and have
mercy on us, and save us: for our eyes look to
you, for you, O God, are a gracious and
merciful king.

Blessed are you, Lord, for you build Jerusalem.
Amen.[29]

The Berakhah Hammazon concludes with a blessing of God,
"our father, our king, our creator, our redeemer, good
and beneficent king, who day by day is concerned to
benefit us in many ways."

Now it is evident from this berakhah that Hebrew
anamnesis has ingredient within it a whole conception of
temporality which is bound up with its notion of memory.
The prayer posits a relationship between what is past,
present, and future which belies the very pastness of the
past. While it is outside the scope of our inquiry to go
into any detailed analysis of this Hebrew conception of
temporality, we must attend to it at least briefly if we
are to understand the temporal mode of the Eucharistic
anamnesis.

In the history of ideas, it is a commonplace to note
the fundamental distinction between the Hebrew and
Hellenic understandings of temporality. One of the most
striking differences between these two modes of thought
is the significance each sees in the process of history.
While the Greeks viewed history as the endless repetition
of a closed circle, for the Hebrews history had a
definite beginning and ending. The beginning of time and
history was the Lord's free creation of the world out of
nothing; the ending, what the Hebrew Scriptures call the
"Day of the Lord," when time and history would end with
the ending of this world. Both before the beginning and
after the end, however, there is Yahweh, who is the
source of all that comes to be and who is still ruling in
the age to come.[30]

This conception grants to history a purpose,
direction, and meaning--given to it by God's eternal will
toward the whole creation and toward humanity in
particular. It is this will of God which guides history

toward its final purpose. While we, who are in the midst of this temporal process, cannot grasp its meaning and purpose as a whole, in the last time (or eschaton) when the meaning of history is complete, the kingdom of God will be manifested. In later Hebrew thought, it is the Messiah (the Anointed One of Yahweh) who will bring about this completion of history which reveals its whole purpose, thus manifesting the Kingdom of the Lord in everything that has ever happened in time.

Now it is important to note that this eschatological conception of history does not imply the rejection of or escape from temporality as if it were something corrupt or phantasmagoric. Rather, in the Hebrew conception, all of temporality is eschatological in the sense that those events develop and happen in it by means of which it is given its significance, those events which direct it toward its consummation in the final event which will be revelatory of its whole meaning.[31] Temporality is transformed into history proper; it has a directedness, not toward mere cessation, but toward completion. As Dom Dix writes:

> This completion of history, "the End" which manifests the "kingdom" of God throughout history in all its parts, does not interrupt history or destroy it; it fulfills it. All the divine values implicit and fragmentary in history are gathered up and revealed in the eschaton, which is "the End" to which history moves. In this sense the "Day of the Lord" involves a "judgment" of history as a whole and of all that goes to make up history. "The End" is at once within history and beyond it, the consummation of time and its transmutation into what is beyond time, the "Age to come."[32]

The eschaton, quite contrary to being simply an end to time and history, is rather the fulfillment of what has happened in time. Nor is it as if there are two times, a natural and a human. Since the whole of creation is taken up into this eschatological understanding, the cycles of natural time (days, seasons, etc.) are no more self-sufficient or self-enclosed in their meaning than are the human beings who live in history--all of creation is wholly subordinate to Yahweh. Thus the Semitic Paul sees the whole creation as eagerly waiting for God's revelation, "groaning in one great act of giving birth" (Rom. 8:22). The entire cosmos is taken up into the body of the Christ who "is everything and is in everything."

He [God] has let us know the mystery of his
purpose, the hidden plan he so kindly made in
Christ from the beginning to act upon when the
times had run their course to the end: that he
would bring everything together under Christ,
as head, everything in the heavens and
everything on the earth (Eph. 1:9-10).

In the Hebrew Scriptures (and especially in the
prophets), this age to come is imaged as an age of
blessings of all kinds and the vindication of the
Covenant between Yahweh and the chosen people, to which
Israel found itself being unfaithful time and again,
despite all its strivings. With the coming of the
Messiah, the age of the New Covenant will dawn, carrying
with it the power for a heretofore faithless Israel to
remain faithful. Through the Messiah who will bring this
New Covenant, Yahweh will redeem Israel from its own
sinfulness as well as from the pain of temporal history.

As Cullman has shown in his <u>Christ and Time</u>, this
same understanding of temporality is shared by the New
Testament. Without it we cannot understand either early
Christian eschatology or the temporal dimension of the
Eucharist, for the central understanding of Christianity
is that the Messiah so long awaited has come, the event
toward which the whole history of Israel and in relation
to which the whole cosmos has been directed.[33] The
peculiar turn of Jewish Christianity is precisely the
belief that in the life, death, and resurrection of
Jesus, the fulfillment of history is achieved and
manifested. According to Schmemann,

> The difference between Christianity and Judaism
> is not in their understanding or theology of
> time, but in their conception of the events by
> which this time is spiritually measured.
> Judaistic time is eschatological in the sense
> that it is still directed towards the coming of
> the Messiah and the messianic Kingdom. In
> Christian time the Messiah has already come, is
> already revealed, the Kingdom of Yahweh is at
> hand.[34]

It is no longer possible to understand eschatology only
in a futuristic sense, for, as Cullman notes. "the norm
is not something which is still coming in the future, but
that One who has already come."[35] Christianity does not
offer a new conception of temporality; it simply affirms
that that event toward which temporality has been
directed from the beginning has already begun. The

Christ-event is eschatological in that it reveals and defines the meaning of everything in time.

It is in this sense that we must understand the Pauline notion of living "in Christ." As the Body of Christ, the Church is the New Covenant of all those who by living in him have entered into the Kingdom of God.

> When we were dead through our sins, he brought us to life in Christ--it is through grace that you have been saved--and raised us up with him and gave us a place with him in heaven, in Christ Jesus (Eph. 2:5-6).

Even so cursory a discussion will have served its purpose if it helps us to understand the mode of temporality of the Eucharistic anamnesis, for it is in the light of this eschatological notion of temporality that we must situate the Christian community's eucharistizing. The language of the earliest Eucharistic prayers is full of eschatological reminiscences. The Hippolytan Great Eucharistic Prayer, for example, begins by recalling that "in the last times" God sent God's child to be a savior and redeemer (1); the Addai and Mari ends with communion "for new life in the kingdom of heaven"; and the Anaphora of Basil of Caesarea praises the "God existing before the ages and reigning until the ages."[36] Indeed, the whole notion of anamnesis is eschatological, for, in the words of one commentator,

> in the eucharist the church perpetually reconstitutes the crisis in which the kingdom of God came in history. It never gets beyond this. At each eucharist we are <u>there</u>. . . . Sacramental communion is not a purely mystical experience, to which history . . . would be in the last resort irrelevant; it is bound up with a corporate memory of real events.[37]

Once again, we are led to reflect upon the poverty of our ordinary notion of memory as the recollection of what is past, for in the Eucharist what the Church remembers is partly beyond our human history. Anamnesis is the remembering of meta-historical events as well as of the historical past and future. It is not as if the eschaton is composed of two parts, both totally within our temporality, one in the historical past and one in the historical future, but that both past and future are comprised within an eternal present and Presence. There is only one eschaton, the coming of all creation to God in Christ, of which the Eucharist is the anamnesis. In this anamnesis, the Church in all its temporality and incompletion is continually entering into its own being in the Kingdom of God, in Christ, through his act.

Alexander Schmemann expresses well this complexity of temporality contained in the Eucharistic anamnesis. I quote from his discussion at some length:

> The event which is "actualized" in the Eucharist is an event of the past when viewed within the categories of time, but by virtue of its eschatological, determining, completing significance, it is also an event which is taking place eternally. The coming of the Messiah is a single event of the past, but in His coming, in His life, death, and resurrection, His Kingdom has entered into the world, becoming the new life in the Spirit given by Him as life within Himself. This messianic Kingdom or life in the new aeon is "actualized"--becomes real--in the assembly of the Church, in the ἐκκλησία, when believers come together to have communion in the Lord's body. The Eucharist is therefore the manifestation of the Church as the new aeon; it is participation in the Kingdom as the <u>parousia</u>, as the presence of the Resurrected and Resurrecting Lord. It is not the "repetition" of his advent or coming into the world, but the lifting up of the Church into His <u>parousia</u>, the Church's participation in His heavenly glory. Later Christian thought will begin to interpret the nature of the Sacrament--of this repetition of the unrepeatable--in concepts borrowed from Greek philosophy.[38]

The community of believers lives in the world and yet its life is hid with Christ in God. The Church is in the world without being of the world, in time without being time-bound. So too, as the Body of Christ, the Eucharist is the actualization of the new time within the old, not the actualization of the future within the past, but of the present of God within which is contained one's own past, present, and future. By participating in it, the members of the worshipping community receive into themselves his life and kingdom.

The Eucharist is essentially an action of anamnesis, done in conformity to Christ's expressed command, done by the community of believers which is his body. Thus it is necessarily his action, what is offered is what he offered, its consequences are what he named: This is my body. In and through the anamnesis, Christ's and the

Church's actions are so closely identified that the Eucharist is not a mere repetition of the past, but a re-present-ing of the same offering of Christ by the Church which is his body. Through participation in Christ's own offering to the Father, the Church remembers forward, transforming pastness into presence and promise, openness to future. In the third century, Cyprian writes, "The passion is the Lord's sacrifice, which we offer."[39] And Chrysostom notes with characteristic eloquence:

> What then? Do we not offer daily? Certainly we offer thus, making an anamnesis of his death. How is it one and not many? Because it was offered once, like that which was carried into the Holy of Holies. . . For we ever offer the same person. Therefore the sacrifice is one. By this argument then, since the offering is made in many places, does it follow that there are many Christs? Not at all, for Christ is everywhere one, complete here and complete there, a single Body. We offer even now that which was then offered, which cannot be exhausted. This is done for an anamnesis of that which was then done, for "Do this" said He "for the anamnesis of Me." We do not offer a different sacrifice like the high-priest of old, but we ever offer the same. Or rather we offer the anamnesis of the sacrifice.[40]

These, indeed, are the recurrent motifs through the patristic writings on the Eucharist: the uniqueness and unity of Christ's offering and its presence in that uniqueness and unity here and now through the Eucharistic anamnesis. Such paradox reveals that it is not by any mediation on the Church's part or by some peculiar power of the believer's memory that the saving action of the Christ-event is actualized now in the world, but rather by the unique present mediation of Christ, by the response to God which he gave and continues to give. Such at least is the theological understanding. The peculiarly Protestant distortion of this understanding of anamnesis sees salvation as something past to which return is made by faith, understood as an act of remembering what is past. In contrast to this intellectualizing and sentimentalizing drift is the typical Catholic automatistic tendency expressed in the notion of ex opere operato which emphasizes an infinite sacramental repetition of redemptive acts through a kind of heredity of power from the apostles to the priests of the Church.

But it is in Christ--and in the actualization of that indwelling in the Eucharist--that the historical act of salvation is made present. By doing his anamnesis, the Church, united now to Christ in the Eucharist, makes present the historical act of redemption. The Eucharistic anamnesis is the activity of Christ in God without ceasing to be the most personal and self-involving of rememberings on the part of the community; it is public worship which, at the same time, shapes the interiority of the worshippers; it gathers into itself and forms the believer's subjectivity even as it is the manifestation of the meaning of all creation in the Kingdom of God.

In our reflection on the Eucharistic anamnesis, we have been led to uncover certain features peculiar to the remembering that goes on in the Christian liturgy, and, by implication, in Christian life experience.

These features challenge and enlarge the philosophical tradition's notions of memory as an interior mental state which can do no more than reiterate what is past. In its narrative and imaginative qualities, its self-constituting character, and its temporal density, the liturgical anamnesis opens up to us a more robust understanding of the human activity of remembering than is commonly available either in the philosophical tradition or in our commonsense notions.

Now since the word "anamnesis" is contextual, its meaning determined by its use in certain circumstances, we cannot simply generalize from these features some meta-theory which would be true of all rememberings. These features, however, can give us clues and provide us with certain avenues of exploration into the activity of remembering in other life-contexts. How, then, shall we get on with our hermeneutical inquiry? If we allow the Eucharistic symbol with all its embodied richness to give rise to our thought, perhaps we can find other evidences for a richer notion of remembering. This will be our task in part II.

NOTES TO CHAPTER II

[1] Cited in R.C.D. Jasper and G. J. Cuming, eds., Prayers of the Eucharist: Early and Reformed (London: Collins Publishers, 1975), pp. 22-23. All other references to this prayer are given within the text according to the numbering of verses in this edition.

[2] Gregory Dix, The Shape of the Liturgy (London: Dacre Press, 1945; reprint ed. 1964), p. 160. I am indebted to this and to Thurian's Eucharistic Memorial throughout this chapter.

[3] Ibid.

[4] J. A. Jungmann, The Eucharistic Prayer (London: Challoner Books, 1956), p. 6.

[5] Max Thurian, The Eucharistic Memorial, Part II, trans. J. G. Davies (Richmond, Va.: John Knox Press, 1961), p. 38.

[6] Dix, p. 243.

[7] C. Spicq, L'Epitre aux Hebreux, II, 1953, p. 103, cited by Thurian, p. 6.

[8] The New Catholic Encyclopedia, 1967 ed., s.v. "Anamnesis."

[9] Dix, p. 156. Plato most likely borrowed the term "anamnesis" from the mystery cult lexicon with which he was familiar.

[10] Cassell's Latin/English, English/Latin Dictionary, by D. P. Simpson (London: Cassell & Co., n.d.).

[11] Dix, passim.

[12] The ensuing argument relies heavily on Paul Ricoeur's work on narrative. See especially "The Narrative Function," Semeia and World 12 (1979):123-141; and "Narrative and the Paradoxes of Time," Yale University Taylor Lectures (Feb. 1979).

[13] See Hayden White, Metahistory: The Historical Imagination in Nineteenth-Century Europe (Baltimore: Johns Hopkins U. Press, 1973) and "The Historical Text as Literary Object," Clio 3 (1974) :277-303.

[14]Ricoeur, "The Narrative Function," p. 183.

[15]Edward S. Casey, "Imagining and Remembering: In Time and Beyond Time," unpublished paper, p. 7.

[16]Ricoeur, "The Narrative Function," p. 192.

[17]Mircea Eliade, Patterns in Comparative Religion, trans. Rosemary Sheed (Cleveland and New York: The World Publishing Company, 1958).

[18]Alexander Jones, gen. ed., The Jerusalem Bible (Garden City: Doubleday & Co., Inc., 1966), Exodus 12[a], p. 91.

[19]Ibid., 12[k], p. 93.

[20]Ricoeur, Interpretation Theory: Discourse and the Surplus of Meaning (Fort Worth: The Texas Christian University Press, 1976), p. 64.

[21]This passage gathers into itself as well a whole New Testament enlargement of the metaphor. In its stories and sayings, John's gospel constructs a fabric of association between Jesus and bread. This is also true of the other gospels. See, for examples, John 2:1-12; 4:13-34; 12:1-8; 21:9-14; Mt. 4:4; 9:10-13; 11:18-19; 26:6-13; Mk. 2:15-17; 14:3-9; Lk. 5:29-32; 7:36-50; 24:28-35; 24:41-43.

[22]Mary Douglas, Natural Symbols: Explorations in Cosmology (N.Y.: Vintage Books, 1973), p. 69.

[23]Don E. Saliers, "Theology and Prayer: Some Conceptual Reminders," Worship 48:233.

[24]Ibid, p. 234.

[25]Thurian, pp. 35-36.

[26]Augustine Sermons 57.7 and 227, cited by Dix, pp. 247-248.

[27]Jungmann, p. 6.

[28]Jasper and Cuming, p. 9.

[29]Ibid., p. 10.

[30]Dix, pp. 256-258.

[31]Alexander Schmemann, <u>Introduction to Liturgical Theology</u>, trans. Asheleigh E. Moorhouse (N.Y.: St. Vladimir's Seminary Press, 1966), p. 55.

[32]Dix, p. 258.

[33]Schmemann, pp. 58-59, develops these notions from O. Cullman's <u>Christ and Time</u>.

[34]Schmemann, p. 56.

[35]Cullman, cited by Schmemann, p. 57.

[36]Jasper and Cuming, pp. 28, 29-30.

[37]Dr. Dodd, cited by Dix, p. 263.

[38]Schmemann, p. 57.

[39]Cyprian <u>Ep</u>. 63, 17, cited by Dix, p. 162.

[40]S. John Chrysostom, <u>Heb. Hom</u>. 17, 3, cited by Dix, pp. 243-244.

PART II

FEATURES OF REMEMBERING

Let us pause to take stock of where we have been in chapters I and II so that we can clarify the task at hand. First we examined some paradigms for memory in the history of philosophy, lifting out of that tradition certain prevailing themes. We noticed how the spatialization of time, a tendency prevalent in the philosophical tradition until the twentieth century, has radically denigratory effects on our conception of memory. Such a notion of human time shows an overweening predilection for the present and relegates memory to an act of mind derivative from perception. In chapter II, as an antidote to this impoverishing view of memory, we placed before us a symbolic "text": the Eucharistic anamnesis. For the purposes of comparison and contrast with the philosophical tradition on memory, the case of liturgical anamnesis has the virtue of longevity. Its history parallels that of philosophy, and yet its practice has remained fundamentally unchanged by philosophical thinking about memory precisely because it is connected with fundamental human ritual capacities.[1]

The two cases present a striking juxtaposition. Contrasted with the quite lamentable and uncreative history of philosophical theories about memory, the conceptually determinate practice of Eucharistic anamnesis presents us with one specialized instance of a densely embodied, creative, and ritualized remembering. In the setting of liturgical anamnesis, remembering emerges as a surprisingly central human activity, tied to the form of life and shape of experience of a whole community of persons. We noticed that such a remembering has the power to shape a community's consciousness, as it continually brings to life the narratives which formed that consciousness in its beginnings. Can this be the same phenomenon of memory which the philosophical tradition has most often relegated to a lowly act of mind which can do little more than revive past perceptions? What are we to make of this contrast?

On the one hand, as confessional, first level discourse, the Eucharistic anamnesis certainly cannot provide us with sufficient evidence upon which to construct yet another theory about the objective or real nature of remembering. On the other hand, we must take seriously active memory's capacity, within that context, to do a whole range of things the philosophical tradition would never have led us to believe possible. We need a mediating discourse between our symbolic "text" and philosophical thought.

103

Following Paul Ricoeur's suggestive project, let us take it as our task to allow the symbol to give rise to thought, eliciting our reflection on memory out of the fullness of "meaning already there" in the liturgical anamnesis.[2] I must now try to articulate and defend what we glimpsed of memory's creative capacities in the Eucharistic anamnesis, generalizing from that to a level of discourse which will offer a way of understanding and appreciating memory's more generic activity. Without purporting to be a full-blown theory, such a discourse may be a viable alternative to the philosophical tradition.

But this way of framing the issue of the first part of our study is already an oversimplification and thus a distortion of the case. In Plato and in the moderns, we have seen the philosophical tradition's struggling with its own tendency to denigrate memory. In his concept of Recollection, Plato does this by completely freeing certain rememberings from time. The unfortunate result of this is the bifurcation of memory itself. Nevertheless, in Plato we see a philosopher's deep fascination with and appreciation for the role remembering plays in a person's interior life. While eschewing his dualist metaphysic, we welcome his intuition of memory's importance. Twenty-five centuries later, Bergson attacks a reductive notion of memory by challenging the spatialized conception of time on which it is founded. And most importantly for our purposes, Husserl, in his turn, offers an analysis of the structure of internal time-consciousness which generates a temporality rich with retentional sedimentations of the past and protentional intimations of the future. In his thought, memory becomes a distinct mode of consciousness itself, the human capacity which frees us from entrapment in the immediate present.

Drawing on these allies in the philosophical tradition, and allowing the Eucharistic symbol with all its embodied richness to give rise to our thought, let us explore whether a further reflection on the human activity of remembering can lead us toward an understanding of memory per se. Can we argue, now at a second level of discourse, that the significance remembering enjoys in the liturgy is neither spurious nor strictly limited to a ritual confessional mode, but rather may have to do with the fundamental character of memory itself and the role it plays in our human lives?

Such a task is, however, limited in its claims. I think that memory is an important human activity, and more important than philosophy has credited it with

being. I want, first of all, to offer certain hypotheses
for how memory functions as a human activity; and,
secondly, to propose some reasons for taking these
hypotheses seriously--reasons which will appear as convergences between the phenomenological literature and the
liturgical material. By thus giving content to the
hypotheses in the form of certain evidences for a richer
notion of memory than we find in the mainline
philosophical tradition, we will be confirming that such
a view may indeed be true and is at least worth testing
as a fresh basis for hermeneutical inquiry into fictional
narratives.

There are, however, two caveats. I am neither
offering analytical proof of the truth of the hypotheses,
nor giving an exhaustive account of the nature or content
of memory by, for example, doing a phenomenology of
memory acts to show exactly how human memory works.[3]
While drawing on phenomenological insights into the
intentionality of consciousness and its temporal phases,
I am not employing a strict phenomenological method with
its successive stages of reduction, thematization, and
imaginative variation. Rather, we will be lifting out
certain features of the human activity of remembering in
support of our intuition about memory's importance. This
is so because of the nature of the project itself. We
are simply looking to gather enough support for our
intuition to do practical literary criticism. It
remains, in the final chapters, to put this description
of memory's activity to the test in the face of concrete
literary texts.

How can we set about such a task? Let me suggest
something of memory's importance by showing its inherent
relationship to two life-questions which are generally
agreed to be important, particularly to philosophical
reflection itself. We can frame these questions at this
point most simply as: (1) Who am I? or Who are we?, and
(2) What is the nature of ultimate reality? Put another
common way, they are the questions of the self and the
world.

Chapters IV and V will explore how memory relates to
these two questions. Before addressing them, however, we
must find some way to concretize our discussion while at
the same time getting beyond the first level discourse of
our symbolic text. We need a more common and more
commonly available discourse which preserves concretion
and yet transcends the confessional mode. Still taking
my lead from our reflection on the features of
remembering in the Eucharistic anamnesis and keeping in
mind the literary critical nature of the project, I have

chosen <u>narrative</u> for this purpose. While the final chapters of this essay will address themselves to specific narrative fictions, here our focus will be on narrative activity per se.

Narrativity provides us with a handle by means of which we can get hold of memory in action, for creative memory expresses itself in both story-telling and story-following. In narrative activity, creative memory becomes, in Ricoeur's word, distantiated, and is made accessible to us.[4] As the sedimentation and objectification of rememberings, the human activity of narrative offers us a place to take hold in order to see how memory is actually and functionally related to our two questions. The present chapter on narrative, then, will equip us for what follows. Finally, chapter VI will explore the relationship of memory and imagination.

Since we are searching for a mode of discourse which can effectively mediate philosophical analysis and ritual expression, the style of this chapter will necessarily be eclectic. While I shall be appealing to a variety of disciplines and thinkers in my exploration, no one of them ought to be identified exclusively with the particular aspect at hand. Indeed, we shall find along the way that one given thinker or area of inquiry may have implications for several of the issues we are exploring. This is so because the issues are not themselves unrelated to one another. In our search for a gestalt, we shall be looking to a variety of sources which may support our hypotheses about memory.

NOTES TO PART II, INTRODUCTION

[1]The history of liturgical anamnesis is at least as long as the Western philosophical tradition, if we take Hebrew liturgical practices into account.

[2]Ricoeur, The Symbolism of Evil, trans. Emerson Buchanan (Boston: Beacon Press, 1967), p. 352.

[3]Since the present manuscript was written, this significant and necessary work has been completed by phenomenologist Edward S. Casey. See his Remembering: A Phenomenological Study (Bloomington and Indianapolis: Indiana University Press, 1987).

[4]Ricoeur, Interpretation Theory, p. 43 and passim.

CHAPTER III

REMEMBERING AND NARRATIVE

In our reflection on the liturgical anamnesis'
narrative quality, we discovered one particular case in
which to remember means to tell a story. We do not
intend to argue on that basis a thesis that all rememberings entail telling stories. Language analysis has
effectively cautioned us against any such universal
claims about the nature and content of rememberings. Our
hypothesis about remembering and narratizing is the at
once more circumspect and resonant one that the two human
activities enjoy a close connectedness. If in the
liturgy remembering involves telling stories, could it be
that this cooperation manifests itself elsewhere in our
human lives as well?

Now, at one level, this connection between the
activities of story-telling and remembering is patently
obvious. It has long been recognized, for example, by
literary criticism. As indication of this wide
acceptance of the collusion between narrative and memory
among literary critics, let me cite two examples. The
first is from a current fiction anthology commonly used
in college-level introductory courses; the second, from
E. M. Forster's influential study, _Aspects of the Novel_.

In the Preface to _The Norton Introduction to
Fiction_, the editor makes this observation in his
discussion of plot.

> Our reading between the first sentence of a
> story and the last, though sequential, is
> actually multidimensional: as we read on, we
> remember all or some of what went before, so
> that by the middle of the story we are not
> reading quite the same way we were at the
> beginning, and at the end, we are reading in
> still another manner.[1]

He makes an even stronger claim for memory's role in the
narrative experience when he asserts that "attention,
anticipation, and retention are the activities . . . that
inform our understanding of and response to all elements
of fiction."[2]

While editorial prefaces to college anthologies do
not represent the cutting edge of critical scholarship,

they do provide a dependable litmus for the state of the art as it is generally understood and practiced. In his assertions, this editor is simply echoing the principles of fiction laid down by E. M. Forster some fifty years earlier. Forster makes a distinction between story and plot in a fictive work. A plot, like a story, is a narrative of events arranged in their time sequence, but plot adds to this an emphasis on causality. If story responds to our elemental curiosity, plot responds, says Forster, to our intelligence and our memory. Memory and intelligence are closely connected because unless we remember we cannot understand. If we are to understand the meaning of the narrative, then, we must exercise our memories, for only our memories allow us to perceive the pattern in the sequence.[3]

There is common agreement among literary critics that our <u>story-following competencies</u> require memory. There is even widespread agreement that our <u>story-telling competencies</u> are founded on memory. So long as we reject an extreme Romanticist aesthetic of spontaneous <u>ex nihilo</u> creativity, we can readily assent that the story-teller speaks and writes out of her own remembered experience in constructing her tale.[4] One notable exception is, of course, the minstrel or teller of traditional tales who, though he does not draw his material from his own history, is dependent on formulaic phrases in the rendition of his song. Here memory's role in story telling is no less extensive; for as Scholes and Kellogg have shown in <u>The Nature of Narrative</u>, the singer is utterly dependent on his tradition.[5]

Let these few examples suffice to show that literary criticism recognizes some connection between memory and narrative in the acts of story-telling and story-following. If we were to put this connection in traditional terms, we might say that the faculty of memory is necessary in order to tell and to follow stories with comprehension. Having granted this, we can explore the relationship further, suggesting that the logic of memory and narrative's connection is even more complex and fundamental. Coming from diverse sources, there have been suggestive proposals in support of such an hypothesis. Let us examine three of them here, selected for the very range of approaches they display. While we cannot hope to do full justice to the divergent contexts in which these theories are embedded, we can glean support for our hypothesis about memory and narrative's interconnectedness from the convergences they do exhibit.

All three proposals run counter to the mainline philosophical understanding, and display certain correspondences to the liturgical understanding, of memory. Each rejects a faculty psychology approach, seeing memory rather as a relatively autonomous and intersubjective human activity with its roots in the social character of human existence. What is even more striking, each understands human memory fundamentally in terms of narrativity, and for each narrativity itself is an inherently human and not an artificial act.

Arendt on Narration

Hannah Arendt offers a profound analysis of action and narration within the context of political philosophy. In The Human Condition, she argues that narrative is the most distinctively human action because it, and it alone, responds to the question of who, rather than what, we are. What is more, the human action that finds expression in stories must be memorable; thus narratives, in the form of history, conserve not only the individual human being but the whole rich and variegated tradition of being human. In terms of our interests, Arendt suggests that our remembering capacities discover their deepest significance not in the simple recall of information or images from the past but in the stories we tell and by which we seek to understand what it means to be human. The narrative function, which she sees as so central to the human condition, is a function of memory. Let us briefly rehearse the terms of her argument.

In The Human Condition, Arendt distinguishes among the three fundamental human activities of labor, work, and action. She calls these three fundamental because "each corresponds to one of the basic conditions under which life on earth has been 'given' to human beings."[6] Labor corresponds to the biological processes of the human body; it assures the survival of both the individual and the species in the struggle between human beings and nature. Its product is oriented toward consumption. Work, in its turn, corresponds to the unnaturalness, the artificiality, of human existence. It provides the world of made things, different from our natural surroundings. Its product, the human artifact, grants some sense of permanence and durability to the futility of mortal life, for by our work we leave some mark in the world which can survive us.

Distinguished from labor and work, action is the only activity that goes on directly between persons without the mediation of nature or matter. It corresponds to our social condition; and, insofar as it engages in founding and preserving political bodies, creates the condition for human remembrance, i.e., history. Precisely because it corresponds to our social condition, no other human performances require speech to the same extent as action. In speech and action, human beings reveal who--not just what--they are. This disclosure of "who" someone is is implicit in everything she says and does, though it tends to remain hidden from the person herself. This revelatory character of speech and action, by which persons disclose themselves as subjects, always falls into the already existing web of human relationships. Together, speech and action begin a process which emerges as a life-story, which in its turn, will affect uniquely the life-stories of those with whom one comes into contact. "It is because of this already existing web of human relationships . . . in which action alone is real that it produces stories with or without intention as naturally as fabrication [work] produces tangible things."[7]

Action goes beyond leaving a mark; it aims rather toward being recollected in stories. The function of such life-stories is to provide an identity, a narrative identity, to the doer. Not only do stories provide such an identity, but only stories can do so. The manifestation of "who" confounds all efforts toward univocal verbal expression. Only the complexity of narration can reveal the intricate interplay of self and world, of freedom and necessity, in which one's identity is grounded. History then becomes the storybook of humankind, "with many actors and speakers and yet without any tangible authors," precisely because it is the outcome of action.[8] It repeats action which is memorable in the form of narration.

From her vantage in political philosophy, Arendt draws certain links between memory, narrative, and identity. (1) She understands memory as an autonomous and distinctive human activity and not simply a derivative faculty of mind; (2) sees the profound engagement of remembering in narrative; (3) claims that narrativity is fundamental in intersubjective human experience; and (4) places this memory/narrative nexus at the heart of human identity.

Crites and the Narrative Quality of Experience

Approaching these issues with a different set of interests, Stephen Crites recapitulates similar conclusions in his description of "The Narrative Quality of Experience."[9] More tentative and exploratory than Arendt, Crites does not attempt to place his argument within a larger systematic framework, such as her theory of political behavior. For our purposes, however, it too is suggestive. Crites comes at the issues polemically. He wants to argue for phenomenological insights against faculty psychology with its mind/body bifurcation and concomitant predilection for mind and abstraction. And he wants to argue against an understanding of narrative which is rooted in such predilection.

There has been a definite vogue recently to consider all narratives (whether literary, historical, or autobiographical) as fictions. According to this understanding, human experience is chaotic and inchoate, and only our fictive powers can make sense out of an inherently senseless reality.[10] Such sense-making is never more than artifice, however: the imposition of pattern on fundamental chaos. Such a defensive theory of narrative is constructed at least partially, whether knowingly or not, on a model of mind drawn from the mainline philosophical tradition. According to this model, the mind imposes sense on the world through narration. Stories order an otherwise inchoate temporal experience by the imposition of beginnings, middles, and ends. Crites believes this conception of narrative serves to reinforce an already philosophically bankrupt self/world dichotomy. If we take Husserl's phenomenology of inner time-consciousness seriously, he suggests, we generate a quite different model for narrative activity, one that makes convincing claims for that activity's inherency in our experience.

Crites is our ally on several counts: (1) he draws out the implications of Husserl's phenomenology for a thesis about narrative; (2) this leads him to make the strongest possible claim for narrative activity in our human experience: that experience itself has an inherently narrative shape; (3) he locates this narrative quality both in the world and in consciousness itself; and (4) he bases his argument on memory as an autonomous act of consciousness. Strangely enough, however, Crites blends his phenomenological material with a model of memory which owes more to Augustine than to Husserl. He describes memory as the storehouse of our ideas and impressions. His thesis, however, does not depend on this image theory of memory and, indeed, counters it in serious ways. It is his very polemicism which leads him into this mistake, for in his efforts to save narrativity from being mere artifice, he too easily adopts a retentionist theory of memory. If Husserl has taught us anything, however, it is that memory cannot be rightly

113

understood along the model of a recording machine. With these provisos in mind, let us look at Crites' proposal.

Crites combines his reflection on inner time-consciousness with certain notions of the function of myth and ritual in traditional cultures. He begins by proposing a distinction between what he calls "sacred stories" and "mundane stories." A reflection on traditional cultures leads us to surmise that there must be certain narratives which form a civilization's very sense of itself and its world. Embedded in the ritual practices of the culture, such stories have special resonances. They seem to be allusive versions of deeper stories which cannot be fully and directly told, for they are not so much the objects of consciousness as the formings of consciousness itself. The culture seems to be the telling rather than the teller of such deep, untold stories: they inform a people's sense of the story in which their lives participate. Because a culture's very sense of itself and its world are given in such ineffable narratives, Crites proposes to call them "sacred stories." They function as Ur-myths, from which spring the myths which traditional cultures celebrate in ritual. While they are themselves "too deep for words," they seek expression more directly in the ritualized myths of the society. As we have seen in the liturgical anamnesis, such an expression is necessarily intersubjective, praxological, and self-involving.

Once expressed, a "sacred story" becomes a "mundane story"--it both gives a world and is set in a world. Every story that has been told is a mundane story. There is a distinction, then, but not a separation, between sacred and mundane stories. Every mundane story is somehow implicit in a people's sacred story and points to it.

What mediates between them is the form of the experiencing consciousness itself. It is not only that consciousness is moulded by the communal sacred story to which it awakens and in its turn finds its own expression in the mundane stories which are the articulation of that sense of reality. Consciousness does this precisely because its own form is at least incipiently narrative. Here Crites is following Kant's lead in The Critique of Pure Reason where he shows that consciousness must have its own form if experience is to be coherent and intelligible. But his conclusion about what that form must be differs from Kant's. Using Husserl, Crites grounds his own hypothesis that the form of the experiencing consciousness is narrative on consciousness' temporal structure. He aims to show that both remembering and anticipatory phases of consciousness display a rudimentary narrative interest and shape.

Our expectations of the future may be empty and vague, but they are by no means formless. Reflection on our own experience of anticipation convinces us that we anticipate by framing little stories or scenarios of how things may turn out. Our hunches, guesses, predictions, dreams, worries, and wishes are often thin stories indeed, but they are never simply random. It is by means of such scenarios that we orient ourselves toward the future.

Contrasted with these frail anticipatory stories, the chronicle of memory tends to be much denser and sharper in detail. Already in memory there is sequence, the simple temporality of before and after. For Crites, if I retrace my steps in search of my keys, my mind may not be doing anything particular in which my effort to remember consists, but my whole person is, by my very action, implying the remembered sequence of my past experience. Without the simple chronicle of memory, experience would be incoherent. Locked in a bare present, we could have no more than a disconnected succession of perceptions. The sense of temporal succession in experience and the power to formulate coherent unities from this succession are powers of memory.

Taking his lead from Augustine's renowned ruminations on memory in Book X of the _Confessions_, Crites wants to distinguish between these two functions. For him, "memory proper" simply records a succession of experiences, whereas "recollection" grasps these experiences together into patterns. Experience is illuminated and made intelligible by the subtle processes of recollection, through which consciousness makes new configurations and thus re-orders the past. It is in this sense, Crites suggests, that we can affirm Plato's dictum that all knowledge is Recollection.

Anticipation and memory do not exist in isolation in experience but are rather inseparably joined in the present itself. Only the present exists, but it exists only in the tensed modalities of memory, attention, and anticipation. The inner form of any possible experience is determined by this union of past, present, and future modalities in every moment of experience. This tensed unity, already story-shaped in some rudimentary sense, requires narrative forms both for its expression (what Crites calls "mundane stories") and for its own sense of the meaning of its internal coherence ("sacred stories").

But if consciousness thus molds experience by narrative forms, its expression is obviously not limited to story-telling. The raw narrative materials of consciousness can be recollected into non-narrative forms. Indeed, thought seems to have its own powerful inner drive to overcome the relentless temporality of experience. Archetypal myths, the spatial articulation of painting and sculpture, meditation, and such theoretical endeavors as philosophy are all examples of consciousness' capacities for breaking the sense of narrative time.

In the modern period, the strategies of abstraction and contraction serve this purpose. By abstraction, we detach ourselves from our temporal experience in order to formulate generalized principles and techniques. By contraction, narrative temporality is fragmented into dissociated immediacies. Crites argues that such contraction to the present is wrongly assumed to be what is concrete and irreducible in experience. These two time-defying strategies, in detaching us from the narrative movement which is really concrete in experience, have generated the mind/body dualism endemic to modern philosophy which Crites so decries. As he writes,

> [W]e state the matter backwards if we say that something called mind abstracts from experience to produce generality, or if we say that "the body" has feelings and sensations. It is the activity of abstracting from the narrative concreteness of experience that leads us to posit the idea of mind as a distinct faculty. And it is the concentration of consciousness into feeling and sensation that gives rise to the idea of body. Both mind and body are reifications of particular functions that have been wrenched from the concrete temporality of the conscious self.[11]

By contrast, in stories the self is given whole, as an activity in time. Remembering, likewise, is not simply a process in the head, as the recalling of our own painful past experiences tells us!

If experience does indeed have a narrative quality, then, suggests Crites, both the self's identity and its "world" are implicit in a person's multidimensional story. Transformation or conversion (of the kind we see, for example, in Augustine) must involve undermining the stories within which someone has been awakened to consciousness. She must be able to re-member, re-collect, and re-cognize herself into a new story. This new story which she tells must, however, in some sense preserve her continuity with herself. We see here once again how a thesis about the narrative quality of experience will have radical implications for a theory of identity.

Crites and Arendt, from their varying perspectives, both speak to memory's constitutive function in narrative activity; and both understand such narrativity to be fundamental to human experience. Crites makes an even stronger claim when he argues that all experience has an inherent narrative shape, mediated by the temporal character of the experiencing consciousness itself.

Freudian Psychoanalysis

For further support for our hypothesis we turn finally to our strongest ally, psychoanalysis. Until now, we have been tracing certain theories about the links between memory and narrative in human experience. In psychoanalysis, we shall be reflecting not simply on another theory, but on how certain theoretical understandings--not just about memory but about the nature of human experience itself--are drawn from a long tradition of praxis. In the case of psychoanalysis, the praxis is what actually happens in the psychoanalytic situation, especially as regards remembering and story-telling. Now since we are more concerned with remembering as a human activity--with how it works, than with what it is--this rootedness of psychoanalytic theory in practice is especially significant for our purposes.

In terms of our argument thus far, psychoanalysis shares with Arendt an interest in the intersubjective and linguistic character of remembering and narrative; and with Crites it shares an attention to the temporal character of our experience. It advances our argument, however, in three significant ways: (1) Psychoanalysis offers us a concrete case in which to remember is to narratize and storytelling is itself an anamnesis. (2) Memory emerges here with striking clarity as an autonomous act, not derivative from other acts of consciousness. (3) Psychoanalysis presents the strongest and most consistent challenge from experience to the Aristotelian and empiricist views of memory which have dominated philosophical thinking until this century and still predominate in our commonsense understanding.

Because of the very complexity of psychoanalysis' treatment of these issues, our exposition must necessarily be correspondingly lengthy. It will divide itself into three sections: (I) We shall first attend to the theory/practice character of psychoanalysis and its implications for us. (II) Next we shall lay out Freud's discoveries about memory, using a concrete case history to ground our discussion. (III) Finally, we shall discuss the implications of these discoveries for the narrative commitment of psychoanalysis.

I

Psychoanalysis is not simply a name given to a theory. According to Freud himself,

> Psychoanalysis is the name (1) of a procedure for the investigation of mental processes; (2) of a method (based upon that investigation) for the treatment of neurotic disorders; and (3) of a collection of psychological information attained along those lines, which is gradually being accumulated into a new scientific discipline.[12]

This three-fold relationship of a procedure for investigation, a method of treatment, and a theory, as well as the order Freud establishes among them, has been too commonly overlooked in the psychoanalytic literature. While such exaggerated attention to psychoanalytic theory is understandable in the light of Freud's own theoretical inclinations in his writings, recent commentators as diverse as Edward Casey, Jurgen Habermas, James Hillman, Paul Ricoeur, and Michael Sherwood have begun to challenge what they see as a skewed focus.[13] It is, after all, on the basis of his analytic experience that Freud develops and revises his theories. If we are to assess psychoanalysis adequately, we must recognize that the theory is, fundamentally, the codification of what takes place in the analytic situation and more precisely in the relationship between analyst and analysand. Psychoanalytic theory takes into account not raw scientific data but data already selected by the nature of the analytic situation itself.

What is the nature of that situation? In his examination of "The Question of Proof in Freud's Writings," Ricoeur notes four interrelated aspects of the analytic situation which condition the selection of relevant data for psychoanalytic theory.[14] They include: (1) The talking-cure character of psychoanalysis. Facts in psychoanalysis are not items of observable behavior so much as reports or accounts. Only what is capable of

being said can enter into the psychoanalytic experience.
(2) <u>The intersubjective character of psychoanalysis</u>. It
is not only a question of what can be said, but of what
is said <u>to another person</u>. It is here that the Freudian
notion of transference, discussed below, becomes
significant. (3) <u>The relevance of psychical reality in
contrast to material reality</u>. Through his work with
hysterics Freud discovers that fantasies frequently pose
as memories, possessing "a psychical reality opposed to
material reality . . . ; in the world of neurosis, this
psychical reality plays the dominant role."[15] This
discovery will, of course, lead him to a profound
skepticism regarding memory's truth claims. (4) <u>The
narrative character of the psychoanalytic experience</u>.
The account given by the analysand has a narrative shape.
The analytic situation selects from the analysand's
experience only that which is capable of entering into a
story. This narrative element is fundamental in psychoanalysis; and, in this sense, case histories constitute
psychoanalysis' primary texts. (It has even been
suggested recently that Freud's theory may not be
adequate to his reported case histories).[16] Although
Freud does not discuss this narrative character directly,
he does refer to it indirectly in his considerations
about memory.

II

As Edward Casey notes, memory is important for Freud
because he recognizes in early childhood memories the
germ of all later psychopathology.[17] We are familiar with
his famous dictum from <u>Studies in Hysteria</u> that "my
hysterical patients suffer principally from
reminiscences."[18] Of course, he later decides that such
memories are not real memories at all but rather screen
memories and fantasies. He always considers such screen
memories in relation to remembering and forgetting,
however, precisely because of their connection with
resistance and repetition. In the 1914 essay on
"Remembering, Repeating, and Working-Through," he
articulates this connection.

When the memory of a past event is too painful and
traumatic, it is replaced by a compulsion to repeat which
has the effect of blocking the remembering. "The
analysee repeats himself rather than remember and does
this by means of resistance."[19] The transference
generated by the "playground" quality of the analytic
situation between analyst and analysand serves to curb
this compulsion by turning it into a motive for

remembering. As Freud explains it, "The part of the patient's emotional life which he can no longer recall to memory is re-experienced by him in his relation to the physician; and it is only this re-experiencing in the 'transference' that convinces him of the existence and of the power of these unconscious sexual impulses."[20] The only aim of such a struggle against resistance (called working-through by Freud) is to reopen the path of memory itself. Repetition needs to be replaced by remembering if analysis is to have a therapeutic effect. Remembering is thus the therapeutic goal of psychoanalysis. We can already begin to see how psychoanalysis will have radical effects on our tendency to consider memory a mere lowly act of the mind. Let us examine these Freudian notions more concretely by seeing how they are operative within a particular case history.

In the same year as he published his essay on "Remembering, Repeating, and Working-Through," Freud first wrote the details of the wolf-man case history.[21] The patient had been in analysis for four years by this time. While it is well beyond our present scope to rehearse the case in its entirety, let me focus on those two events which most fascinated Freud about it and which Edward Casey singles out for examination in "Piaget and Freud on Childhood Memory".[22] These events are the wolf-dream itself, from which the case takes its popular name, and the observation of the primal scene. Since Casey's argument is so pertinent for our own concerns, let me paraphrase it here in some detail.

Casey argues that a close examination of the wolf-dream's subsequent influence on the patient and its manifest content led Freud to suppose that it represented, by means of reversal, the wolf-man's witnessing of his parents' love-making some two and a half years prior to the dream's occurrence. The wolves' fearsome immobility is a screen for his parents' violent actions during intercourse; the wolves' staring at him replaces his staring at them; their bushy tails symbolize his fear of castration (by way of a story told him by his grandfather in the meantime). Casey notes the importance of remembering that the supposed originary event, the observation of the primal scene, is never recollected by the wolf-man in therapy. Rather, it is a reconstruction within the psychoanalytic situation of what must have happened, since such an event alone is able to make sense of the man's shattered psyche in the light of other evidence provided in the wolf-man's conversations with Freud. As Freud writes in the case history, "so far as my experience hitherto goes, these scenes from infancy are not reproduced during the treatment as <u>recollections</u>, they are the products of <u>construction</u>."[23]

In the wolf-man case history, Casey identifies the three forms of memory central to the analytic experience: <u>recollection</u> (of the wolf-dream), <u>repetition</u> (of the primal scene by the dream, which is a disguised memory of that event), and <u>reconstruction</u> (of the primal scene itself). For Freud dreaming is "another kind of remembering, though one that is subject to the conditions that rule at night and to the laws of dream-formation."[24]

Casey helps us to see here a quite complicated memory pattern. The wolf-man not only recollects the dream itself but is tormented for years afterward by a wolf phobia. The dream memory, that is, continues to be <u>enacted</u> in the phobia in which wolves function as mnemic symbols. What is more, if Freud's reconstruction is correct, there is a pattern of double symbolic repetition in the memories. The dream symbolically reenacts the observation of the primal scene and the phobia in its turn symbolically reenacts the dream. A further density of memory events obtains in that both dream and phobia are recollected by the wolf-man in the present analytic situation, several years after they themselves have been replaced by other repetition compulsions.

Of what significance are these discoveries by Freud about remembering? Early on in his analyses, he finds that memory, far from being merely a copy of a past event, has its own causal efficacy which may be greater than that of the original event itself. As he asserts in <u>Studies in Hysteria</u>, "in every analysis of a case of hysteria based on sexual traumas, we find that impressions from the pre-sexual period which produced no effect on the child attain traumatic power at a later date as memories."[25] <u>Memory, that is, has the power to exert a significant effect long after the original event, and most importantly, the power resides in the memory and not in the original impression</u>. Such an understanding of memory clearly runs counter to the mainline philosophical tradition we traced from Aristotle to the empiricists. Freud rejects the Aristotelian paradigm of efficient causality as a valid model for memory. In analytic situation after situation, he finds that memory displays "a power which was completely lacking from the event itself. [It] will operate as though it were a contemporary event."[26] Memory, the effect of an event, itself becomes an event, through what he calls "deferred action."

In *Vocabulary of Psychoanalysis*, Jacques Lacan describes this after-the-event phenomenon in these terms: "Expressions, impressions, mnesic traces, are recast later in function of new experiences of the access to a new stage of development, and . . . they may assume, not only a new meaning, but a new efficiency."[27] In the process of working-through, Freud discovers that certain experiences could not be integrated into a meaningful context when they were experienced. Thus in the case of the wolf-man, it is only at the age of four that he can remember and understand the event he witnessed when he was one and a half. But how remember and understand? In the form of a dream, which is to say, in Casey's provocative phrasing, as a "symbolically disguised understanding, an understanding unknown to itself.[28] Dreaming is a form of understanding precisely because it is a form of remembering, i.e., it is of the past. As Freud writes,

> [The wolf-dream] is simply another instance of deferred action. At the age of one and a half the child receives an impression to which he is unable to react adequately; he is only able to understand it and to be moved by it when the impression is revived in him at the age of four; and only twenty years later, during the analysis, is he able to grasp with his conscious mental processes what was going on in him.[29]

The subsequent reworking of such early experiences requires new events and new situations. In the case of the wolf-man, it is a second sexually significant scene, the seduction by his sister, which confers upon the first its effectiveness and opens the way for the wolf-dream. What is more, it is only much later, in the context of the analytic situation with its fourfold aspects, that the wolf-man brings this understanding to conscious awareness.

But if many repressed memories become traumatic only after the event, it cannot be that memory simply reproduces real events by a kind of perception of the past. Rather, memory is a work, indeed a working-through, which goes over and over extremely complex structurations in the psyche. It seems that there are certain significant rememberings which require such a gradual deferment to reach the depths of understanding. Freud's discovery about memory is closer to Plato than to Aristotle, for Plato understood knowledge as an anamnesis, a gradually regained Recollection of Forms.

So, in psychoanalysis, the long and painful process of understanding is an anamnesis, achieved intersubjectively in the dialogue between analyst and analysand. The analyst takes the place of Plato's midwife. He is also a kind of literary critic of life-fictions.

III

This working-through by means of memory in the psychoanalytic situation is achieved by virtue of the narrative character of the psychoanalytic experience. The subject matter of psychoanalysis is neither more nor less than an individual patient, a single human being. And the ultimate basis of psychoanalytic explanation is a long narrative account applicable to that person as a whole and not to isolated bits of his behavior.[30] Freud recognizes this when he says that the explanation of "a single symptom would in fact amount to the task of relating an entire case history."[31] In the psychoanalytic situation, remembering is not simply recalling certain isolated events from the past. It is, rather, discovering the capacity to form ordered connections and meaningful sequences out of those events. That is why a particular interpretation's truth resides in its fruitfulness, its power to engender new memories which were previously unconscious, and to shape out of those a life story. In the words of Ricoeur, in psychoanalysis to remember is "to be able to constitute one's own existence in the form of a story where a memory as such is only a fragment of the story. It is the narrative structure of such life-stories that makes a case a case history."[32] The problem in psychoanalysis is to build a story which makes sense of his existence to the analysand. He comes into analysis with a story to tell (an anamnesis typically leading up to: "And that's why I came to see you, Doctor"), but it is a story which makes no sense, which is unbearable to him.[33] It is in the psychoanalytic situation, with its four interrelated aspects, that he must learn to build an acceptable story out of his memory, to construct a coherent narrative out of the tatters of his experience. The new story he learns to tell, through the dynamics of remembering, repeating, and working-through, must finally be able to make sense of who he is. Indeed, it is the very telling of his new story which discloses, in Arendt's sense, not what but who the agent is.

Psychoanalysis begins with the exploration of memory and its expression in language. Memories must first of all be spoken if they are ever to be liberated or

123

liberating. Psychoanalysis, according to Freud, "brings to an end the operative force of the [traumatic experience] which was not abreacted in the first instance, by allowing its strangulated affect to find a way out through speech."[34] The wolf-man's understanding of his tormented childhood comes only in the narrative discourse he has with Freud in analysis.

The story, however, is not a monologue; rather, through the cooperation of analyst and analysand in transference and reconstruction, a new story is pieced together intersubjectively. As Habermas writes, the therapist "makes interpretive suggestions for a story that the patient cannot tell. Yet they can be verified in fact only if the patient adopts them and tells his own story with their aid."[35]

On what basis does the therapist make such interpretive suggestions? As Habermas contends, it is only "the metapsychologically founded and systematically generalized history of infantile development" which puts the therapist in the position to combine the fragments of the patient's story in such a way as to reconstruct the gaps in his memory.[36] In other words, to put it somewhat crudely, it is Freud's meta-story about the nature of human existence which allows him to elicit from his patients their own story. The masterplot, however, that theory of human behavior, is arrived at by Freud on the basis of his psychoanalytic experience; and that experience, in its turn, necessitates constant revisions in the theory. In this sense, psychoanalytic theory is simply a story told about human existence on the basis of single human beings' quite specific stories.

Here we confront the thorny issue which has plagued psychoanalysis from the start, "the question of proof" in Ricoeur's terms. If psychoanalysis is indeed a "new scientific discipline," then what are the criteria which ground its truth claims? Failing to articulate such scientific criteria, Freud opens himself to the accusation that it is the account's acceptability to the patient which is therapeutically effective, an acceptability manipulated by the analyst's suggestions. Beyond this suspicion is the more serious one that the criterion of success in psychoanalysis is simply the patient's capacity to adapt to a given social milieu, the values of which are represented by the therapist. Then psychoanalysis becomes equivalent to a fascist propaganda, psychoanalytic explanations to the socially repressive rhetoric of persuasion.

These accusations, and the issues they raise, are outside the scope of our inquiry. Habermas and Ricoeur address them by elaborating complex epistemological bases for psychoanalysis' truth claims. Sherwood holds that even if the therapeutic efficacy of psychoanalytic explanations is not correlated with the truth or accuracy of psychoanalytic narratives, it is related to their adequacy, their capacity to provide a coherent pattern to the patient's tangled and tormented life story. Hillman makes a virtue of suspicion by wrenching psychoanalysis from "its supposedly empirical framework" and connecting it with the tradition of poesis, of fictive tellings.[37]

We need not go so far as Hillman does to recognize psychoanalysis' significance for our hypothesis about memory and narrative's inherent connection. It seems clear that what these diverse commentators agree upon, the "narrative commitment of psychoanalysis,"[38] is inextricably bound up with the psychoanalytic situation's character as an anamnesis, a complex and intersubjective activity of remembering.

Let us recall what we said, following Ricoeur, about emplotment in our discussion of the liturgical anamnesis' narrative quality. All plots, whether historical or fictional, combine in varying degrees sequence and pattern. Sequence responds to our fundamental story-following curiosity. We listen to a story to find out what happens next. But stories satisfy as well our sense-making propensities. We want to know why it happens, what the connection among the events is. Plot emerges in this paradoxical competition between sequence and pattern.

A person enters therapy with a story to tell, but it is a mere chronicle, a dark and disturbing sequence. It has no plot. This is the leitmotif, if you will, of psychoanalysis: the patient enters therapy. Therapy itself then becomes the theme, the means of focusing and selecting incidents from the chronicle of life, as we can see in Freud's case histories. We do not learn everything there is to know about the wolf-man, but only those details of his experience which serve in the construction of a plot. The analyst's successive interpretations, or diagnoses if you will, are little suggestive stories aimed at nurturing in the analysand the memorial capacity to retell his own intolerable story in a more adequate way. Successful therapy is really a collaboration between the stories of analyst and analysand by virtue of which the analysand is able to recast his memories in such a way as to discover a pattern in his story and thus to find a plot which allows him to live. It is the paradoxical interplay of sequence and pattern, central to all plots, which elicits the new story.

Hillman identifies three senses in which Freud's psychoanalytic case histories are fictions or imaginative tellings.[39] (1) They are, first of all, themselves stories told by Freud on the basis of his memory of the psychoanalytic situation. They are neither verbatim records of these sessions, nor are they biographies or autobiographies. Freud the storyteller, in writing case histories, creates a new narrative genre which is as different from the typical medical case history as it is from a novel.

(2) The stories case histories present are more concerned, as we have seen, with psychical reality than with factual reality. Freud's crucial discovery that the stories he was being told were often psychological happenings dressed up as history and experienced as remembered events was the first recognition in modern psychology of the independence of memory from history and vice versa. Forgetting, distortion, denial, and repression reveal that there is a history which escapes memory; and, conversely, screen memories, confabulations, and tales told of early sexual traumas and seductions reveal that there are memories which are not historical. Memory does not simply record the past. It originates as well, presenting its productions as reproductions. Even screen memories, however, are tied to and grow out of the past. Freud discovered that memory recasts the past in imaginative tellings which are nonetheless psychologically true accounts.

(3) Because of this independence of psychical reality from factual reality, and, more importantly, because of the case history's independence from verifiability, a case history is a fiction in the philosophical sense, i.e., a construct beyond the scientific criteria of true or false. In this sense, case histories belong to Vaihinger's category of the "as if." They are not subject to proof or disconfirmation, but simply to neglect should they lose their operational effectiveness. This is one reason why Ricoeur insists that "if the ultimate truth-claim of psychoanalysis resides in case histories, the means of proof reside in the articulation of the entire network," of which narration is simply one aspect.[40]

If psychoanalytic case histories are in some senses fictions, they are therapeutic fictions and anamnetic fictions. Psychoanalysis' narrative commitment is based on Freud's conviction that, through story-telling and story-following, memory can escape its own fatedness. At the foundation of psychoanalysis' imaginative tellings is memory's capacity to engender in the analysand a way of reconnecting with his life story, of making for himself a new story which, without any longer denying or escaping the past, opens that past up to fresh possibilities.

We have gathered support for our hypothesis about memory and narrative's integral relation from a number of spokespersons in diverse fields of inquiry. The picture of remembering we are piecing together with their help is remarkable in its divergence from the philosophical tradition and its resemblances to the liturgical practice of anamnesis. In speaking about their "way of picturing remembering," I do not mean to suggest that there emerges for us any univocal understanding of what exactly memory is or what happens when we remember; no do I mean to suggest unanimity among them. There is no need to rehearse their differences here. What is significant, however, is that each is interested less in the precise nature of memory than in how our remembering capacities are woven into the fabric of our human lives. Consequently, they offer us a more robust and fully embodied picture of remembering than we were able to find among the philosophers.

I have tried to clarify in the course of our discussion the specific fashions in which Arendt, Crites, and Freud are allies in our search for a gestalt. At the risk of repetitiveness, let me reiterate the salient points of agreement among them. (1) Memory is not merely derivative from perception but actually enjoys an autonomy among conscious acts. (2) We gain a more accurate understanding of memory if we consider it not as a mental faculty but as a human activity. (3) As a human activity, memory exhibits inherent interdependencies with narrativity. (4) Memory is wrongly understood as a mere repetition or recording of the past. Indeed, because we remember, the past is never simply past, never simply "dead and gone." Memory reorders and reconstructs the past, opening it up to change. Memory, that is, has imaginative powers.

Beyond this, we have noted in each instance how such an understanding of remembering and its relation to narrativity invariably opens into notions about how both activities are engaged in our fundamental understandings of the self. Our narrative and remembering capacities are not unrelated, it appears, to our fascination with the question "Who am (are) I (we)?, the question of identity. While this was evident in Arendt and Crites, it is especially the case with psychoanalysis. All our talk about the analysand's construction of a story to live by can be recast quite readily in terms of identity.

Before we address this question, however, let us recall that other fundamental issue raised at the start of this chapter. The self's question of "who am I?" has as its corollary a question addressed to the world that self intends: "What is the nature of reality?" Now phenomenology has always insisted on the correlation between these two questions. As Merleau-Ponty puts it, "Truth does not 'inhabit' only 'the inner man,' or more accurately, there is no inner man, man is in the world, and only in the world does he know himself."[41] In other words, we are not simply faced with two fundamental questions. Phenomenology suggests not only that we know a self through its world, but that we can best understand the self by approaching it indirectly in this manner.

Doesn't this correspond to our ordinary experience? Each of us has anxieties, hopes, and expectations directed toward our world. What is it all about? Is it capricious, benevolent, absurd? We know too that we often get a clearer sense of another not by listening to his self-description but by hearing how he describes the world. We sense a person's bitterness, for example, by seeing what the world is like for him, not because he tells us of his bitter emotions.

Literature recognizes this. Characters are not revealed to us exclusively or principally through their ruminations on the question of identity, but rather through their stories. When Crites calls all tellable stories "mundane," this is just what he is getting at. Stories are mundane because they display a world. As Arendt says, we come to know who a person is by seeing how his actions serve to construct a world in story form. Tragedy, says Aristotle, is the imitation not of persons but of action and of life. Character comes in as a subsidiary to action. We learn who the character is by discovering what her world is like.

Surely each of us is concerned about how things are, about the way things are going, but why? Are we not concerned about the world precisely because things are, indeed, going, are constantly changing? Our existence is not secure. We are subject to a future which is inscrutable to us, thrown into a world and toward a destiny we do not understand. It is in the face of this world that the self understands itself. The world question--"What is the nature of reality?"--and the self question--"Who am I?"--are actually two poles of the same reality. We are selves who have worlds. We are in the world, and only in the world can we know ourselves.

In addressing these two ultimate questions and their relation to remembering, we shall turn first to the question of world. But we shall take our very personal concern about our world as a clue. Why, indeed, are we so concerned? We have just said that our concern is the correlate of the insecurity of our existence, our being situated in a world which is constantly changing. Is not, then, temporality the very aspect of the world which causes our concern? When we address the question of our world, we are addressing the temporal condition of our being.

Now this way of talking about the issues, of linking our concern with our being-in-the-world and with temporality, is Heidegger's. No one has spoken so eloquently and so provocatively about our temporal condition and its reverberations in our being. If we thought with Husserl about the nature of inner time-consciousness, we shall think with Heidegger about our temporality. Husserl's description of consciousness' temporal character has the clarity of philosophical argument; Heidegger's denser language is at once more visceral and more profound. His reflections are more embodied; they give us the world which Husserl's temporal consciousness intends. Our task, however, is not simply to reflect with Heidegger on temporality, but to consider memory's place in it.

Our temporality is not simply a matter of our concern about the future. As Ray Hart insists, following Merleau-Ponty, "We live out of the future but understand out of the past."[42] Our commonsense way of thinking about temporality, drawn from the philosophical tradition, is that we move from the past into the future. The underlying conception, as we have seen, is of time as a line. But there is a very real, albeit paradoxical, sense in which we move out of the future into the past. By virtue of our vulnerability vis-à-vis the uncertain future, we reach back to and draw on our past. Such a reaching back is not simply to retrieve data stored in some memory bank, as Aristotle might have us believe. Through the activity of remembering, our use of the past is an active interpreting. It is in that very process that the past becomes meaningful. When we "understand out of the past," what we are understanding is precisely who we are and what our world is like.

Much of what we have to say about the temporal condition of being is already implicit in our discussion of memory's relation to narrativity. It remains for us to explicate the issues thematically. In the next chapters, then, we shall be examining memory and narrative's relation to the questions of temporality and identity.

[1]Jerome Beaty, ed. The Norton Introduction to Literature: Fiction (N.Y.: W. W. Norton & Co., Inc., 1973), p. xvii.

[2]Ibid., p. xvi.

[3]E. M. Forster, Aspects of the Novel (N.Y.: Harcourt, Brace & Co., 1927), pp. 130-132.

[4]Wordsworth, of course, is the prime instance of a Romantic with a "remembering" aesthetic. For him, poetry is "emotion recollected in tranquility." (Preface to Lyrical Ballads, (1800), in The Literature of England, ed. G. B. Woods et al., vol. II (Chicago: Scott, Foresman & Co., 1941), p. 340.

[5]Robert Scholes & Robert Kellog, The Nature of Narrative (London: Oxford U. Press, 1966; reprint ed. 1971), p. 22.

[6]Hannah Arendt, The Human Condition (Chicago: Chicago U. Press, 1958), p. 7.

[7]Ibid, p. 184.

[8]Ibid.

[9]Stephen Crites, "The Narrative Quality of Experience," JAAR 39 (Sept. 1971):291-311. For yet another version of the inherent relationship between remembering and narrative, see French social psychologist Pierre Janet's phylogenetic and ontogenetic accounts of human temporal behavior in L'Evolution de la Memoire et de la notion due temps.

[10]Among the proponents of this theory, perhaps the most notable is Frank Kermode. See The Sense of an Ending (London: Oxford U. Press, 1967).

[11]Crites, p. 309.

[12]Sigmund Freud, S.E., 18, 235, cited by Ricoeur, "The Question of Proof in Freud's Writings," The Philosophy of Paul Ricoeur: An Anthology of His Work, ed. Charles E. Reagan & David Stewart (Boston: Beacon Press, 1978), p. 192.

[13]Each of these writers has been influential in my own thinking about remembering and psychoanalysis. I have found Ricoeur and Casey of particular help. See Jurgen Habermas, Knowledge and Human Interests, trans. Jeremy J. Shapiro (Boston: Beacon Press, 1971); Ricoeur, Freud and Philosophy: An Essay on Interpretation, trans. Denis Savage (New Haven: Yale U. Press, 1970), "A Philosophical Interpretation of Freud" and "The Question of Proof in Freud's Writings," The Philosophy of Paul Ricoeur; Michael Sherwood, The Logic of Explanation in PsychoAnalysis (Evanston: Northwestern U. Press, 1972), "The Fiction of Case History: A Round," Religion as Story, ed. James B. Wiggins (N. Y.: Harper & Row, Publishers, 1975); Edward S. Casey, "Piaget and Freud on Childhood Memory," unpublished paper, "Imagining and Remembering," Review of Metaphysics 31 (Dec. 1977).

[14]Ricoeur, "Question of Proof," pp. 185-191.

[15]Freud, Introductory Lectures on Psychoanalysis, cited by Ricoeur, "Question of Proof," p. 188.

[16]By Ricoeur in an informal question and answer session after a public lecture at Emory University, Nov. 1977. The lecture was later published in revised form as "The Narrative Function."

[17]Casey, "Piaget and Freud," p. 4.

[18]Freud, Studies in Hysteria, cited by Ricoeur, "Question of Proof," p. 190.

[19]Freud, S.E. 12, 154, cited by Ricoeur, "Question of Proof," p. 186.

[20]Freud, S. E. 11, 51, cited by Sherwood, The Logic of Explanation. p. 104.

[21]Freud, "From the History of an Infantile Neurosis," in Freud: Three Case Histories (N. Y.: Collier Books, 1963), pp. 187-316.

[22]My own discussion follows Casey's argument closely.

[23]Freud, S. E. 17, 50-1, cited by Casey, "Piaget and Freud," p. 6.

[24]Freud, "Infantile Neurosis," p. 239.

[25]Freud, S.E. 2, 133, cited by Casey, "Piaget and Freud," p. 5.

[26]Freud, _S.E._ 3, 154, cited by Casey, "Piaget and Freud," p. 9.

[27]Jacques Lacan, _Vocabulary of Psychoanalysis_, p. 33, cited by Ricoeur, "Question of Proof," p. 191.

[28]Casey, "Piaget and Freud," p. 12.

[29]Freud, _S.E._ 17, 45 n, cited by Casey, "Piaget and Freud," p. 11.

[30]This is Michael Sherwood's thesis in _The Logic of Explanation in Psychoanalysis_. See esp. pp. 188-191.

[31]Cited by Sherwood, p. 191.

[32]Ricoeur, "Question of Proof," p. 190.

[33]Hillman, "The Fiction of Case History," p. 135.

[34]Cited by Casey, "Piaget and Freud," p. 34.

[35]Habermas, _Knowledge and Human Interests_, p. 260.

[36]Ibid.

[37]See Hillman, _The Myth of Analysis_ and "The Fiction of Case History."

[38]This is Sherwood's phrase in _The Logic of Explanation_.

[39]Hillman, "The Fiction of Case History," pp. 133-136.

[40]Ricoeur, "The Question of Proof," p. 205.

[41]Maurice Merleau-Ponty, _The Primacy of Perception_, ed. James Edie (Evanston: Northwestern U. Press, 1964), p. xi.

[42]Ray Hart, _Unfinished Man and the Imagination_ (N. Y.: Herder & Herder, 1968), p. 11.

CHAPTER IV

REMEMBERING AND TEMPORALITY

Many twentieth century philosophers have concerned themselves with the question of time, including Bergson, James, Dewey, and Whitehead. If we focus on Heiddeger in our discussion, it is because no one has rethought the meaning of time with more vigor, originality, and coherence of detail.[1] These very qualities make it impossible to do justice to his thought here. We shall attend, therefore, to three relevant aspects of Heidegger's reflection on temporality and its development in the thought of other phenomenologists: (1) his critical response to the understanding of time in the philosophical tradition; (2) the constructive description of temporality; and (3) its implications for our interest in memory.

The Critical Response

Heidegger attacks the traditional interpretation of time and its aspects through a root analysis. Let us set before us once again the salient features of that tradition. From Aristotle on, time has been understood as being related to the movement of physical objects. This leads to a conceptualization of time as objective, spatial, and quantifiable. Time is something we can calculate and measure. The effect of such a mathematical notion of time is to conceive of it as a linear succession, with a concomitant preoccupation with the present. Thus the present enjoys a privileged status as the locus of truth and reality. The past and future become two sorts of unreality, the no-longer and the not-yet.

This set of propositions represents traditional Western philosophy's answer to the question, "What is time?" Heidegger wages his attack on the traditional theory by, first of all, reformulating the question. He asks not "What is time?", but "What does it mean to be in time?" "Man is in the world, and only in the world does he know himself." This notion of human being as a being-in-the-world is central to Heidegger's understanding.

Now one of the first things we can say about human being is that it is being in the world. So, however, are lots of other things. Are we beings in the world the same way as chairs and trees are? Are human beings in the world like sardines in a can? This is certainly true in a limited sense, e.g., my being in my study right now. I am, however, more than one object among others. For objects to be given at all, there has to be a subject to perceive and understand. The subject is that being to whom alone the world reveals itself. For phenomenology, there can be no meaning to the notion of a self which is not in a world. Heidegger's Dasein is _inherently_ being-in-the-world. Human beings do not just happen to be in the world, rather it is our essence to be in the world. Dasein, that is, is essentially a relation, not a Cartesian substance. Rather than identifying Dasein with the Cartesian subject, it would be more accurate to interpret it as this very relation, this gap which both separates and unites subject and object. We are the "in-between" subject and object; we are beings dwelling in and familiar with the world[3].

Even this way of conceiving of Dasein is misleading, for it is couched in spatial terms. Dasein is not in the world like a thing. Dasein happens. The relation between subject and object which is Dasein is an event, not a fact. It is profoundly temporal.

Such a notion of being-in-the-world challenges radically the traditional way of thinking about time. It reveals, for example, that time is temporal and not the other way around. Human temporality, that is, is the basis of time. Heidegger shows that the Aristotelian mathematical conception of time is inherently derivative in character.[4] It already presupposes the human capacities of calculating and measuring. Human temporality is the basis of every possible projection of time in science and in our everyday understanding of the world.[5] What is more, such temporality is not an actual succession. Time, which arises from our relation to things, is less a line than a network of intentionalities, less a system of objective positions through which we pass, than, as Merleau-Ponty will insist, a mobile setting which moves away from us like the land from a train window.[6]

When he places time and its essential relationship to being at the center of philosophy, Heidegger is not only countering the long tradition which begins with Aristotle; he is rejecting Plato as well. For Plato believed that it was philosophy's task to provide us with an escape from the bondage of time, but for Heidegger, there is no human being apart from temporality. Our only being is being-in-the-world, and our being-in-the-world is being-temporal. To assert this is to reject both sorts of claims: (a) that time has some objective meaning prior to our being, and (b) that our true being is somehow atemporal. Since temporality is inextricably bound up with our being, we must understand the one in terms of the other.

Constructive Redescription

In Being and Time, Heidegger thus derives his analysis of temporality from his foregoing analysis of Dasein as Care. As he writes, "Dasein is an entity for which in its Being, that Being is an issue. . . . Being-in-the-world is essentially Care" (pp. 192, 193/236-237). What precisely is this Care which is the Being of Dasein?

Our ordinary understandings of care can help us here. In our common usage, care signifies a kind of openness toward the world. All of my interests, concerns, excitements, and disappointments can be seen as a kind of care. An attitude of care is the contrary of indifference. When I care, I am vulnerable. I can both care about and care for; my caring, that is, encompasses both the things and the persons in my world. What is more, however, whenever I am caring about and for the other, my careful attitude manifests a kind of caring for my own existence. My caring can range from concern, worry, and anxiety to solicitude, cherishing, and reverencing. This range in the common usage of the term is roughly equivalent to the emphases in the early and later Heidegger. In Being and Time, care is closely akin to anxiety and dread; in the late works, care conveys reverence, even a piety of thinking. Thus he will come to speak of Dasein as the shepherd, the husbandman of Being; it is our task and our privilege to take care of Being.[7]

The ordinary understandings of "care" are certainly contained in Heidegger's choice of term. He is not unaware of such ready-to-hand meanings which might lead us to an intuitive acceptance of his claim that Care is the Being of Dasein. As supportive as these common usages are, however, they do not constitute the explicit ground of his claim.

Such multifarious carings are episodic in character. But Heideggerian Care is not simply an emotional or psychological category. It is not only that we experience care in our everyday lives but that Care is the relation we described as our being-in-the-world. Our carings are ontic clues, if you will, to our ontological condition. Dasein is Care, not the subjective experience of our relation to the world but that relationality itself. By calling Care ontological, we mean to say that it has to do with the very structure of our human existence. We are related to the world by virtue of Care, and that relationality is temporal.

Heidegger's claim is that it is our essence to care about the world. Why? Because our ontological condition is unheimlich--insecure, off-balance, if you will. We are not self-contained or self-sufficient in a present we can grasp and hold on to. The vulnerability of our being is that we are oriented. Our being-in-the-world is a being-possible.

We are oriented toward a future which is empty and silent. Try as we might to formulate secure futures for ourselves, our future remains an open question. Indeed, the only certainty we have about that future is the nothingness of our own death. The rub is that the very orientation of our being does not and cannot provide us with self-definition. Care, as the ontological condition of our being, both causes and manifests our intrinsic vulnerability, the unfinished character of our human existence.[8]

Heidegger calls the authentic mode of our Being-toward-possibility "anticipatory resoluteness" (pp. 267/312ff.). In anticipatory resoluteness, we recognize the enigmas of the future and proceed to act out of this lucidity. We can begin to see how it is that time is the ground of our existence. If we inquire how such anticipatory resoluteness is possible, how it is possible to be toward anything at all, the answer is that we have a future.

To have a future cannot mean that the future is merely a not-yet waiting for us to come to meet it on the path of time. A mere not-yet is not meaningful. Time is not a road along which we are traveling toward certain future objects already there. Heidegger defines the future as "coming-toward." We come toward the future and it comes toward us. What it means to have a future is that I look forward to, I anticipate, I expect. We always confront ourselves as engaged in projects to realize ourselves in the future. In other words, the future has meaning precisely because it is one of the ways in which I exist. My ability to have possible ways of being is what future means. I am as coming-toward. Existence has a futural character. Dasein essentially expects and anticipates its being. The future is human existence in the mode of self-anticipation.

Now since Heidegger grants priority to this human capacity for possibility, he asserts that it is the future, not the present, which bears the locus of our existence. Understood as the way of existing characterized as my Being-toward-possibility, the future is the ultimate presupposition of authentic existence. It is the primary phenomenon of temporality precisely because our care for ourselves is first of all care for the future.

But we do not confront the future as an openness which makes all our projects equally possible. We are already cast in a situation; what is to come is modified by what has been. The future is simply one way in which I exist, always already limited by the past. All my thinkings and awareness presuppose attitudes of both being-toward the future and being-from the past. Just as the future is not simply a not-yet, so the past is not a mere no-longer. Like the future, the past must be interpreted in terms of my human existing. What the past means is my having-been. As Dasein's having-been, the past does not signify some now-gone realm of facts or events. I do not possess my past like a thing; I carry my past with me. It is not something that used to be; rather, my having-been is what I, as an individual being, am. (Likewise, our historical past is what we, as human beings, are.) I cannot escape from my past into an open future, since both are constitutive of my very being. Though I certainly can estrange myself from my past, to do so is to lose myself, since I am so intimately wedded to it. It is precisely because the future is so mute that, as Ray Hart says, "We live out of the future but understand out of the past." By virtue of our vulnerability vis-à-vis the uncertain future, we reach back to and draw on the past.

My capacities for remembering and forgetting are what make the past significant. My self is no less a remembering-and-forgetting-self than it is a self-anticipation. It is not enough to note that memory is the function by which the past is presented to me. In order that it be remembered, the past must be conceived in terms of my human existing. I am as having been, just as I am as coming toward. Dasein can possess itself only as the journey from past to future.[9]

If I am as being-toward and being-from, what then of the present? Heidegger does not repudiate the present, but he does put it in its place by showing that the now-point in the philosophical tradition does not render an accurate existential account of the present. Less a point than a span, the present is not that in which something occurs but a making-present. The present signifies my rendering-myself-present in decision and resolute action. My capacities to perform actions and to be in situations are what the present means.

As Care, Dasein has three characteristics, onto-logically grounded in these three modes of temporality. By virtue of the future, it is ahead of itself in terms of possibility; by virtue of the past, it is already in the world; and by virtue of the present, it is alongside others in concern and solicitude. Thus temporality is the fundamental basis of all human self-relation. It is not a thing, not something we add to human existence, but an essential mode of being, integral to human existing and to the cognitions and actions which are elements of that existing. My being ahead of myself in projective understanding _is_ my future; my already being myself _is_ my past, my having-been; and my rendering myself present in action _is_ my present. "Let us no longer say," writes Merleau-Ponty, "that time is a 'datum of consciousness'; let us be more precise and say that consciousness unfolds or constitutes time."[10]

Temporality is not a line but a network of intentionalities; the present is not a point but a moving field of focus. It is the essence of temporality to be in the process of self-production. The very process is dynamic, non-serial, and unitive. Temporal experience is not an addition or series of separate past, present, and future modes. Past, present, and future are mutually implicated in the temporal form of our being. Anticipation and memory are necessarily and integrally involved in any actual present I make.

In place of the traditionally conceived linear structure of time, Heidegger posits this structure of human temporality, which he calls "ecstatic." "Ecstasis" means literally "standing out." Each of our temporal dimensions of past, present, and future is an ecstasis, a standing out from the primordial temporal flow of human existence. Thus our very temporal being is a flight out of itself, a "self stretching in the world."[11] As he writes,

Temporality does not signify that ecstases come in a "succession." The future is _not later_ than having been, and having been is _not earlier_ than the Present. Temporality for Dasein temporalizes itself as a future which makes present in the process of having been (p. 350/401).

When time moves, that is, it moves throughout its whole length. As the upsurge of the temporalizing process, the present is the passage of future to present and former present to past. Each projection issues from the other, and each is simply one aspect of a total unitary movement. This is what we mean when we say that temporality is not a series of objective positions through which we pass. Each future becoming present on its way to being past carries this movement with it. For the present to become past does not mean it is thereby "bereft of its being," in Merleau-Ponty's phrase.[12] Its disintegration as present is the very consequence of its coming to maturity. The future cannot but become past as it moves into and through being present. By definition, the present transcends itself toward both future and past, for each present reasserts the presence of the past which it supplants and anticipates the future coming to be. The present is not self-enclosed. In becoming past, the event does not cease to be, since being and passing are coinherent in the temporalizing process. It is Heidegger's original contribution to our understanding of time to have shown that time is not best conceived of as a noun but rather as a verb. Not time but temporalizing.[13]

I cannot hold on to my present. It is always already an ecstasis, a flight out of itself toward future and past. Now this ecstatic nature of our temporality has paradoxical consequences. On the one hand, it is in these temporal ecstases that our life's cohesion is given. I do not _witness_ time passing; I _perform_ its passage.[14] On the other hand, understood in its temporality, Dasein is seen not to be at one with itself. It is already ahead of itself toward the future, lagging behind itself toward the past, and encountering other persons and things in the present. As Care, Dasein is essentially outside itself. It is this ecstatic character of Dasein which precludes our making it into a fact. When we characterize Dasein as Care, we emphasize this temporal openness of our human existence. Since we are not given to ourselves as whole, we are constantly confronted with the task of having to be ourselves. This very incompleteness is constitutive of Dasein. Ecstatic temporality reveals the sense in which Dasein is essentially care-for-itself. The meaning of Care _is_ temporality.

We are now in a position to confront once again, at another level, the accusation of subjectivism raised at the start of our discussion. As the Being of Dasein, temporality cannot be rightly understood as either

141

subjective or objective. Time is not objective in the sense of being an independent entity or of having a significance apart from human existence. Nor, however, is it subjective in the sense of being identifiable with the faculty by which change is measured. Temporality is insofar as we are. It is not enough to understand time epistemologically, for it is the ontological condition for our being-in-the-world.

Still less can Heidegger's temporality be identified with our ordinary conception of subjective time. In our commonsense understanding, we tend to identify the objectified, spatialized conception of time in the philosophical tradition with reality. We may, indeed, then go on to posit a subjective, psychological time, but this "sense of time" is deprived of any fundamental bearing on reality.[16] To use a crude example, the clock may confirm that my friend is only twenty minutes late, but to me it feels like an hour. My subjective sense of time-lengthening (or foreshortening) may be the result of a host of factors: in this case, for example, I am standing in the cold; I have another appointment; I tend to be impatient; and I know she tends to be tardy.

Literary critics often use such rough-hewn and misleading distinctions between objective and subjective time in their analyses of a novel's sense of time. Even in recent theories of narrative, it is taken for granted that the kind of time in which stories unfold is linear, a succession of nows separated by measurable intervals. Faced with this reduction of narrative time to mere chronology, the structuralist alternative in its turn reduces narrative fictions to achronological models in which the locus of transformation is deprived of any chronological dimension. Since the traditional interpretation overlooks the genuine specificity of human time, one is forced to choose between mere chronology on the one side and atemporal models of transformation on the other.[17] The problem, far from being solved, is exacerbated when it is granted that there is besides this chronological time a subjective, psychological time which is deprived of any fundamental bearing on reality. Thus literary critics often speak of "real" vs. "psychological" time in a novel and generate their discussion of narrative time on the basis of the interaction between these two time-senses. This amounts to no more than throwing a sop to our discomfort with the objective characterization of time in the philosophical tradition and in our everyday understanding. Out of one side of our mouths we insist that the novel is about time; out of the other, we articulate a conception of time which is highly unnovelistic, a conception imported from an

142

extraneous philosophical understanding which takes no note of the peculiarly human character of time.

Such tactics simply serve to strengthen the monopoly objective time has on our thinking and get us no further in our appreciation of the genuine specificity of human time and the inherently temporal character of our human existence. For all the re-visioning of temporality in contemporary philosophy, literary criticism persists in its basic paradigm of time as linear succession. For Heidegger, as we have seen, it is because temporality has its meaning in Dasein's ecstatical way of existing that it is the basis of our conceptualizations of time in the everyday world. A thetic consciousness of time destroys the essence of temporality, which is to be always in the process of self-constituting and never completely constituted.

To assert, as Heidegger does, that human temporality is essentially finite is not the equivalent of ruling out the possibility of an infinite. It does, however, rule out separating the essence of Dasein from its temporality and arguing that human being has been cast from eternal being into the flux of time. Heidegger's thought fundamentally counters Platonism.[18] Does it then rule out as well any possibility of transcendence?

If his description of human temporality has validity, it certainly reveals the finitude of our being-in-the-world. Our future is limited and finite. Not only is everything not possible (we are all too familiar with the tragedy of the excluded alternative!), but we have our being as a being-unto-death. As ecstatic being-in-the-world, Dasein's ground is nothingness. Being-toward-death, Dasein is in dread. It is Heidegger's genius, however, to have grounded the very possibility of transcendence, not in some pre-existent eternity, but in this finite character of our being. Dasein is transcendent in that the very possibility of meaning is a function of our finitude. It is because we face the certainty of nothingness that our existence is so important to us. It is, as we noted above, because we are not given to ourselves as whole that we are offered the task of having to be ourselves.

Now this presence of transcendence-within-finitude vis-à-vis our future is clearly evident in <u>Being and Time</u>. What, however, of our past? There is no denying Heidegger's tendency in <u>Being and Time</u> to conceive of the past primarily in terms of facticity. In his attack on the classical idolatry of the present, Heidegger neglects the past in favor of the future. Having-been is seen

143

principally under the dimension of the limitations of Dasein's possibilities. This facticity of our having-been is indicative of our finitude. In the later Heidegger, however, there is a growing tendency to understand the very givenness of our being-in-the-world as a being-from as providing the occasion for meaning's disclosure. In the early Heidegger, our past is the lagging behind of being. In the later Heidegger, however, our having-been is seen less as the givenness of Dasein which constricts and limits its being-toward and more as the gift of being, given to us to nurture, care for, and cherish. It is in this sense that Dasein is the shepherd of Being. It is not surprising, then, that remembering becomes a major theme in Heidegger's later thought.

Key Implications for Remembering

Already in Being and Time, of course, Heidegger is concerned with memory and its misunderstanding in the philosophical tradition, a misunderstanding rooted in that tradition's conception of time. As soon as we understand time not as a noun but as a verb (temporalizing), then memory must be understood not as a substantive but as a human activity. Although Heidegger does not attend to the consequences of such a shift of understanding for memory in Being and Time, we can make them explicit by focusing on this conception of the past.

As we have seen in our discussion thus far, it is not enough to identify memory as the function by which the past is presented again to consciousness. If the past is not a mere no-longer but a way we have of existing, then our capacities for remembering and forgetting are precisely what make the past significant. Since my having-been is who I already am, it is constitutive of Dasein. Thus human being means being a remembering and forgetting self. This means that we must take memory seriously not simply as a mode of cognition but as a fundamental way of being human.

Memory, that is, is the condition of personal being. Our now-being is a being both from and toward the past. Our past has constitutive reverberations in our being precisely because memory is this very condition of personal being. The past in memory is the foundation of my present acts. It is, as Hart argues, because in memory the discontinuous object is profoundly blended with the continuity of the self that the meaning of the past changes as I change. We live out of the future but understand out of the past. Such an understanding is not a simple retrieval of data stored in some memory bank. Through the activity of remembering, our use of the past is an active interpreting. It is in that very process that the past becomes meaningful. The kind of life had out of the future determines, in its turn, the mode of the past that is accessible to understanding.[19] Insofar as we live our lives in the power of a finished past, we are in bondage to a future which is merely repetitive. And if we refuse to the past our active complicity, we abjure responsibility for our present. This, of course, is the insight of psychoanalysis, cast now in phenomenological terms.

What on the surface seems impossible is thus revealed to be possible: future is able to impinge upon, press into, and change the past. There is no access to the past as pastness in itself, as facticity and fate. In that sense, it is truly irrevocable. But our rememberings are always already conditioned by our anticipations. If we approach the past with a different set of possibilities, we creatively transform it. In remembering, the present returns to the past "dwelling in its own depth" and reveals that pastness as a dimension of human being in the process of developing ahead into future.[20] It is our human being's very qualities of accumulating and deepening, i.e., our temporality, which paradoxically open it up to novelty. When we understand out of the past, when we remember, what we are understanding is precisely who we are and what our world is like.

Once again we see how a reflection faithful to remembering's character as a fundamental human activity invariably leads us to the threshold of a consideration of the interconnectedness between our remembering capacities and our identity. Once again, however, we shall postpone that consideration until two further points have been clarified. The first is to retrieve the notion of forgetting and place it in its proper context; the second, to consider what Heidegger himself says about memory in his later writings. These points are not digressions, since both will put us in a better position for the discussion of memory and identity which follows.

In our reflection on Dasein's temporality, we have just characterized human being as being a remembering-and-forgetting-self no less than a self-anticipation. We included forgetting in our formulation as a corrective to making exaggerated claims for memory. In our efforts to redress memory's denigration, we must guard against a tendency to construct an omnivorous conception of our remembering capacities. There is, after all, a great deal of our past (both personal and collective) which is unavailable to our memories. We cannot seriously suppose that the happened past and the recollected past are one and the same thing. Some past events are simply not memorable; they open up, in Hart's phrase, a negligible field of future-projecting potency.[21] In Heidegger's language, they are part of our within-timeness, past instances of our preoccupation with everyday life. The appropriate response to much of what is past is to forget it. This on the one hand. On the other hand, we cannot suppose either that the recollected past exhausts my present and anticipatory being's concern with the past. There are aspects of the past which are ontologically relevant even though they are not recollected. Such unrecollected, ontologically relevant past events disclose the potentiality of the past for fate.[22] We need, then, to place both types of forgetting into the context of our past.

Remembering does not function like a camera-eye, recording the whole of the past for future consultation. Rather, it preserves the economy and harmony of the psyche. It is constructive of a world and a biography-- ordered wholes which have a shape and form, albeit one which is always being modified. Memory itself must be formed. Psychology, of course, recognizes this; the whole psychoanalytic project, as we have seen, is constructed on this foundation. That task aims at self- knowledge and integration not through the mere piling up of memories--such total recall would be futility itself. Rather, psychoanalytic remembering tries to discover a new, more integrating gestalt for the past by disclosing key memories which have been neglected or repressed. Rather than accumulating memories it alters the entire perspective of remembering.[23] Thus it offers an analogue to the liturgical anamnesis which is, as we have seen, a selective, directed, and transforming remembering enacted by a community.

To remember everything and anything would be literal madness. We remember--and want to remember--some things and not others. Forgetting is not a mere lapse or absence so much as a condition of the life of the mind. As Gadamer notes,

> Only by forgetting does the mind have the chance of total renewal, the capacity to see everything with fresh eyes, so that what is long familiar combines with the new into a many leveled unity.[24]

Forgetting belongs within the context of remembering in a kind of dialectic of losing-in-order-to-find. Their dynamic relationship within the dramatic and narrative quality of a human life opens up the possibility of a "second naiveté," in Ricoeur's happy phrasing. Viewed in this way, forgetting reveals itself, not as an incapacity to remember, but as the positive human capacity which grounds memory's constructive and integrative character. This is, however, only one side of the story.

There is a second way of understanding the relationship between remembering and forgetting. We are already familiar with it from Freud. While psychoanalysis does not aim at being total recall, it is nonetheless constructed on the principle that forgetting has destructive consequences in human life. In this second view, then, forgetting represents surrender to time as fate. Remembering is then seen as the struggle against forgetting, the force which counters such a surrender to a fated existence. Remembering, that is, becomes a form of critique.

It is this understanding of remembering which undergirds Heidegger's whole project. We would be remiss in our discussion of Heidegger on memory if we overlooked this point, which serves to link the early and the later writings. Being and Time opens with the assertion that we have forgotten the question of being. Heidegger believes it is this very forgetfulness which is at the heart of our modern existential crisis. The question of being, which provided the stimulus for Plato and Aristotle at the beginnings of Western philosophy, subsided from then on as a theme for philosophical investigation. The result, according to Heidegger, is that the history of Western philosophy is the perilous history of the forgetfulness of being. All the counter examples in our exposition of time and memory are examples of this very forgetfulness. In Being and Time, Heidegger thus understands his whole philosophical project as a highly individual anamnesis. It is, for example, because of the forgetfulness of the question of being that he must attack the traditional conception of time by a root analysis. Philosophy's forgetfulness of being leads to its fascination with the question "what is time?" As one who understands his task as the remembrance of being, Heidegger asks instead, "What does it mean to be in time?"

A comparable understanding of the relationship between remembering and forgetting is at the heart of Critical Theory. As its name suggests, Critical Theory sees its project as a critique of Western thought and civilization, a critique which must take the form of a remembrance if it is to counter effectively the notions of evolutionary progress which constitute repressive societies. Such remembrance must be a deliberate, painstaking, and painful task in the face of civilization's tendency toward forgetfulness. Herbert Marcuse articulates well this foundational issue for Critical Theory:

> This ability to forget--itself the result of a long and terrible education by experience--is an indispensable requirement of mental and physical hygiene without which civilized life would be unbearable; but it is also the mental faculty which sustains submissiveness and renunciation. To forget is also to forgive what should not be forgiven if justice and freedom are to prevail. Such forgiveness reproduces the conditions which reproduce injustice and enslavement; to forget past suffering is to forgive the forces that caused it--without defeating these forces. The wounds that heal in time are also the wounds that contain the poison. Against this surrender to time, the restoration of remembrance to its rights, as a vehicle of liberation, is one of the noblest tasks of thought.[25]

Historically repressive societies indulge in a timelessness which is the collective counterpart to the individual's repression of pain, disease, and death. Where forgetfulness closes history, remembrance keeps it open to both the past and the future. As the critical task par excellence, remembrance is the womb of freedom and justice. Such remembering cannot be taken for granted, according to Critical Theory, but must be cultivated. How is such remembering-against-forgetting cultivated? Long before we are able to name our oppression in rational discourse, John O'Neill argues, we nurture our liberty in the collective creative expressions of ritual, art, and music.[26] Now it is worth noting here how this notion of remembrance in Critical Theory sheds light on the liturgical anamnesis we have already examined. In performing the anamnesis, the Hebrew community, and the Christian community after it, is overcoming its past slavery in the very enactment of its foundational liberty.

Such an understanding of memory (as the womb of freedom in face of the temptation to forget who we are) is closely allied with the Greek notion of Mnemosyne, the mother of the Muses, source of all the arts, rhetoric,

148

history, and science. This alliance provides us with a link to Heidegger's later thinking about memory, to which we will turn in conclusion of our discussion of temporality.

Let us first summarize what we have been saying about remembering and forgetting. It is not enough to understand forgetting as the mere lapse of memory, for, as Heidegger says, "remembering is possible only on [the basis] of forgetting" (p. 339/389). What is more, neither can be rightly understood merely as psychological occurrences. Forgetting belongs with remembering positively as the pre-condition for memory's ordering function; and negatively it can be seen as Dasein's propensity to forget itself at its roots. In both cases, forgetting is as ontological as remembering; both belong to the very structure of our existence.

We have already seen that Heidegger places the activity of remembering at the heart of _Being and Time_ insofar as his central concern in that work is to redress the forgetfulness of Being. Twenty-five years later, in _What Is Called Thinking?_, originally a lecture course delivered in 1951-52, he gives himself over to an explicit elaboration of this central role of remembering in his life-work. In this relatively accessible little book, Heidegger generates his reflection on memory by the sort of etymological word-play which always fascinated him. The word for "remembering" in German is a derivative of the word for "thinking." Of the many different kinds of thinking that are possible, Heidegger has come to recognize as the one closest to his central concern a thinking which he characterizes as "recollected" or "gathered."[27]

Recollected thinking, according to Heidegger, is a process in which we so give ourselves over to what is thought that we are in direct contact with it. In such a process, "to think" is no longer an intransitive verb but has a transitive sense. We no longer think about something, in the way of scholars, mastering our subject matter and drawing conclusions from it. Rather we think something in the sense that we settle down and live in our thought. In this highest kind of thinking, that is, we belong to our thought; we go with it where it goes. Such intimacy between ourselves and our thinking cuts two ways. First of all, we must prepare ourselves to receive thoughts. Heidegger writes in a poem, "We never come to thoughts. They come to us."[28] Secondly, we must give our thoughts a genuine response, a response which takes the form of a questioning in which we put ourselves in question.

Heidegger finds support for such a notion of "recollected thinking" in the Greek characterization of memory as Mnemosyne. Decrying the reductive understanding of memory to which we are heirs, he wants to recover this originary richer meaning. He writes,

> Mnemosyne, daughter of Heaven and Earth, bride of Zeus, in nine nights becomes the mother of the nine Muses. Drama and music, dance and poetry are of the womb of Mnemosyne, Dame Memory. It is plain that the word means something else than merely the psychologically demonstrable ability to retain a mental representation, an idea of something which is past. Memory--from Latin memor, mindful--has in mind something that is in the mind, thought. But when it is the name of the Mother of the Muses, "Memory" does not mean just any thought of anything that can be thought. Memory is the gathering and convergence of thought upon what everywhere demands to be thought about first of all. Memory is the gathering of Recollection, thinking back. It safely keeps and keeps concealed within it that to which at any given time thought must be given before all else, in everything that essentially is, everything that appeals to us as what has being and has been in being.[29]

J. Glenn Gray argues that this understanding of memory as Mnemosyne came to assume for Heidegger "the role that productive imagination played in the German idealists."[30] This would explain his virtual silence about imagination, for the synthetic power of imagination is assimilated by him to memory. We will return to this question in chapter VI in our discussion of Memory and Imagination.

For Heidegger, "what everywhere demands to be thought about first of all" is, of course, Being. Memory keeps and keeps concealed within it everything that has being and has been in being. This intimacy between thinking and remembering in Being leads him to take his reflection a step further. In old English, the etymology for "think" is "thanc." Heidegger interprets both thinking and remembering as a form of thanking, "a commemorating and celebrating of our human existence."[31] In recollective thinking, we concentrate with devotion on Being. As he writes,

> "Memory" initially did not at all mean the power to recall. The word designates the whole

disposition in the sense of a steadfast intimate concentration upon the things that essentially speak to us in every thoughtful meditation. Originally "memory" means as much as devotion: a constant concentrated abiding with something--not just with something that has passed, but in the same way with what is present and with what may come. What is past, present, and to come appears in the oneness of its own <u>present</u> being.[32]

This is the piety of thinking we mentioned earlier as Heidegger's later expression of the Care which is Dasein. There are obvious analogies with what we have seen in the Eucharistic anamnesis, a ritualized form of thanking and remembering. Memory as <u>Mnemosyne</u> is the way we fulfill our human task of caring for Being. As such, it belongs to a more comprehensive activity called thanking, our gratitude both for Being and for the capacity to think Being. In recollective thinking, we gather ourselves in concentration on what is to be thought, realizing at the same time that we ourselves, as Dasein, belong to that which we think, Being itself. This kind of remembering discloses our capacity to gather our past and future into a pregnant present which is the unity of time and Being. In such a recollective present, Being presences in us, allowing us to escape our fallenness into time, our sense of being stretched along a temporal continuum.

Our usual state of mind, however, is forgetfulness, living distractedly in within-timeness. Such forgetfulness is only partially within our ability to transcend; it is also our destiny. This is why, as Heidegger insists in <u>What Is Called Thinking?</u>, nothing is harder than to learn to think. Being at once reveals and conceals itself. When it chooses to reveal itself in our recollective thinking it gives us the realization of the sense of our lives. In remembering-thinking-thanking, we are enabled to listen and belong to Being and so discover our place in the world we inhabit. But our attempts to gather the ecstases of time into such presence are never fully realized. Since in our temporality we are always a flight out of ourselves, we invariably forget who we truly are.

If the Heidegger of <u>Being and Time</u> tends to neglect the past in his efforts to redress the traditional idolatry of the present, the later Heidegger redresses his earlier neglect. What I have tried to show, however, is that his later thinking about remembering and its significance for Dasein is already implicit in the

fundamental task he undertakes in <u>Being and Time</u>.
Heidegger always thinks in dialogue with the past. In
both the early and later works, the unity of Being and
Time toward which Dasein struggles is never a given and
always the most fundamental human task. That task, as
his later writings make clear, is an anamnesis in which
what we remember is inseparable from who we are. If
Dasein is the shepherd of Being, it is in the activity of
remembering, understood as comprising thinking and being
comprised by thanking, that we enact our Care for Being.
In <u>The End of Philosophy</u>, he declares:

> Being and truth belong to each other just as
> they belong intertwining to a still concealed
> rootedness in the origin whose origination
> opening up remains that which comes.
> That which is original . . . never
> perishes, it is never something past. Thus we
> also never find what is Original in the
> historical retrospect of what is past, but
> rather only in remembrance which thinks at the
> same time upon presencing Being (what has been
> in being), and upon the destined truth of
> Being.[33]

In this section, we have been thinking with
Heidegger and those influenced by him about the question,
"What does it mean to be in time?" We took this question
to be central to our concern about our world. In order
to address that fundamental question ("What is the nature
of reality?"), we addressed the temporal condition of our
being, wagering that our very concern was the correlate
of the insecurity of our existence. We have seen how our
being-in-the-world is essentially temporal, understood
not as linear succession but as the ecstases of
being-toward, being-from, and being-alongside. Finally,
we have shown how remembering, understood now not simply
as a cognitive faculty but as a fundamental way of being
human, is essential to our finite historical being. It
is because the "ecology and interiority" of human
experience are thoroughly temporal that we must understand remembering-and-forgetting as constitutive of our
very being.

In all this, we have been following the
phenomenological double insight that we have our being as
a being-in-the-world and that it is only in the world
that we know ourselves. In addressing the issue of
world, we have also been addressing, albeit indirectly,
the issue of identity. It remains for us now to turn
directly to this issue. Our task, as stated in the

introduction to part II, is to show memory's inherent relationship to the question, "Who am (are) I (we)?"

NOTES TO CHAPTER IV

[1]Michael Murray, <u>Modern Critical Theory: A Phenomenological Introduction</u> (The Hague: Martinus Nijhoff, 1975), pp. 163-164.

[2]Karsten Harries, "Martin Heidegger: The Search for Meaning," in <u>Existentialist Philosophers: Kierkegaard to Merleau-Ponty</u>, ed. George Alfred Schrader, Jr. (N.Y.: McGraw Hill, 1967), p. 170.

[3]Ibid., pp. 170-171.

[4]Heidegger, <u>Being and Time</u>, trans. John Macquarrie and Edward Robinson (N.Y.: Harper & Brothers, 1962), sec. 78-83, pp. 456ff. Other references to <u>Being and Time</u> given in the text of this essay note the page reference to the German edition followed by the page reference to this edition.

[5]Murray, p. 166.

[6]Merleau-Ponty, <u>The Primacy of Perception</u>, pp. 419-420.

[7]This notion from the later Heidegger will be discussed below in <u>Key Implications for Remembering</u>.

[8]Thus the title of Hart's study: <u>Unfinished Man and the Imagination</u>.

[9]My exposition of Heidegger's phenomenology of temporality draws heavily on the following sources: Michael Gelven, <u>A Commentary on Heidegger's "Being and Time"</u> (N.Y.: Harper & Row, 1970); Karsten Harries, "Martin Heidegger: The Search for Meaning"; Ray Hart, <u>Unfinished Man and the Imagination</u>; Michael Murray, <u>Modern Critical Theory: A Phenomenological Introduction</u>, pp. 163-169.

[10]Merleau-Ponty, <u>The Primacy of Perception</u>, p. 414.

[11]Ibid., p. 419.

[12]Ibid., p. 420.

[13]Paul Ricoeur, "The Paradox of Time in Augustine and Heidegger," taped lecture, Yale University Taylor Lectures, Feb. 1979.

[14]Merleau-Ponty, p. 421.

[15]Harries, p. 188.

[16]Murray, p. 165.

[17]Ricoeur, "Narrative and the Paradoxes of Time," taped lecture, Yale U. Taylor Lectures, Feb. 1979.

[18]Harries, p. 187.

[19]Ray Hart, p. 197-198.

[20]H. Ganse Little, Jr., Decision and Responsibility: A Wrinkle in Time (Tallahassee, Fla.: AAR, 1974), p. 15.

[21]Hart, p. 190.

[22]Ibid., p. 191.

[23]Louis Dupre, "Alienation and Redemption through Time and Memory: An Essay on Religious Time Consciousness," JAAR (Dec. 1975), p. 676.

[24]Hans-Georg Gadamer, Truth and Method (New York: Seabury Press, 1975), p. 16.

[25]Herbert Marcuse, Eros and Civilization: A Philosophical Inquiry into Freud (N.Y.: Vintage Books, 1962), p. 212.

[26]John O'Neill, "Critique and Remembrance," in On Critical Theory, ed. John O'Neill (N.Y.: Seabury Press, 1976), p. 4.

[27]Heidegger, What Is Called Thinking?, trans. J. Glenn Gray & F. Wieck (N.Y.: Harper & Row, 1968), p. 143 and passim. See also J. Glenn Gray, "Heidegger on Remembering and Remembering Heidegger," Man and World 10 (1977), p. 62-78.

[28]Heidegger, "The Thinker as Poet," cited by Gray, p. 64.

[29]Heidegger, What Is Called Thinking? p. 11.

[30]Gray, "Heidegger on Remembering," p. 65.

[31]Ibid., p. 66.

[32]Heidegger, What Is Called Thinking? p. 140.

[33]Heidegger, The End of Philosophy, trans. Joan Stanbaugh (N.Y.: Harper and Row, 1973), p. 75.

CHAPTER V

REMEMBERING AND IDENTITY

Our theme has been the interrelationship between self and world. We have argued, following the phenomenologists, not only that we know ourselves through our world, but that we can best understand the self by approaching it indirectly in this manner. We took temporality as the key to this self/world relation because in temporality we can see our concern for the world actualized. In fact, in our reflection on temporality, we have been speaking about "self" as much as about "world." Everything we have said about temporality could quite easily be recast now in terms of identity.

Heidegger's project intends to drive a wedge between human temporal experience and the objectified mathematical point of the traditional philosophical understanding of time. His fundamental mistrust of the present conceived as now-point and time conceived as an infinite succession of such nows is precisely that it leads to a description of human beings in terms of things. In opposition to this tendency, he argues that our distinctively human mode of being displays decisive criteria which have no parallel in things. We have our being as a being-toward-death, and we discover ourselves as already situated in the world. Dasein is a journey from birth to death. We are not <u>on</u> a journey; we <u>are</u> the journey.[1] To picture time as an objectified infinite succession is inauthentic in the face of our finite temporal being. Thus for the three substantive categories of past, present, and future, Heidegger substitutes three modes of Dasein's Care. Human temporality is simply Care directed toward our future possibilities, our having-been, and our making-present.[2] To speak authentically about human time, we must speak in verbs and gerunds rather than in nouns. Our temporalizing is an activity, not a series of objective now-points.

The very words "temporality" and "temporalizing" distill the self/world relation which is Dasein. It is precisely because speaking about temporality is speaking about both self and world--or better, about the self-world relation--that it would be possible for us to repeat all we have said about temporality with an altered emphasis to set forth the issue of identity. Thus, for example, instead of defining the future as

157

Being-toward-possibility and the past as Being as having-been, we could define the self as she who is concerned about what is to come and she who is concerned about what has been. Indeed, we have already spoken in this way when, for example, we argued that we are remembering-and-forgetting selves no less than we are anticipatory selves.[3]

In sum, to speak phenomenologically about temporality is already necessarily to speak about identity. But I do not want simply to repeat myself in a different key; nor do I want to rest my discussion of memory and identity at the level of indirection. In this section, I want to highlight this interconnectedness between our remembering capacities and our identity while remaining true to my phenomenological theme of the self/world relation.

As an alternative to a simple repetition of our reflection on temporality, we could think with psychology about the interrelationship of memory and identity. We have already pointed toward this coherence in our discussion of the narrative commitment of psychoanalysis. There the analysand reconstructs his life story through fresh rememberings of his past. The intent is not to rediscover the past in its pastness but to open a new way of understanding oneself and new possibilities for living one's life. The new story the analysand is enabled to tell has no other point than to make better, more workable sense of who he is. Such a project would not be possible if remembering were no more than a mental faculty which reproduced past perceptions. It is because of the temporal condition of our being that remembering is a way we have of existing. We are selves precisely because we remember. Psychoanalysis' way of talking about memory and narrative offers a striking correlation with phenomenology's insight into the coinherence of temporality and identity.

A third alternative would be to approach the issue of personal identity in the grand philosophical manner. There is nothing new philosophically about positing a connection between memory and identity. At least since the British empiricists, philosophy has been directly concerned with their interconnection. But despite their long history and despite their refinements in argument, philosophical controversies about personal identity and the criteria for it have remained persistently unresolved. Among the many distinct questions at issue in such philosophical controversy, there has been little or no agreement about which are central. Various philosophies of personal identity concern themselves with establishing criteria for: (1) how persons are to be distinguished

158

from other classes of beings (e.g., apes, robots, corpses, fetuses, corporations); (2) how one person is to be distinguished from another; (3) how a person is to be defined as essentially who she is; and (4) how a person is to be identified as the same individual in different contexts and at different times.[4]

It is especially in response to this fourth issue that the involvement of memory in personal identity has been explored. The locus classicus for this connection is found in John Locke. Locke wanted to determine the conditions under which various stages of a person can be asserted to belong to the same person. In other words, on what basis can we posit an identity between the I who used to be and the I who is, such that "I" can be said to have a personal identity? He concludes that such identity obtains only if the person I am now can contain a memory experience of an earlier conscious experience which was contained in who I used to be. He concludes, that is, that personal identity can be defined in terms of memory. What is interesting about this solution in relation to our concerns is that it confronts the problem of identity in terms of time and posits memory as that faculty which grounds personal identity.[5]

One obvious problem with such a theory, however, is that it requires our being able to remember everything that ever happened to us. Philosophers of personal identity who follow Locke have tried to give more plausible accounts of the connection between memory and identity by weakening his necessary condition for an earlier experience to belong to a person.[6] We are not, however, going to re-trace their arguments here for two reasons. First, the terms of their arguments are inadequate for reasons that are by now all too familiar to us. The conceptions of time and memory which underlie them remain immured within the very philosophical tradition we have found wanting. Because they presuppose time to be linear succession and memory to be an act of mind derivative from perception, their question about personal identity sooner or later redounds to Aristotle's question about memory: How is it possible for something that is past to be present? Thus in their thought we find ourselves back in objectified time, grappling still with image theories and feelings of familiarity and pastness. Locke's way of picturing memory, for example, is as a container of past experience, with rememberings being the contents of the container.

Secondly, at least partially as a result of this, their interests in the question of identity are not congruent with ours. We are committed to the phenomenological theme of self/world relation and thus to the relation between temporality and identity. Our concern with the issue of personal identity is thus to show how our remembering capacities are related to the fundamental life-question, "Who am I?" This, in its turn, is simply a part of our hermeneutical inquiry. We are trying to tease out a more robust understanding of remembering than is available in traditional philosophical thinking to help us in the task of practical literary criticism.

Thus we shall not address the question of personal identity in the grand philosophical manner; nor shall we try to articulate any systematic ontology of the self apart from a phenomenology of human temporality. In keeping with the hermeneutical nature of our project, we shall elaborate the connection between our remembering capacities and our identity out of what we have already described about narrative and temporality. We intend to show how the temporal structure of the self/world relation is reflected in texts and our relationship to texts.

Our hermeneutical inquiry will proceed in four stages. (1) We shall think with Hans-Georg Gadamer and Paul Ricoeur about the dialectical movement characteristic of text-interpretation. This dialectic will be seen to parallel what we have just been observing in the phenomenological movement from world to self. (2) We shall move from a general discussion of texts to a focus on narrative texts to show how, at the level of sense, narrative discourse witnesses to the phenomenology of temporal identity. (3) We shall see how history and fiction, as two modes of narrative discourse with differing referential claims, intersect on the plane of our temporality. Such an intersection will entail the claim that history is more imaginative than is ordinarily supposed; and fiction, more anamnetic. (4) Finally, we shall test this claim in the face of a concrete narrative of the self, Augustine's Confessions. We will notice how Augustine's reflection on the nature of memory is an organic component of his narrative project. His theory of memory has peculiar significance for us precisely because it is generated out of his articulation of a narrative identity. Our reflections on the Confessions correlate with some of the most suggestive work being done now in theology and identity.[7] The new emphasis in the ethical inquiry into character represents a positive revaluation of the past and suggests the importance of our remembering capacities in how the self acquires unity and duration. In each of these stages of our inquiry, the task at hand is basically a hermeneutical retrieval. We will be gathering together the thinking we have already been doing on narrative, temporality, and remembering in

order to show how it is already directed toward the
question "Who am (are) I (we)?"

Dialectical Movement in Text-Interpretation

When we reflect on texts and our relationship to
them, we discover a definite movement in interpretation,
a movement which is grounded in the being of the text
itself. As Gadamer writes in Truth and Method,

> The experience of the work of art includes
> understanding, and thus itself represents a
> hermeneutical phenomenon . . . The under-
> standing belongs to the encounter with the work
> of art itself, so that this connection can be
> illuminated only on the basis of the mode of
> being of the work of art itself.[8]

Gadamer grounds his phenomenological hermeneutic of the
ontology of the work of art in the Aristotelian notion of
mimesis. Art, like play, is an activity that is
meaningful in itself; its mode of being is self-representation. Art, however, intends its self-representation
for someone; its mimesis is directed toward the
recognition of an audience. Openness toward the audience
is ingredient, we might say, in the closedness of art.
The classical notion of mimesis can describe art only if
the word retains the element of knowledge. What is
represented in a text must be there to be recognized.
But what is recognition? What is cognized--recognized--
in the self-representation of a text? For Gadamer, what
one experiences in a work of art and what one is directed
toward is "how true it is, i.e., to what extent one knows
and recognizes something and oneself" (p. 102).

Let us linger over this notion of recognition which
is, according to Gadamer, ingredient in the work of art
itself. By "recognition" we do not understand simply
that what we already knew is known again. Recognition
involves more than familiarity. In the act of recognizing, we know more than we already knew. What we know
emerges in its essence from all the variables that
condition it--we know something. Gadamer shows that this
profound sense of recognition is the central motif of
Plato's theory of Recollection.

> In his theory of anamnesis Plato combined the
> mythical idea of remembrance with his
> dialectic, which sought in the logos, i.e., the
> ideality of language, the truth of being. In
> fact this kind of idealism of being is already

suggested in the phenomenon of recognition. The "known" enters into its true being and manifests itself as what it is only when it is recognized. As recognized it is grasped in its essence (p. 103).

In the mimetic play of art, what is represented is recognized in its own validity and truth.

> The basic mimic situation that we are discussing not only involves what is being represented being there, but also that it has in this way come to exist more fully. Imitation and representation are not merely a second version, a copy, but a recognition of the essence. Because they are not merely repetition, but a "bringing forth," the spectator is also involved in them. They contain the essential relation to everyone for whom the representation exists (p. 103).

Mimesis, rather than implying "mere imitation," is necessarily creative and revelatory. The mode of this revelation is anamnesis (recognition). <u>Anamnesis is ingredient in the mimesis of art</u>. For Plato, of course, all knowledge of being is anamnesis. For Aristotle, it is this anamnetic quality of mimesis which grounds his claim that poetry is more philosophical than history. Mimesis thus has a clear cognitive function. Implicit in a mimetic theory of art is the significance of art as knowledge of the true. The mode of being of the work of art is representation-intended-as-recognition.

Gadamer uses the Aristotelian theory of tragedy as an example of this structure of aesthetic being. In Aristotle's inclusion of the effects of the spectacle on the audience in his definition of tragedy, Gadamer finds confirmation of his own understanding of the being of the work of art as self-representation intended as recognition. Now this effect requires of the audience a dialectic of distance and identification. The distance that the spectator retains from the drama is not an optional attitude, but the essential relation whose ground lies in the meaningful unity of the play itself. Tragedy is the unity of a tragic succession of events. According to Aristotle, the representation of the tragic works through <u>eleo</u> and <u>phobos</u>, distress and apprehension. Both are modes of <u>ecstasis</u>, of being outside oneself, which testify to the power of what is taking place before us. The dialectic of distance and ecstatic emotions has such a curve to it that it carries us back to ourselves in a kind of affirmation. For Gadamer, the tragic emotion is a response to an order of being that is "true for [us] all" (p. 117). To see that "this is how it is" is a kind of self-knowledge for the spectator who emerges with new insight from the illusions in which he lives.

By understanding the work of art as a self-representation which intends itself toward an audience, Gadamer saves recognition--and art itself--from all purely subjectivist theories. This mode of being of the work of art has as its corollary a distinctive attitude required of the audience. Recognition, as we have seen, is not purely subjective. Rather, being present as an audience to a text is determining of the being of the audience. To be present is not simply to be in the presence of something else which is present. To be present means to share. As a subjective act of a human attitude, to be present means to be outside oneself for the positive possibility of being wholly with something else. This kind of presence to the text is a self-forgetfulness. The reader forgets herself in the activity of reading the text; the text makes claims on her.

The text's self-representation to the reader does not, however, play itself out in the moment of reading. It has what Gadamer calls "a claim of permanence and the permanence of a claim" (p. 112). The reader as reader has no separate legitimacy in the face of the being of the text. But precisely that in which she loses herself requires her own continuity.

> It is the truth of his own world, the religious and moral truth in which he lives, which presents itself to him and in which he recognizes himself. Just as the parousia, absolute presence, describes the ontological mode of aesthetic being, and a work of art is the same whenever it becomes such a presence, so the absolute moment in which a spectator stands is at once self-forgetfulness and reconciliation with self. That which detaches him from everything also gives him back the whole of his being (p. 113).

In "texting" herself, the reader deepens her own continuity with herself. Literature's claim has the characteristic of a genuine communion. To recognize the truth of the text is a kind of self-recognition for the reader who emerges with new insight from the illusions in which she lives--insights, that is, into herself as well as her world. At the heart of Gadamer's hermeneutic of the text lies this dialectic of self-forgetfulness for

163

the sake of self-recognition, continuity, and reconciliation.

In his <u>Interpretation Theory</u>, Paul Ricoeur develops a parallel notion of the reciprocity between text-inter-pretation and self-interpretation. He is as eager as Gadamer to rescue hermeneutics from a Romanticist subjectivity by restoring to the text its character as mimesis. At the same time, he too wants to take seriously the event character of the act of reading by exploring the nature of understanding a text. For Ricoeur, mimesis is the Greek name for what he calls the unostensive reference of the literary work, or, in other words, the Greek name for world disclosure.

> The text speaks of a possible world and of a possible way of orienting oneself within it. The dimensions of this world are properly opened up by and disclosed by the text. Discourse is the equivalent for written language of ostensive reference for spoken language. It goes beyond the mere function of pointing out and showing what already exists and, in this sense, transcends the function of the ostensive reference linked to spoken language. <u>Here showing is at the same time creating a new mode of being.</u>[9]

Interpretation then becomes the kind of inquiry appropriate to the power of a work to project a world of its own and to initiate the hermeneutical circle between the apprehension of such projected worlds and the expansion of self-understanding in front of these novel worlds. As he states, "If a subject is called upon to understand himself in the presence of the text, it is to the extent that the text is not closed on itself, but open to the world which it redescribes and refashions."[10] This is like the claim of permanence and the permanence of a claim in Gadamer. The reading event has implications for the very being of the reader. The dialectic we saw in Gadamer of self-forgetfulness for the sake of self-continuity and reconciliation with the self becomes in Ricoeur the dialectic of distanciation and appropriation.

> To appropriate means to make "one's own" what was "alien." Because there is a general need for making our own what is foreign to us, there is a general problem of distanciation. Distance, then, is not simply a fact, a given, just the actual spatial and temporal gap between us and the appearance of such and such

work of art or discourse. It is a dialectical trait, the principle of a struggle between the otherness that transforms all spatial and temporal distance into cultural estrangement and the ownness by which all understanding aims at the extension of self-understanding. Distanciation is not a quantitative phenomenon; it is the dynamic counterpart of our need, our interest, and our effort to overcome cultural estrangement (p. 43).

Appropriation is the concept for the actualization of meaning as addressed to someone. Potentially a text is addressed to anyone who can read. Actually it is addressed to me, here and now. Interpretation is completed as appropriation when reading yields something like an event, an event of discourse, which is an event in the present moment. As appropriation, interpretation becomes an event.

The reader understands herself before the text, before the world of the work. To understand oneself before, in front of, a world is the contrary of projecting oneself and one's beliefs and prejudices; it is to let the work and its world enlarge the horizon of one's own self-understanding.

Far from saying that a subject already mastering his own way of being in the world projects the a priori of his self-understanding on the text and reads it into the text, I say that interpretation is the process by which disclosure of new modes of being--or if you prefer Wittgenstein to Heidegger, of new forms of life--gives to the subject a new capacity for knowing himself. If the reference of the text is the project of a world, then it is not the reader who primarily projects himself. The reader rather is enlarged in his capacity of self-projection by receiving a new mode of being from the text itself (p. 94).

Both Gadamer and Ricoeur identify two dialectical moments in text-interpretation. Letting the work and its world enlarge the horizon of my own self-understanding requires that I first of all forget myself in the presence of the text. But this self-forgetfulness (Gadamer) or principle of distanciation (Ricoeur) is always for the sake of a new remembering, a recognition and reconciliation with myself. The work's mimetic power to project a world is the enabler of the reader's anamnetic capacity to receive a new mode of being from the text.

The dialectical process of text-interpretation reveals how remembering is engaged in the hermeneutical act. As Hart says, "One cannot stray from memory so long as he is considering anything involving interpretation."[11] This remembering is neither a purely subjective act on the one hand nor an act separate from the self on the other. The anamnesis is both ingredient in the text's mimesis and profoundly directed toward self-continuity. What is more, the remembering proper to the text is certainly no mere repetition of the past, any more than the text's mimesis is a mere copy of reality. Both mimesis and anamnesis are creative activities; what they enlarge is our imagination, our capacities to dwell in other worlds and construct new modes of being. In hermeneutical theory, anamnesis emerges as ingredient in the dialectical process of text-interpretation, as the moment in which text-interpretation is completed as self-interpretation before the text.

Gadamer and Ricoeur make the same claim, now on hermeneutical grounds, which we have been making with phenomenology about temporality and identity. That claim, in its simplest form, is that we discover and create ourselves in relation to a world. Phenomenology, as we have been arguing, insists that we can best understand the self by approaching it indirectly in this manner. Following from this, we have been addressing the self-question, "Who am I?", by way of the world-question, "What is the nature of reality?" And we have claimed that these are not two separate questions but rather two sides of the same question. In each case, the dialectical movement is the same: self-interpretation through text-interpretation, identity by way of temporality. In each instance, we are led to the self by way of its world, and we can only understand it in terms of this relation. Indeed, we have claimed with Heidegger that Dasein is this relation, this being-in-the-world. From a hermeneutical perspective, can we not say that the world itself is a text; and remembering, a primary hermeneutic of the "text" of our temporal human lives.?[12] In Arendt's terms, we construct our biographies by an anamnetic "texting" of ourselves in the world.

The Witness of Narrative Discourse to Temporal Identity

In the last chapter, we described our being-in-the-world as fundamentally a temporal relation. We must now inquire how temporality fits in with our present hermeneutical inquiry into the self-text relation. To do so, we shall move our discussion from the general level of the text to a focus on the narrative text. I can justify such a focus in the light of the specific literary critical intention of our project, i.e., our interest in a fresh hermeneutic for the novel. I wish, however, to make a stronger claim. I am choosing to reflect on narrative discourse not simply because it offers an example which is close to my own interests. I will argue, rather, following Ricoeur, that narrative is that mode of discourse which manifests the form of our temporality. To do so, I shall retrieve what I have already said about narrative in my discussion of the liturgical anamnesis.

There we argued that history and fiction share a common narrative structure at the level of sense. We identified plot, understood as the paradoxical competition of sequence and pattern, as the structural factor grounding the family resemblance between history and fiction. On that basis we concluded that, thanks to their unity of structure, history and fiction constitute what Wittgenstein calls a language-game. We now intend the further claim, again in Wittgensteinian terms, that speaking this language is a form of life, or, in Heideggerian language, a mode of being. We have identified our temporality as that aspect of our human life to which narrative discourse refers.

As we have already mentioned in our discussion of temporality, current epistemologies of narrative generally take for granted that the kind of time in which stories and histories unfold is linear time. Such a reduction of narrative time to mere chronicity, a succession of nows separated by measurable intervals, is precisely what the phenomenology of temporality denies. Is it possible to bring the two together? On the one hand, we need an epistemology of narrative which, by recognizing the complexity of narrative time, will be more faithful to the phenomenology of temporality. On the other, we need to demonstrate to phenomenology that narrative activity offers us privileged access to the articulation of its own understanding of human temporality. In his recent work, Ricoeur undertakes just such a rapprochement through a reflection on plot as the matrix of narrative structure.[13] I summarize his argument here.

Let us grant, with current narrative theories, that a phenomenology of narrative must first of all recognize that stories are bound to a chronological order. By virtue of its episodic dimension, a plot makes a series of events into a story. This elementary function of narrative emplotment establishes the characters within everyday time. What is more, the very act of telling the story presupposes time as succession. Adverbial expressions are endemic to stories: "and then . . . and then." In following the story, we are satisfying our basic curiosity to know what happens next. Because it is thus bound to chronology, a story reveals the blind complexity of the present moment as it is experienced by the characters. If we consider only the episodic dimension of plot, we may be led to conclude that narrative does, indeed, give us simply a linear image of time.

Even at this level, however, narrative activity shows that the truth of everyday time is genuine Care, in the Heideggerian sense. There is a datable and public character to the time of the characters' preoccupation, but this very preoccupation cannot be overlooked. Characters reckon with time, and this struggle reveals that we measure time because we reckon with it and not the other way around.[14] Stories and histories show that even public time, the time of hours, days, and seasons, is human time. There is time to do something; characters have time, take time, waste time, run out of time. A character's being in everyday time is first of all a grappling with time. It is this reckoning with time which causes our need to calculate and measure it. Stories and histories show that the popular image of time as a linear succession is true enough as far as it goes, but that even it must be understood as proceeding from our Care. The character's present invariably temporalizes in union with memory and expectation. Stories do not allow us to remain at an abstract conceptualization of time as an infinite succession of nows. The very succession of events draws us forward in expectation toward the story's conclusion. Stories thus reveal how even a blind present proceeds from and is embedded in our historicity, our stretching along from birth to death. The present's significance in a story is necessarily connected with the ecstatic character of our temporal being, with Dasein as a journey.

Thus even at the episodic level of emplotment, stories and histories display the truth of the phenomenology of human temporality. But even the humblest plots, as we have seen, combine in varying proportions an episodic dimension and a configurational one. By virtue of its configurational dimension, a plot does not merely pile up episodes but forms them into meaningful wholes. To follow a plot is to elicit a pattern out of the sequence, to construe meaningful wholes out of the succession of events. If the episodic dimension of plot responds to our question "and then? and then?", the configurational dimension responds to our question "why?" It tells us the point; it gives us the theme of the story or the thought which unifies the history. As such it is a reflective act; it displays, as Ricoeur shows, the character of a Kantian judgment. To tell and follow stories is already to reflect upon events in order to grasp their unity, coherence, and directedness.[15]

In answering the "why" question, this configurational dimension which correlates sequence with thought supersedes mere chronicity. Such pattern is not, however, achronological. On the openendedness of mere succession, narratives impose what Kermode calls "the sense of an ending." This teleological strategy does not abolish time but rather brings it back to what Heidegger calls historicity or repetition and what we have been calling recollection. To understand the story, we must read it as a whole, ruled by its ending. In a way analogous to listening to a symphony, we grasp the work's patterns and themes as a whole, in the light of the entire story. The self-representation proper to a story is that of a structure of meaning-as-temporality. Its self-disclosure discloses new possibilities of reality through the creation of a world as an image of temporal experience.

As a moving structure of temporality, a story or history provides a clear alternative to the picture of time as flowing from the past through the present into the future. To follow the story, we must read the end in the beginning and the beginning in the end. Through its configurational dimension, plot establishes human action in memory. By virtue of the anamnesis proper to text-interpretation, we as story-followers retrieve the course of events according to an inner order. In reading a story or following a history, we are in a sense re-enacting our own historicity, since our own being-from the past is a retrieval of our ownmost potentialities in the form of a personal destiny. If remembering is ingredient in the acts of story-telling and story-following, this is the case not simply because we have to know what comes before and what comes after if we are to understand the point of it all. Rather it is so because the structure of the narrative itself, thanks to the sequential and configurational dimensions of plot, is a memorial structure, a simulacrum of our human temporality.

History, Fiction, and the "Narrative"
Dimension of Temporality

We have been arguing that at the level of sense, narrative discourse, comprising both history and fiction, displays a unity of structure which justifies our calling it a language-game. The structural factor of emplotment reveals how that language-game bespeaks our human temporality. Narratives articulate a time which is more than an objective succession of now-moments. In narrative discourse, time reveals itself as the care of our being, a care evidenced both in the succession of events (sequence) and in our grasping them together in a tightly interdependent network of moving meaning (pattern). Already at the level of sense, then, we have been claiming that narrative discourse articulates our temporal identity and thus engages our capacities for remembering. Indeed, our capacities have their native habitat there, once learned.

If history and fiction display a unity at the level of sense, however, this is not so immediately apparent at the level of reference. Sense is the "what" of discourse; reference, the "about what." Here we are confronted with a striking dissimilarity between history and fiction, and no such unity seems to obtain. For its part, history claims to tell a story which is true in the sense that it refers to something which actually happened in the past. It is immediately evident that history makes memory claims vis-à-vis the past. Fiction, on the other hand, is not bound by such evidential claims. History purports to give us the real as past (as does memory); fiction, the imaginary unreal. Granted this discontinuity at the referential level, how can we talk about narrative discourse's capacity to refer to a unified form of life? And how can we assert that all narratives involve remembering even at the referential level? This issue is crucial for us because we are grounding our argument for memory's role in identity in this correspondence between narrative discourse and temporality in texts.

To answer this objection, we must show that the remembering proper to history is more imaginative than is ordinarily supposed; and the imagination proper to fiction, more anamnetic. In making this argument, we are preparing the ground for our next chapter's reflection on the connection between memory and imagination. I do not intend to suppress the differing referential claims of history and fiction, but rather to show that they intersect in a particular way on the plane of our temporality. My claim, following Ricoeur, is that our temporal identity is such that it requires the narrative strategies of both history and fiction for its full expression.[16]

Let us begin with history because the involvement of memory there is immediately apparent. Our aim is to show that the remembering proper to history cannot be accounted for by the traditional notion of memory as the passive reiteration of what is past. A controlling theme in our discussion of temporality has been that we live out of the future but understand out of the past. We have been calling such understanding out of the past a remembering activity. It is, as well, a description of the motivation of history. If we inquire into history's interest in the past, we are led to assert that history is concerned with the past to the extent that it ought not to be forgotten, to the extent, i.e., that it is memorable.[17] Prior to the emergence of history as a scientific discipline is memory as the concern for our having-been.

In order that it be remembered, the past must be conceived of in terms of our human existing. We possess ourselves only as the journey from birth to death, from past to future. Faced with a silent and inscrutable future, we orient ourselves toward it out of a thrownness which is also a well of possibilities. We draw on our past in our projections of purposive action. As the human activity which articulates our Care as having-been, remembering is grounded in our historical condition. As Wittgenstein puts it, we "learn the concept of the past by remembering."[18] Thus, as we have repeatedly insisted, recollection is not a mere replication of the past but the retrieval of Care. The first application of this retrieval in the structure of Care is thus not history as science but remembering as a human activity constitutive of the self.[19] In its turn, history is not simply a story we tell about the past but rather the gathering of our heritage of possibilities. Its interests correspond to the fact that we _are_ as having-been. The movement from personal retrieval to collective retrieval is the movement from memory to tradition, from "Who am I?" to "Who are we?" We would be unable to be-toward, to project any purposive actions, were we not able to draw on this supply of inherited possibilities. History cannot be a merely passive transmission of data any more than memory itself is.

We have said that history repeats the past insofar as that past is memorable. To its methodological concern with facts, history adds a concern for communication. What is memorable about the past? In Ricoeur's words,

> What is most worthy of being kept in our
> memories are the _values_ which ruled the
> individual actions, the life of the
> institutions and the social struggles of the
> past. Thanks to the objective work of the
> historian, these values are added to the common
> treasure of mankind.[20]

Or as T. S. Eliot expresses it in "Tradition and the
Individual Talent," if we think we know so much more than
those who came before us, it behooves us to remember that
"they are what we know."[21]

Our present interests are what motivate history. In
this we see an exact parallel with memory. A traditional
view of history as a complete set of facts which tell us
"how it _really_ was when it happened" simply does not make
sense.[22] We can speak of the past only when it is revived
in somebody's present reflection. Such reflection is
dependent on documents which represent depositories of
memories and relics of the past. All such evidence is
oblique. What is more, while history does give us
certain things which count as facts, these facts must be
arranged in larger contexts of meaning. Such contexts
are the configurational dimension of the historical plot.
In providing an integrating context for the relevant
data, the historian is giving her story a theme which
corresponds to her particular theories and the values in
which they are embedded.

Here we need to remind ourselves of the distinction
we made in our discussion of the liturgical anamnesis
between an event which merely happens and that event as
told. History, we claimed, lives in that gap. It does
not just _tell_ a story; rather, it _makes_ events into a
story. On the basis of eyewitness reports, memoirs,
documents, archives, relics, and the like, the historian
produces a work which is, in Collingwood's phrase, an
"imaginative reconstruction" of the past.[23] As such,
history is both a literary artifact in the sense that it
imaginatively reconstructs the past _and_ a representation
of reality in the sense that the world it reconstructs is
assumed to refer to actual past occurrences.

History is no more a set of dusty facts than the
past is dead and gone. But neither is history a reliable
testimony to "how it _really_ was when it happened," any
more than the past is a relic carried along untouched by
time. What gives the lie to each of these ways of
picturing history and the past is the human activity of
remembering. It is because there is no authentic
objective past "back there" waiting to be retrieved

172

wholly in its pastness that we must reconstruct it through our present remembering and historicizing. It is because the past is part and parcel of the living present, continually affected by our Care, that each age writes its own history of the past.

We reconstruct our past, both individually and collectively, in the histories and stories we tell as we live the ecstases of temporality. What is retrieved of that past is subject to continual modification and substantial transformation by our present interests. The kind of life had out of the future affects the possible kinds of understanding had out of the past. This is as true of history as of personal rememberings. As Frederick Wyatt writes,

> The past as history, as a coherent account of events, their sequence, interdependence, and significance comes into being only when it is reconstructed in an ever-renewed present.[24]

That such reconstructions are continually subject to change means that they transcend themselves in the light of new data, new experiences, and new understandings. In this sense, it is not only the case that the past makes us but that we make it, by putting it together through our creative narrative rememberings.[25] By such remembering activity, we reconstruct not only the past but our very selves. The past is only really retrieved again in our present reconstructions. And our identity is only really given in this way: when we creatively remember ourselves, a re-membering which preserves our self-continuity in fidelity to our Being-toward-possibility. It is, as we have argued before, the narrative quality of our experience that keeps these paradoxes alive.

Such remembering, both in history and in life, cannot be a passive function. It is a creative act, engaging our imaginative capacities. This kind of remembering follows the dialectical curve which we have seen to be characteristic of text-interpretation. Resuming the forgotten past requires as its counterpart the capacity to suspend one's own situation, to bracket one's own desires. It is the dialectic of self-forgetfulness for the sake of self-continuity which history reveals as a dialectic between the foreign and the familiar, the remote and the proximate. When we speak of history as "imaginative reconstruction" we do not intend to imply a pure subjectivism. It is not that we re-make history in our own image, to bolster our own preconceptions. To be present to the historical past, like being present before the world of the text, is the opposite of reading our a priori self-understandings and formulations into the past. What we recognize about the values of the past is precisely their difference. Such recognition, proper to history, has the effect of opening "the real to the possible," in Ricoeur's phrase.[26] Through its "true" stories of the past, history reveals the potentialities of the present. Thus history allows us to transcend an immured present by inviting us to recognize other possible ways of being human.

We have been arguing that the remembering proper to history is more imaginative than is ordinarily supposed. By virtue of its narrative structure, history is both a literary artifact and a representation of reality. That fiction, on the other hand, does not purport to describe actual occurrences does not, however, mean that it is antithetical to the representation of reality. As we have already seen in our discussion of text-interpretation, the paradigm for this conjunction between fiction and reality is given in Aristotle's Poetics. Aristotle understands art as combining both mythos and mimesis. By virtue of its mimetic character, art imitates reality, not in the sense of producing a copy of it, but rather in the sense of showing forth the significance of events. Art's mimesis is creative imitation; it offers a metaphor of reality. This, then, is the basis of fiction's referential claim. Fictions refer to reality, not to replicate it, but to disclose new readings of it. It is in this sense that Aristotle can claim that art is more philosophical than history. Not tied as history must be to the contingent and the particular, art can address itself directly to what is essential and universal in human experience. Fiction both discloses and creates, both makes and remakes, reality. In offering models for perceiving in a new way, it suppresses the referential claim of conventional language, but such suppression is at the service of its very redescription of that reality in its essence. Fiction's suspension of the ordinary world is simply the negative counterpart to its positive referential claim.[27] In Jakobson's language, fiction is not without reference; rather, its reference is "split."[28] If, as Ricoeur puts it, history opens us to the possible by opening us to the different, then fiction brings us back to the essential by opening us to the unreal. Now we have already argued that such a "bringing back" is a creative anamnesis, a recognition by which we are freed from self-projection, freed for new understandings of ourselves and our worlds.

Fiction involves a texture of anamneses, if you will. (1) As a text, it intends its self-representation toward the recognition of its audience. (2) What we recognize before the world of the text are the essential and universal aspects of the human condition. (3) As an image of meaning-as-temporality, its rhetoric of temporality comprises recollection at the level of emplotment's sequential and configurational dimensions, or more exactly, in the paradoxical competition between the two. (4) Typically, a story shows how the character constructs her identity in and through her actions in the world. Such a construction of biography entails remembering. (5) While characters may be mired in their own prejudices and false interpretations of self and world, fictions do not confine the reader to their perspectives regarding their own actions. Fictions give us both a story and a story-teller.

Scholes and Kellogg go so far as to claim that "in the relationship between the teller and the tale and in that other relationship between the teller and the audience lies the essence of narrative art."[29] Narrative point of view provides a dialectic between narrator and story and narrator and reader which they label "ineluctably ironical."[30] Narrative irony is a function of the disparity of understanding among the points of view of characters, narrator, and audience. As a result of this disparity of viewpoints, fictions enable us to participate in events without being subject to their consequences. The pattern elicited by the reader, for example, need not be recognized by the character, and may or may not be recognized by the narrator.

Part of what we recognize about ourselves in reading stories is precisely how difficult it is to grasp the pattern of events as we live them. Such a recognition, about the characters and about ourselves, challenges our ordinary presuppositions of having mastered our own way of being in the world. Paradoxically, that certain superiority we feel toward the characters in the story, because they are involved in the events in a way we are not, opens us to receive new insights into our own self-enclosed worlds and meanings. This kind of recognition, built into the narrative strategies themselves, forms the basis of fiction's moral claims. The notion of fictional character is not unrelated to an ethics of character. Both address the capacity or incapacity of the self to achieve unity and duration in the face of a temporality which is a flight out of itself. Thus both involve our capacities for remembering and forgetting, for recognition and amnesia.

Our aim in this section has been to complicate a simple and misleading picture of history as the reiteration of past facts and fiction as the creation of imaginary unreals. As long as we persist in such dichotomies, we will tend to place memory on the side of history and imagination on the side of fiction. Such neat categorizing correlates with the philosophical tradition's tendency to see memory and imagination as twin faculties derivative of perception and of lesser value and importance than thought and perception. In such a view, thought and perception enjoy a primacy stemming from their reciprocal relationship in the synchronic dimension of time. Both give us the _real_ by a kind of escape from time as stretching along: thought's objects are "eternal"; perception's, instantaneous. Memory and imagination by contrast correspond to our fall into time.[31] Memory can only give us what is past, what is no longer; imagination, what is not or is not yet. An attention to history confirms, however, that memory cannot be rightly understood as a storehouse of the past. In history, memory is a construing motivated by present interests. A comparable attention to fiction reveals that it cannot be comprised under the category of imagination as the unreal, thanks to its multifarious engagement of various remembering activities.

Now the philosophical tradition's denigration of memory and imagination is simply the consequence of a tendency to see time itself as a lesser value, a fall from eternal being, in Plato's terms, a decay of sensual immediacy, in Hobbes'. Once we accept a phenomenology of human temporality, however, we are committed to revising our understanding of memory and imagination. In such a revision, we need not go so far as Crites, who sees thought and perception as strategies of abstraction and contraction which defy our temporal existence and generate the mind/body dualism. We would rather claim that all four acts--thought, perception, memory, and imagination--as the expression of our being-in-the-world, are inherently temporal. Here we can recall Heidegger's conviction that the highest kind of thinking is a recollecting. And an epistemology of narrative discourse reveals how the thought proper to both history and fiction already requires our capacities for remembering and imagining.

Our own focus has been on remembering rather than imagining. We have been arguing that our remembering capacities are complicit in and constitutive of our present identity. Thanks to the temporality of Dasein, we can say that both memory and imagination are crucial components of every present. This cannot mean that history, as memory, simply correlates with our having-been and fiction, as imagination, with our being-toward. Our reflection on the sense and reference of narrative discourse has shown that each narrative form and each human activity participates in the other.

In arguing for history's imaginative dimension and fiction's anamnetic dimension, we do not intend to collapse their differing referential claims. We do, however, want to argue that these claims intersect on the plane of our historical condition. The intersecting references of history and fiction are the key to the relation between narrative and temporality. As a language-game, narrative discourse has two distinct but mutually implicated forms. Both work together to display our temporal form of life. It seems that our historical condition is so deeply rooted that it cannot be said directly by either history or fiction in isolation. As story-tellers and historians, we are ourselves "members of the historical field."[32] If our temporality cannot be said directly, it is because we belong to the story we tell before we tell it. We always already <u>are</u> as having-been and being-toward. We need both narrative strategies, both history and fiction, to grasp ourselves as this journey. To repeat Ricoeur's formulation: history opens us to the possible by opening us to the different; fiction brings us back to the essential by opening us to the imaginary. It is because we are always already temporal beings that we are always already remembering and anticipating selves, and it is because of both these facts that narrative discourse, in the form of history and fiction, is the privileged articulation of our temporal identity. Our self-understanding has a narrative structure. Memory and narrative are mutually constitutive of the self.

Autobiography: Augustine's Confessions

In our hermeneutical inquiry into memory's implication in the question "Who am (are) I (we)?", we have moved from the general level of text-interpretation to the structure of narrative discourse, and, finally, to history and fiction as species of narrative with differing but intersecting referential claims. In conclusion, we shall focus on autobiography as a special case in which this collusion between memory and identity in narrative is peculiarly manifest.

Autobiography is a narrative form well suited to our purposes because it recapitulates within itself all the connections we have been arguing for in our previous

three sections on identity. (1) As a narrative of the
self, its self-representation is not only intended toward
the reader's anamnesis; it is itself an anamnesis of the
autobiographer's identity. (2) Its structure combines
sequence and pattern in the construction of plot, but in
autobiography what is emplotted is the self. (3) As a
version of the narratable self, autobiography gives
incontrovertible evidence of memory's complicity in our
temporal self-knowledge and self-identity. (4) As such,
it is both historical and fictive; or, rather it is in a
certain sense beyond the difference between the empirical
and the fictional.

The term "autobiography" means literally the
description (graphia) of an individual life (bios) by the
individual himself (auto). The Oxford English Dictionary
cites its earliest known use in English in the first
issue of the Quarterly Review, published in 1809.[33] It
appears to be a translation of the German word which had
appeared in the title of a collection of "lives" ten
years earlier.[34] When it came into common currency during
the course of the nineteenth century, it replaced the
earlier customary name for such writings, "memoirs."
While this latter term now generally refers to informal
and loosely constructed writings of no great literary
pretensions which convey the sense of a period through
the perspective of a significant participant, originally
"memoirs" preserved an understanding not conveyed by the
more technical contemporary term "autobiography." That
understanding is the classical view, which we have
already discussed, that not only history but poetry
itself has its source in Memory, the mother of the muses.
A "memoir" was thus a work both of history and of poesis.
Understood in this richer sense of memoir, autobiography
is seen to possess its own peculiar power to attain the
truthfulness of art without losing its empirical hold.
As Georg Misch, one of the earliest writers about
autobiography as a genre, states in his definitive two-
volume History of Autobiography in Antiquity,

> Empirical contemplation of reality affords a
> comprehensive view only at moments of
> exaltation: this heightened awareness, shaping
> its story, while re-living it from the present
> and past seen as a whole, produces a creative
> objectivation of the autobiographer's mind that
> cannot be other than true. The more style his
> work has, the farther it is from mere stylized
> narrative.[35]

Misch first published this in 1907, but what he is
getting at in his own rather florid style is a conception

of autobiography which continues to fascinate autobiographical theorists today. It is related to a point we have already made in our discussion of history and fiction.

There we argued, following Ricoeur, that our historicity is said to the extent that we tell both stories and histories. It is because, as story-tellers and historians, we are always already members of the historical field that we need both forms to articulate our temporal identity. If our experience as historical beings is such that the relation between subject and object is thus undermined, this is especially evident in autobiography. Here, as Dilthey said, "The subject inquiring is also the object inquired into; the historian who tells the story is the same who has already lived it." This identity of author and subject in autobiography led Dilthey to contend that "autobiography is the highest and most instructive form in which the understanding of life comes before us."[36]

In autobiography, the understanding of life is first of all the understanding of the narrator's own particular life. In narrating her own individual experience, however, the autobiographer is also both representing her period and constructing an image of the structure of individuality. In her own life story, she presents a reading of the meaning of human life. Autobiography, that is, presents the particular and contingent in the form of personal history; but in doing so, it witnesses to a universal meaning.

We have already claimed that in a certain sense autobiography is beyond the difference between the empirical and the fictional. In its aim to be a truthful description of the narrator's own experience, autobiography is a species of history, a narration of actual events which typically gives us both a personal history and a history of a certain period. As such, it bears a close family resemblance to that simplest of historical narrative forms, the chronicle. It displays as well the consistency of a good fiction; i.e., it must order itself into a shape which answers what the autobiographer's life means. Such construal of meaning requires selection according to thematic and metaphorical patterns. As V. S. Pritchett comments concerning the autobiographer's art, "The moment one writes the word 'I' one is faced by the problem of settling who or what this 'I' is."[37]

Such "settling" of the "I" happens in the narrative act itself. The meaning of life, the unity of the self, which autobiography discloses is not a prior given which simply needs articulation now in narrative form. It is an imaginative construction. That this is widely recognized to be the case is evidenced by the titles of recent studies of autobiography: <u>Imagining a Self</u>, <u>The Examined Self</u>, <u>Metaphors of Self</u>, <u>Versions of the Self</u>, <u>Recastings of the Self: Interaction of Metaphor and Personal History</u>, <u>Design and Truth in Autobiography</u>.[38] Each of these studies argues or implies that autobiography is an act or process which combines metaphorical self-construction with the rhetoric of temporality. And so, for example, Pritchett comments that "to write well in this way one must feel . . . that one is conducting a search, not traipsing down chronology."[39] Roy Pascal asserts:

> Life is represented in autobiography not as something established but as a process; it is not simply the narration of the voyage but also the voyage itself. There must be in it a sense of discovery.[40]

It is patent that "the voyage itself" in autobiography is a remembering activity. More than any other narrative genre, autobiography testifies to remembering's role in the construction of a narrative identity. What is more, it reveals conclusively that such remembering cannot be limited to a mechanical reproduction but must be understood as a creative process in which what is created is precisely the autobiographer's identity. In the autobiographical act, the narrator does not simply articulate either a past or a present self but actually constructs and reconstructs her self-identity as a journey. Since it is self-consciously directed toward the articulation of a narratable self, autobiography is always about the self as Dasein, as temporal being-in-the-world.

While literary criticism has generally overlooked the role remembering plays in narrative, autobiographical theory has of necessity attended to this connection between creative memory and narrative identity. We do not intend to rehearse such autobiographical theory any further here, however. We shall attend instead to an actual autobiography, Augustine's <u>Confessions</u>.

The <u>Confessions</u> recommends itself to our consideration for several reasons. (1) As an autobiographical act, it exhibits memory's engagement in the narrative articulation of identity. (2) What is more, that very process leads Augustine into a reflection on the nature of time and memory within his narrative.

These philosophical/theological reflections are not extraneous to his life story, but rather intimately bound up with discovering and disclosing his identity in narrative form. (3) Finally, Augustine represents in his person the pre-eminent unification of the classical philosophical tradition with Christianity. Indeed, that very coalescence is in large part the subject of his Confessions. Thus he shows us a way to foster a dialogue between the contradictory tendencies we traced in part I of this study, where we contrasted classical notions of memory with the contemporaneous Judaeo-Christian practice of liturgical anamnesis.

Without going into the kind of detailed analysis which a work of such compelling power invites but which is outside the scope of our inquiry, let me simply focus on two aspects of Augustine's Confessions: (1) what the text discloses about memory and identity, and (2) what Augustine says explicitly about time and memory.

(1) To discuss this relationship between memory and identity we must attend to the Confessions' structure. We have already made the fairly self-evident claim that the autobiographical act is a narrative of remembering which has as its purpose the imaginative formulation of the self. Augustine's Confessions displays a unique structure which serves to reverse the emphasis, as it were, in the relationship between narrative and memory evident in all autobiographies. Here remembering is not at the service of the narrative, but rather the narrative seems to be at the service of remembering. What is more, the peculiarly rich and embodied remembering we find in the text is already familiar to us from our reflection on the Eucharistic anamnesis.

In Augustine, the narrative unity of the self achieved by the autobiographical act is not simply the result of an intellectual and imaginative process. It is as well and primarily a religious act. In the ten years which had elapsed between his conversion and the Confessions, he had thoroughly appropriated and been formed by a Christian anthropology which understands personal identity not as self-achieved but rather as mediated. Augustine's search for identity in memory and experience is revealed in the Confessions as the search for God, in whom the Christian believer has his being. He is quite explicit about this relationship: "Seek for yourself, O man; search for your true self. He who seeks shall find himself in God."[41] The work derives its unity and directedness, as well as its form, from this controlling theme of the two-fold search for God and the self, disclosed to be one and the same search. The book begins with an often quoted prayer which articulates the theme that shapes both the story and the dispositional life of the story-teller: "Thou hast made us for Thyself, O Lord, and our hearts are restless until they rest in Thee."[42]

I stated above that in the Confessions, narrative is at the service of a particular kind of remembering. As his sermons make clear, both the Scriptures and the Eucharist had the profoundest shaping influence on Augustine's formation in the Christian life. It seems apparent that he in turn shaped his Confessions according to the patterns of anamnesis embodied there. As its title indicates, the Confessions is not simply narrative discourse, but primarily a confessional utterance. It is, in fact, a Christian anamnesis which, like the Scriptural and liturgical anamneses we have discussed, places the one who prays in the presence of God. The Confessions is an extended prayer form uttered in the vocative. As such, it recalls past events before God, brings what is past into the present, for the sake of witnessing to and reviving the work of salvation now evident in those events. In the Confessions, that re-enactment of the past is accomplished by the interpenetration of the narrative and vocative modes, an interpenetration which allows Augustine to infuse his past with his present religious conviction without sacrificing the narrative immediacy of the past. One man's personal history thus emerges both as historical process and as witness to the presence and activity of God in that process.[43]

The Confessions' character as a Christian anamnesis provides the narration of that personal history with its structural unity. It has a fixed point of departure (Augustine's sinful condition), a steady progress (God's grace), and a clear conclusion (his conversion and experience of union with God).[44] As an anamnesis, part of its purpose is to recall to the community as well as the author the hidden workings of God in human experience. While Augustine experienced his past as problematic and opaque, an experience of God's distance and absence, his narration of it is always given in the context of prayer, a prayer of anamnesis which never loses sight of God's invitational proximity in that past. The process of remembering, as addressed to God, thus achieves a coherence of his personal identity which transcends the oppositions between the past and present Augustine. In this sense, the Confessions is a powerful example of a conceptual point we made in our discussion of "the narrative quality of experience." Augustine's conversion involved undermining the stories of his past experience, re-membering, re-collecting, and re-cognizing himself into a new story. But this new story preserves his self-continuity. He achieves this in his autobiography precisely by subsuming the narrative into an anamnesis of prayerful recognition.

Let us recall here what we said about the vocative mode in prayer in our discussion of the liturgical anamnesis. To speak in the vocative is peculiarly personal because the knowings and feelings thus expressed are necessarily self-involving. We have claimed that prayer is a rule-keeping and sense-making activity. In the Confessions, Augustine keeps in place certain paradigmatic descriptions of God, the self, and the world by his intricate interweaving of narrative and remembering in addressing God. He makes sense of himself and the world by performing the autobiographical act not simply as a narrative which entails remembering, but as an anamnesis which encompasses narrative within itself. The Confessions articulates the logic of connection between what one says and does when one prays and one's identity and self-understanding. In it, Augustine not only tells the story but enacts the relationship which makes sense of his own existence. The Confessions is a self-constituting act of anamnesis. For such a remembering, the peculiarly constitutive language of the vocative in prayer is pre-eminently appropriate.

In this work, Augustine at once tells his story and constructs his identity in such a way as to reveal the story of salvation history, which is God's story too. In doing so, he reveals the correlation between one's capacities for remembering and one's dispositional life. It is Augustine's history, made accessible and present through memory, which shapes his identity and the morpho-logy of his emotional life. Attitudes of repentance, gratitude, wonder, and praise emerge in him through recollecting his story; they coalesce and are taken up into it. At the same time, such attitudes reveal the openness of the past for transformation.

The Confessions shows us how it is that temporality is inseparable from the structure of the self. What on the surface seems impossible is revealed to be possible: the future is able to impinge upon the present, press into, and change the past. There is no access to the past as pastness in itself. In that sense, it is truly irrevocable. Augustine cannot now undo his theft of the pears. One approaches the past, however, with a different set of possibilities, thereby creatively transforming it. So Augustine, "remembers forward,"[45] and his expectations are already reminiscent. In remembering, the present returns to "the past dwelling in its own depth"[46] and reveals that pastness as a dimension of human being in the process of developing ahead into future. It is the past's very qualities of accumulating and deepening which paradoxically open it up to novelty. In "Repentance and Rebirth," Max Scheler offers what amounts to a gloss on Augustine's text. From the specific case of repentance, he argues a conceptual point about memory. The past is openness to the future because the activity of repentant remembering actually alters the past. The moment of repentance is a moment of freedom out of which issues the rebirth of the essential self.[47]

We have been arguing that Augustine's Confessions is not simply a narrative but a Christian anamnesis, a prayer form uttered in the vocative, addressed to God and enacted in his presence. It is thus a recalling in the fullest sense, i.e., both a remembering and an address. It is this that makes it ineluctably confessional. Its intentionality, nonetheless, is directed not only toward God as hearer, but also to the reading community. Because Augustine grounds what is intensely personal in a universal claim, he invites his audience to discover its own story in his. His aim is to evoke the remembering capacities of his readers toward a recognition which is, in its turn, both autobiographical and "true for us all," to bring his readers to the kind of self-understanding he claims to possess of himself. We would miss the point of this anamnesis, however, if we understood its purpose simply as edification. It is directed rather toward arousing
religious understandings and emotions in the audience, activities of thanking, rejoicing, repentance, and praise.

Like all literary texts, the Confessions can be understood as a self-representation directed toward the audience's recognition. What is striking about this text and the claims it makes on its readers, however, is that the recognition intended explicitly aims itself beyond the level of a fresh understanding of one's self and one's world. The Confessions invites the reader to enact this understanding; it intends nothing less than the reader's own conversion and transformation of identity. Such a conversion on the part of the reader would entail an anamnesis akin to Augustine's own.

Toward the end of a long career of prolific writing, preaching, and teaching, Augustine remarked that none of his works exerted so wide and deep an influence as his Confessions.[48] If this was so and continues to be so some fifteen hundred years later, surely it is due to the

184

text's imaginative, religious, and psychological power to explore the hinterland of the self. Put another way, it is the power of Augustine's prodigious capacity for remembering and the way that remembering actually shapes and structures his narrative. Perhaps more than any other autobiography, the Confessions displays the power of memory to form, unify, and direct one's personal identity. In it, Augustine shows how remembering is constitutive of a life-shape; he reveals the extent to which formation in a Christian life and character-formation generally are formations in capacities for remembering.

(2) While Augustine derives his philosophical understanding of memory and time from the classical tradition, he is led to question that understanding by the very act of writing his Confessions. I suggest this is the case for reasons we have just been discussing: precisely because the Confessions is basically an extended Christian anamnesis in the vocative mode. The dense and intricate self-involving remembering characteristic of the autobiographical act he performs challenges the conceptual notions of time and memory he inherits. As Hans Meyerhoff notes, "Augustine first recognized the nature of memory as a key to the structure of time and the self. He developed his theory of time after the earlier parts of the Confessions had shown, in literary form, how memory functions in the reconstruction of one's life."[49] It is thus not surprising that the philosopher Augustine should interweave reflections on time and memory with the personal history of the believer Augustine, and be led to struggle with the very philosophical tradition he has inherited. The Confessions, of course, is no more philosophical treatise than it is exclusively narrative discourse. Its philosophy and the story it tells must be read together, and both must be seen as comprised within its anamnesis.

Augustine turns to the questions of memory and time (Books X and XI) immediately after the narrative anamnesis of his personal history (Books I-IX). His reflection on their nature is clearly generated out of and flows quite organically from the remembering process in which he has been engaged. His interest in the problems is, as we might expect, religiously and theo-logically motivated. Most of our attention here will focus on what he says about memory, but first it will be worth recalling his famous formulation about time, which itself springs from his interest in memory and the past.

Augustine is puzzled by the question: how can the past and future be said to be, since the past is no longer and the future is not yet? He considers the Aristotelian solution to the problem of time, i.e., that time is the measurement of movement, but he finds this an insufficient account in the light of his own human experience in general and autobiographical activity in particular. In the light of this, he is especially interested in how the past can be no longer and yet be. As present entities which refer to the past and make the past present, recollection and narration contain the key to the problem. Thus he is led to conclude:

> What now is clear and plain is, that neither things to come nor past are. Nor is it properly said, "there be three times, past, present, and to come": yet perchance it might be properly said, "there be three times: a present of things past, a present of things present, and a present of things future." For these three do exist in some sort, in the soul, but otherwise do I not see them; present of things past, memory; present of things present, attention; present of things future, expectation.[50]

This odd formulation signals a drastic change in the common way of conceiving time. By placing the three temporal modes within the mind, Augustine disconnects the human experience of time from the Aristotelian mathematical point. Time is no longer a question of cosmology, but of psychology.[51] We can thus see Augustine's radical internalization of the relations between past, present, and future as the precursor to Heidegger's phenomenology of human temporality.[52]

Augustine devotes thirteen out of forty-three chapters in Book X to the problem of memory and makes substantial references to it throughout the rest of Book X and the whole of the Confessions. This attention to memory alone sets him apart from his predecessors and followers in the philosophical tradition. As he reflects on his own experience, he tells us he was mistaken to search for God outwardly, in the things of the world. The proper search is a search inward, into one's own being. Here he finds the mysterious faculty of memory a special aid to him in his search.

At least initially, his description of memory is recognizably derivative from the classical tradition:

> I come to the fields and spacious palaces of my memory, where are the treasures of innumerable images, brought into it from things of all

sorts perceived by the senses. There is stored
up . . . those things which sense hath come to
(p. 158).

Memory is a place, a storehouse, a "great harbour,"
"fields and palaces," a "vast court," in which are
contained images of past sense impressions. Augustine is
espousing the image theory with which we are already
familiar from the classical loci. But he sees more to
memory than this, going on to identify a second kind
which encompasses now not only images from sense impressions, but realities as well.

Here also is all learnt of the liberal sciences
and as yet unforgotten; removed as it were to
some inner place, which is yet no place: nor
are they the images thereof, but the things
themselves (p. 160).

He insists on this point: unlike memory operating as
described above, "of these things it is not the images
that I carry about, but the things themselves" (p. 160).

In thus positing two types of memory, one which
contains images derived from sense impressions and one
which contains realities themselves, Augustine is clearly
dissociating himself from Aristotle and leaguing himself
with Plato.   Augustine's first kind of memory is akin to
Plato's metaphors of the wax tablet and the aviary in the
Thaetetus; his second, to the Plato of the Meno for whom
all knowledge is Recollection.

We can identify his Platonic preferences as well in
his treatment of the problem of forgetting, a problem to
which Aristotle gives no attention.   Two aspects of
forgetting interest him.   First, that we can remember
forgetfulness.   "When I remember forgetfulness there are
present both memory and forgetfulness--memory, whereby I
remember, forgetfulness, which I remember" (p. 164).
This capacity to remember what is not there to be
remembered greatly puzzles Augustine.   Secondly, he is
fascinated by the forgetfulness which seems necessary for
recollection,

What when the memory itself loses anything, as
falls out when we forget and seek that we may
recollect? Where in the end do we search, but
in the memory itself? and there, if one thing
be perchance offered instead of another, we
reject it, until what we seek meets us; and
when it doth, we say, "This is it;" which we
would   not   unless   we   recognized   it,   nor

recognize it unless we remembered it.
Certainly then we had forgotten it (p. 164).

This dialectical interplay of remembering and
forgetting is so paradoxical to Augustine, that he is led
to exclaim,

> What man will search this out? Who can
> comprehend how it is? I truly labor at this
> task, and I labor upon myself. I have become
> for myself a soil hard to work and demanding
> much sweat.[53]

The intensity in this cry is not simply a philosophical
one; it is deeply personal and religious. It springs
directly from his effort to understand the story he has
just told, the story of his own forgetfulness of God and
thus of himself. The paradox of remembering and forgetting redounds to the question: how can the sinner call
upon God unless he somehow already knew him?

Now we might expect that Augustine should see memory
as a direct and unerring route to God, just as for Plato
the soul (through Recollection) attains the knowledge of
the good it temporarily forgot. Augustine, however,
diverges at this point from Plato and the neoplatonism of
his intellectual formation. As Michael Wyschogrod
comments,

> While Augustine is undoubtedly deeply attracted
> to this view, almost making it his own at
> times, he is also aware that a total acceptance
> of it would tend to weaken his image of man as
> fallen but who can be reconciled to God only by
> means of a more or less miraculous intervention
> on the part of God--in other words, by grace.[54]

Wyschogrod may be overstating his case somewhat, losing
sight of Augustine's insistence on God's unfailing
presence to the soul; but he is certainly on target in
discerning Augustine's discomfort with a wholesale
christianizing of Platonic Recollection. For him no
human capacity, however great, can be the source of the
believer's union with God.

This is not to deny, however, that Augustine
appreciates the extraordinary capacities of memory, shot
through though it be with paradoxes. We will conclude
with one such paradox which brings Augustine to the brink
of a whole new conception of memory.

He sees memory as a world in which colors, sounds, odors, and tastes are experienced without being experienced but only remembered.

I discern the scent of lilies from that of violets while smelling nothing; and I prefer honey to grape-syrup, a smooth thing to a rough, though then I neither taste nor handle, but only remember.[55]

This phenomenon becomes even more striking when he turns to the emotional and dispositional life.

Without being joyous I remember myself to have had joy, and without being sad, I call to mind my sadness; and that of which I was once afraid, I remember without fear; and without desire recall a former desire.[56]

Augustine seems to be suggesting here that through memory we transcend the immediacy of perception and achieve a distance toward the remembered not possible in the original. Phenomenology will later question whether such distance can be rightly understood merely as a matter of degree and intensity, as the British empiricists supposed, or whether there is something distinctive about the activity of remembering itself.[57]

While Augustine does not raise such a question himself, it is implicit in his struggle with this and other paradoxes he finds in memory. Indeed, if there is one theme that characterizes his whole treatment of memory, it is a sense of wonder and amazement at its complexity and its very existence, a wonder which springs less from his philosophical heritage than from his autobiographical activity. It is Augustine, and not Aristotle or even Plato, who first gives his attention to the relationship between memory and the self: "There [in memory] meet I with myself" (p. 159). His significance in the history of philosophy on memory is not so much that he advances our conceptual understanding but that he challenges the denigration of memory typical of his tradition. He approaches the classical notions of memory not simply as a philosopher but as an autobiographer and a Christian believer. From the vantage of his formation in remembering, a formation encompassing his liturgical and prayer life and the shaping of his life-story, he is led to elevate memory from its traditionally low status in philosophy. It is fitting that the greatest encomiums to memory should be his.

Great is the power of memory, a fearful thing,
O my God, a deep and boundless manifoldness;
and this thing is the mind, and this am I
myself. What am I then, O my God? What nature
am I? A life various and manifold, and
exceedingly immense. . . . .
. . . .
I will pass then beyond memory, that I may
arrive at Him who hath separated me from the
four-footed beasts and made me wiser than the
fowls of the air, I will pass beyond memory
also, and where shall I find thee, thou truly
good and certain sweetness? And where shall I
find Thee? If I find Thee without my memory,
then do I not retain Thee in my memory. And
how shall I find Thee, if I remember Thee not?
(pp. 165-166).

In this chapter, our aim has been to argue for
memory's importance by showing how it is entailed in the
fundamental life-question, "Who am (are) I (we)?" In
keeping with the hermeneutical character of our project,
we approached the issue by way of texts. A successive
examination of text-interpretation, narrative discourse,
autobiography, and Augustine's Confessions has revealed
in each instance how the dialectical curve of text-inter-
pretation/self-interpretation involves various
remembering activities oriented toward self-understanding
and the formation of personal identity.

Throughout the course of our discussion in this
chapter and in the previous ones, we have been noticing
various interplays between what we have been calling the
activities of remembering and imagining. It remains for
us now, in the final chapter of part II, to turn directly
to a reflection on these two activities and their
interrelations.

NOTES TO CHAPTER V

[1]Harries, p. 187.

[2]Heidegger, Being and Time, p. 326/374.

[3]Heidegger would probably say we are in danger of reifying Dasein when we speak of "the self," or even of "the self-world relation," and therefore in danger of an "an inauthentic way of understanding time" (Being and Time, p. 326/374). For the sake of speaking in a language more commonly accessible than his own, I have chosen to compromise on these issues, understanding such phrases in a post-Heideggerian sense.

[4]Amelie Oksenberg Rorty, ed., The Identities of Persons (Berkeley: U. of California Press, 1976), pp. 1-2.

[5]John Perry, ed., Personal Identity (Berkeley: U. of California Press, 1975), pp. 12-26.

[6]Ibid., p. 15.

[7]See, for example, Iris Murdoch, The Sovereignty of Good (N.Y.: Schocken Books, 1971).

[8]Hans-Georg Gadamer, Truth and Method (N.Y.: Seabury Press, 1975), p. 90. All other references to this work given in the text of the essay are to this edition.

[9]Paul Ricoeur, Interpretation Theory: Discourse and the Surplus of Meaning (Fort Worth: The Texas Christian University Press, 1976), p. 88. All other references to this work given in the text of the essay are to this edition.

[10]Ricoeur, "Explanation and Understanding: On Some Remarkable Connections Among the Theory of the Text, Theory of Action, and Theory of History," in The Philosophy of Paul Ricoeur, p. 155.

[11]Hart, Unfinished Man, p. 210.

[12]As Prof. David Hesla has pointed out to me, the word "text" has an interesting etymology. A text is (1) what is woven. The "original" text is cloth or a wall or a hut made by weaving sticks and twigs. A poet weaves the strands of history into a plot. A text is also (2) what is fashioned with an axe--timbers, ships, houses,

carpentry. The poem as well-made thing, fitted joints. In Arendt's terms, then, we "weave" ourselves.

[13]Ricoeur, "The Narrative Function."

[14]Ricoeur, "Narrative and the Paradoxes of Time."

[15]Ricoeur, "The Narrative Function," p. 185.

[16]Ricoeur, "The Narrative Function," pp. 195-196.

[17]Ibid., p. 197.

[18]Wittgenstein, Philosophical Investigations, trans. G. E. M. Anscombe (N.Y.: The Macmillan Co., 1958), p. 231.

[19]Ricoeur, "The Paradox of Time in Augustine and Heidegger."

[20]Ricoeur, "The Narrative Function," p. 197.

[21]T. S. Eliot, "Tradition and the Individual Talent," in Selected Essays, ed. T. S. Eliot (N.Y.: Harcourt, Brace & Co., 1950), pp. 3-11.

[22]Frederick Wyatt, "The Reconstruction of the Individual and of the Collective Past," in The Study of Lives, Essays in Honor of Henry A. Murray, ed. Robert W. White (N.Y.: Atherton Press, 1963), p. 307.

[23]R. G. Collingwood, The Idea of History (Oxford: Oxford U. Press, 1946).

[24]Wyatt, p. 319.

[25]Ibid., p. 320.

[26]Ricoeur, "The Narrative Function," p. 198.

[27]Ibid., p. 194.

[28]Roman Jakobson, "Linguistics and Poetics," in Style in Language, ed. T. A. Sebeok (Cambridge, Mass.: MIT Press, 1960), cited by Ricoeur, Interpretation Theory, p. 37.

[29]Scholes and Kellog, The Nature of Narrative, p. 240.

[30]Ibid.

[31]Casey, "Imagining and Remembering: In Time and Beyond Time," p. 2.

[32]Ricoeur, "The Narrative Function," p. 196.

[33]Oxford English Dictionary, 1971 ed., s.v. "Autobiography."

[34]Georg Misch, A History of Autobiography in Antiquity, trans. E. W. Dickes (Cambridge, Mass.: Harvard U. Press, 1951, third ed.), p. 5.

[35]Ibid., p. 12.

[36]Wilhelm Dilthey, from H. A. Hodges, Wilhelm Dilthey: An Introduction (London, 1944), p. 28, cited by Misch, ibid., p. 8.

[37]V. S. Pritchett, Autobiography (London: The English Assoc., 1977). p. 3.

[38]Robert Sayre, The Examined Self (Princeton: Princeton U. Press, 1964); James Olney, Metaphors of Self: The Meaning of Autobiography (Princeton: Princeton U. Press, 1972); J. N. Morris, Versions of the Self (N.Y.: Basic Books, 1966); Patricia Spacks, Imagining a Self (Cambridge: Harvard U. Press, 1976); Ruth Pierson Wardlaw, "Recasting of the Self: Interaction of Metaphor and Personal History," (unpubl. thesis, Emory U., 1976); Roy Pascal, Design and Truth in Autobiography (London: Routledge and Kegan Paul, 1960).

[39]Pritchett, p. 6.

[40]Pascal, p. 82.

[41]Augustine, The Confessions of Saint Augustine, trans. Edward B. Pusey (London: Collier-Macmillan Ltd., 1961), cited on back cover.

[42]Augustine, Confessions I, i, cited by Misch, p. 637.

[43]Misch, pp. 643-644.

[44]Ibid., p. 644.

[45]This is Kierkegaard's phrase in Repetition: An Essay in Experimental Psychology, trans. Walter Lowrie (N.Y.: Harper & Row, 1964), p. 33.

[46]Little, p. 15.

[47]Max Scheler, "Repentance and Rebirth," On the Eternal in Man (London: SCM Press, 1960).

[48]Augustine, De dono perseverantiae, c. 20 (A.D. 429 or 428), cited by Misch, p. 668.

[49]Hans Meyerhoff, Time in Literature (Berkeley: U. of California Press, 1955), p. 42.

[50]Augustine, The Confessions of Saint Augustine, trans. Edward B. Pusey (London: Collier-Macmillan Ltd, 1961), p. 198. References in text are to this edition.

[51]Ricoeur, "The Paradox of Time in Augustine and Heidegger."

[52]Ibid.

[53]Confessions, X, 25, cited by Robert J. O'Connell, St. Augustine's Confessions: The Odyssey of the Soul (Cambridge, Mass.: The Belknap Press of Harvard U. Press, 1969), p. 126.

[54]Wyschogrod, p. 11.

[55]Cited by Wyschogrod, p. 12.

[56]Ibid.

[57]Ibid., p. 13.

CHAPTER VI

REMEMBERING AND IMAGINING

Our discussion thus far has encompassed a broad range of human activities which ordinarily count as rememberings. These have included, among others, personal and historical remembering, recalling, reminiscing, recognizing, recollecting, rehearsing, reliving, and reconstructing. We have reflected on these remembering activities in a variety of contexts and settings. We have not, however, attempted to demarcate boundaries among these act-forms to establish how, precisely, they differ from one another; nor have we subjected them to a rigorous conceptual analysis so as to determine, for example, what counts as remembering, what happens when we remember, or whether remembering is a univocal or multivocal concept. Such tasks belong properly to the philosophy of mind; and while they are sorely needed, they must remain outside the scope of our inquiry.[1]

Our project is at once a more modest, more preliminary, and more wide-ranging one. We are trying to complicate and enrich our ordinary notions of memory, to challenge our Western philosophical tradition's derogatory attitude toward it, and to underline its significance in our lives. Our contention has been that so long as we persist in viewing memory as a mental faculty of low epistemic status, derivative from perception, we miss how essential it is to the interi- ority and ecology of our human experience.

It is for this reason that we contrasted the predominant philosophical paradigms for memory with the practice of liturgical anamnesis, for here we encounter a remembering which is a form of life, a mode of being for a given community of persons. In the liturgical anamnesis, remembering discloses itself to be part of the very fabric of human experience, inextricably bound up with narrative forms, temporality, self-constitution, and imagination. In our search for a way of picturing human remembering that will be rich enough to allow us to use it as a hermeneutical tool for reading literary fictions, we selected these four features which, on the one hand, we take to be more than mere accompaniments but, on the other, have been largely overlooked or misinterpreted by philosophy. Without claiming that these four are exhaustive, we have found them suggestive and comprehensive enough to work for us.

In part II of our inquiry, we have been looking to diverse fields of discourse to see how these features of liturgical remembering are adumbrated outside that specialized religious context. In keeping with our literary critical aim, we have given particular attention to hermeneutical inquiry. What has emerged is a picture of our multifarious rememberings which offers an account adequate enough to allow a fuller hermeneutic than has been readily available to the literary critic.

While we have not focused directly on the interfaces between remembering and imagining, these relations have persistently emerged in the course of our reflection on narrative, temporality, and identity. To conclude this part, we need to examine this issue more explicitly, to lift up those aspects of the relationship between memory and imagination which have already appeared and focus our attention on them. Our reflection will take three steps. We shall (1) review this specific problem as it is addressed in the classical and empiricist traditions; (2) challenge their conclusions in the light of what we have already discovered; and (3) refer to Kant's critical philosophy and its implications to undergird and summarize our contentions.

Memory and Imagination in the Classical and Empiricist Traditions

"Memory," writes Aristotle at the start of the De Memoria, "even the memory of objects of thought, is not without an image. So memory will belong to thought in virtue of an incidental association, but in its own right to the primary perceptive part [of the soul]."[2] We have already laid out in some detail this logic of connection which Aristotle sees between the image theory of memory and perception.[3] All knowledge comes through the senses. It is the faculty of perception which receives into the mind "the sensible forms of things without the matter." There they are worked on by imagination, which changes them into the "mental pictures" which are the material of the intellectual faculty. ("It is not possible to think without an image.")[4] In memory, then, thought works on the images stored from sense perception. Thus, Aristotle concludes, "it is apparent to which part of the soul memory belongs, namely the same part as that to which imagination belongs."[5] Both imagination and memory "belong to" the faculty of perception, and both proceed by means of images of sense data. Thus is launched the whole tradition of faculty psychology which considers (a) perception as the primordial and foundational act of mind and (b) imagination and memory as twin faculties of low epistemic status which are mere outposts or offshoots of perception.

Aristotle's two-pronged thesis becomes a commonplace in medieval and Renaissance thought, and the empiricists' views are really little more than variations on this classical theme.[6] Thomas Hobbes, as we have seen, will go so far as to claim that "Imagination and Memory are but one thing, which for divers considerations hath divers names." For Hobbes, this "one thing" is decaying sense perception.

> This decaying sense, when wee would express the thing it self . . . wee call Imagination. . . But when wee would express the decay and signifie that the Sense is fading, old, and past, it is called Memory.[7]

Following Hobbes, but not going so far as an absolute identification of imagination and memory, David Hume will later assert that their difference is one of degree only. Both imagination and memory "borrow their simple ideas from impressions, and can never go beyond these original perceptions."[8] All imagining (and consequently all remembering) for Hume "amounts to no more than the faculty of compounding, transposing, augmenting, or diminishing the materials afforded us by the senses and experience."[9] The ideas of memory, presumably because they are more closely tied to the original impressions, are less faint, however, than the ideas of imagination. For when an earlier impression reappears and "retains a considerable degree of its first vivacity and is somewhat betwixt an impression and an idea," this is a memory.[10] It is worth highlighting here that Hume's criterion for distinguishing memory from imagination, vivacity, is itself borrowed from the analysis of sense perception, which he sees as their origin and exclusive source.[11]

Even John Locke, who grants to memory a certain privilege of place in his philosophy of mind ("It is of so great moment that, where it is wanting, all the rest of our faculties are in a great measure useless"), still considers perception as the cause and source of memory, which he calls "secondary perception."[12]

These opinions, far from representing the vagaries of a handful of philosophers, are emblematic of the mainline Western philosophical tradition concerning memory and imagination. The two assertions, that memory and imagination have equivalent standing in the mind and that both are strictly derivative from perception, are not unrelated. Once the second is asserted, it follows that memory and imagination are equivalent and equally subservient vis-à-vis their parent act.

In his works on imagination and memory, phenomenologist Edward Casey challenges both tenets.[13] First, that memory and imagination are strictly derivative from perception. Casey argues that we must distinguish between granting the basic indispensability of perception and accepting the more extreme claim stated above. It is one thing to consider perception to be "a general precondition of other, perhaps even of all, acts of mind: if we were not perceivers, we could not also be imaginers, rememberers, or even thinkers."[14] It is quite another to hold that perception is the specific cause of all acts of remembering and imagining and the unique source of their content.

I can remember and imagine without these activities being precipitated by some particular perceptual experience. Even when I can trace particular rememberings and imaginings back to some initial perception, the perception is not necessarily the cause of these activities; it may simply establish their contexts and parameters. It is more obvious still that perception is not the sole source of the content of my imaginings and rememberings. Contra the empiricist view, I can imagine something which is not simply the composite of previous perceptions (Casey's example is a non-existent, fantastical creature), and I can remember such non-perceptual entities as emotions and thoughts.

Second, that memory and imagination are equivalent, i.e., either identical (Hobbes) or of comparable epistemic status and basic operation (Aristotle). Against this assertion, Casey argues for four fundamental differences which emerge in a comparative phenomenology of the two acts. The first is what he calls "the committed character of remembering--committed precisely to stationing its content at some particular point in past experience." While we posit the former existence or occurrence of what we remember, thereby assuming for it a temporal position in the past, imagining entails no such positing activity. Our imaginings may refer to any given time or no time at all. Related to this is the factor of familiarity. While we have the sense of already being acquainted with what we remember, this is not necessarily the case with our imaginings. Thirdly, memories are inherently corrigible; they may be mistaken. Since imaginings do not purport to depict real occurrences, they are non-corrigible; they cannot be held to account for false depictions. Finally, remembering and imagining have different <u>fundamental act-forms</u>. Imagination, according to Casey, is limited to three basic forms:

> imaging (in which quasi-sensuous content is entertained in the guise of simple objects or events), imagining-that (in which states of affairs are envisioned), and imagining-how (wherein we project a situation in which we are ourselves actively involved).[15]

Remembering, by contrast, has a greater multiplicity of act-forms. Corresponding to imagining, there are: remembering in the form of contemplating a simple object or event as past, remembering-that, and remembering-how. But we can also remember-to-do and remember-on-the-occasion-of; an example would be those activities which have no analogue in imagining. Paradoxically, it is as if remembering is in this sense a "more luxuriant phenomenon" than imagining; whereas in the other differences cited, imagination enjoys a freedom denied to memory. We do not need to claim that these differences between memory and imagination are exhaustive in order to grant that they do serve to distinguish the two activities sufficiently to undermine the tendency to lump them together.

Collaboration Between Remembering and Imagining

If the traditional assertions about remembering and imagining do not stand up under close scrutiny, what then of the attitude that underlies them? Suppose that, rather than being merely derivative and lowly mental acts, the two turned out to be fundamental human activities, "part of the very fabric of human experience--including perceptual experience itself?"[16] In the course of this essay, we have been arguing precisely this point regarding remembering. Without now doing the same for imagining, we simply want to recall to our minds those instances in which we have already found the two activities in collaboration with each other and acquiring their significance in their conjoint action. Among those cases in which remembering and imagining function as a single, complex activity, we can cite: (a) history and fiction as species of narrative discourse, (b) screen memories and dreams in psychoanalysis, and (c) the phenomenology of time-consciousness.[17]

(a) The historian's activity of reconstructing the past and the novelist's activity of presenting a mimesis which is a simulacrum of human experience each illustrate what Casey calls the "non-contingent collaboration" of memory and imagination.[18] What is more, in each case it is as if the one act elicits the other, calls the other to its aid.

No amount of sheer documentation can make a history. This is not simply because witnesses' memories are notoriously untrustworthy. Even if they were not, they cannot restore the past totally in all its perspectives. History's need to elicit a pattern from a series of events, to grasp those events as a unified whole and make them into a story, requires the cooperation of imagination. Imagination and memory are the warp and woof of what Collingwood calls "the web of historical reconstruction."[19]

For their part, fictions are imaginations which owe heavy debts to experience and memory, both the author's and the audience's. In recognizing the truth and validity of their mimesis, we are not, of course, measuring them against our memories of actual occurrences; but we are engaging in an anamnesis which brings us back to what is essential and universal. Such an anamnesis trades on our imaginative capacities no less than our remembering ones. The Keatsian certainty of "the truth of the imagination" is closely tied to the Wordsworthian understanding of poetry as "emotion recollected in tranquillity." In art, no less than in history, we find an inbuilt cooperation--and not an opposition--between the two acts.

(b) Freudian psychoanalysis has already provided us with other instances of this collaboration between memory and imagination, in screen memories and dreams. When Freud first realized that his "hysterical patients suffer[ed] principally from reminiscences,"[20] he had not yet discovered the function of screen memories. Casey shows how Freud will later acknowledge that oftentimes such supposedly straightforward memories from childhood are actually complex combinations of rememberings and imaginings in which what is recalled is a cover for phantasies unallowed by consciousness. Such phantasies are imaginations of satisfactions (usually sexual) which did not occur but which are still desired, or imaginations of threats which are still feared. In the case of his women patients who remembered being seduced by their fathers, such memories may screen their desire for sexual relations with their fathers.

Many such screen memories occur in the case history of the wolf-man which we have already discussed. One example is his memory of a butterfly which settles on a flower while he is chasing it, thereby filling him with a dreadful fear. Through an elaborate and complex symbolic analysis which we cannot rehearse here, the memory reveals itself as a screen for his nursemaid's threat of castration in punishment for his urinating before her in a cloaked attempt at seduction. The screen memory, through a series of correspondences among the butterfly scene, the nursemaid event, and the witnessed primal scene, provides an important link between the man's childhood wolf-phobia and later love-compulsions.[21]

In a simpler example from his own autobiography, Freud reports a screen memory in which, as a child, he steals flowers from a female cousin. In this case, the memory conceals his later desire to "deflower" a peasant girl whom he met when he returned as an adolescent to the small town where he spent his early childhood years, the very temporal and physical setting of the screen memory.[22]

In each instance, the screen memory is a vehicle for the fulfillment of an imagination, under the cover of memory. As Freud writes, the screen memory "offers phantasy a point of contact--comes, as it were, half way to meet it."[23] In the resultant compromise-formation, memory and imagination collude with each other to receive satisfaction. By linking itself with a festering imagination, the childhood memory gains recurrence and vivacity; and the imagination needs memory as a cover which can lend substance and credibility to what is otherwise "mere wishful thinking." As is the case in our first example above, the memory may even be falsified to suit the purposes of the imagined wish-fulfillment. This leads Freud to wonder "whether we have any memories at all from our childhood: memories relating to our childhood may be all that we possess."[24] Screen memories disclose how such liaisons between imagination and memory actually reshape our apprehensions of our personal past.

"Dreaming," writes Freud in the wolf-man case history, "is another kind of remembering."[25] Yet he also concludes that "our experience in dreams is only a modified kind of imagining."[26] In both their latent and their manifest content, dreams display the complementary interaction of memory and imagination. The manifest content of dreams derives from short-term memories of the previous day and recent past experiences. Latent repressed wishes from the unconscious attach themselves to this content, modifying and disguising their own content to evade censorship. Dreams are thus only partial expressions of these latent wishes, for the content is only allowed if disguised.[27]

At the latent level of the dream, memory is present in the form of experiences of need and its satisfaction from earliest infancy. Such inchoate memories are filled out by imagination, which converts them into images of satisfaction patterned on these archaic experiences. At the manifest level, the dream scene brings about the satisfaction of the suppressed wish while suppressing it as satisfaction. In this it functions analogously to the screen memory. While the dream scene is highly imagistic, even hallucinatory, in character, it borrows its manifest imagery from recent waking memories. Thus, imagining and remembering interact at both levels of the dream, such that dreaming is seen to be one composite act of remembering-and-imagining.[28]

(c) Since we have already developed Husserl's phenomenology of internal time-consciousness at some length in our treatment of memory in the history of philosophy, here we shall content ourselves with highlighting its main features vis-à-vis memory and imagination. Like our preceding examples, time consciousness reveals the non-contingent collaboration of the two acts, but in it we have a much less isolated instance of that collaboration. Time consciousness, unlike narrative discourse, screen memories, and dreams, is continuously operative in our experience.

Leaguing himself with Bergson and William James over against the historical philosophical tendency to view time as a series of isolated present moments, Husserl asserts that "it belongs to the essence of lived experience to have to be spread out in such a way that there is never an isolated punctual phase."[29] Whereas Bergson and James never describe how this is so, Husserl grounds the assertion in his analysis of internal time-consciousness, which he views as a succession of interrelated phases, one of which is actual while others have elapsed or not yet arrived. While one phase is experienced as actually now, others are experienced as just past, and still others as yet to be. The present as an instantaneous point is thus overcome in one direction by "a continuous streaming backwards of every new experience"[30] in retentional phases and overcome in the other direction by a drawing forward in protentional phases. Consciousness' retentional and protentional phases stretch the initial moment of the act of consciousness, thus granting it duration. Husserl calls the retentional structure of consciousness "primary memory": primary, in that its object is the immediate past;

memory, in that it is the consciousness of something as having already happened. The protentional structure he calls "primary expectation," though we might call it, following Casey, "primary imagination."

> Expectation implies an attitude of anxious awaiting, an expectancy, which is foreign to the spontaneity of protending. This spontaneity is a spontaneity of projecting the proximal future in acts of primary imagining. Just as in primary memory we grasp what has just-come-to-be in the very process of its coming to be. . . The single most characteristic operation of imagination consists in projecting possibilities, among which are those possibilities predelineated on the growing edge of the present. To protend such possibilities is what is primary imagining, which thus allows the present to move forward and to become an ongoing, never-fully-concluded enterprise.[31]

It is this three-fold intentional structure of consciousness' acts (primary impression/retention/protention) which generates what Husserl calls "the living present," a temporality rich with the sedimentations of the immediate past and intimations of the immediate future. Husserl even calls retentions and protentions "the primitive, the first and fundamental, forms of the past and future," though he does not claim that they constitute past and future proper, which are temporal domains in their own right.[32] It is this past proper which is the object of memory in the usual sense, which he sometimes calls "secondary memory." Memory proper is "secondary" not in importance but in the sense that it is posterior to and discontinuous with the experience we are recalling. For an act of remembering, the past must have a certain compression and closure, must have acquired sufficient determination and unity, to be remembered precisely as past, as "once-havingbeen."

Contrastingly, the future lacks the density and contractedness of the remembered past. It is projected "by a form of imagining which, rather than prolonging the present into what is about-to-happen (as in primary imagining), ranges freely over the more remote reaches of the not yet."[33] Acts of what we might call "secondary imagining" concern themselves with pure possibility, since any projection of a future event requires our capacity to imagine it, which is quite different from what we may anticipate.

The structure of internal time-consciousness thus displays two fundamental levels of the cooperation of memory and imagination. At the "primary" level, the two acts cooperate to create the living present which, thanks to them, is never an isolated now-point. At the "secondary" level, they demarcate whole regions of time which are discontinuous with this living present. Since we can never fully possess the past or future, we depend on the activities of remembering and imagining to experience them as our having-been and our being-toward. To be selves at all means being remembering-and-imagining-selves. Once experiences leave the range of the living present, they are available to us only through these activities; and, when they are very distant (as in the cases of history and early childhood), they are often attainable only by the complex interacting of both remembering and imagining.

It is worth restating here that we are not claiming that the two acts are identical or even equivalent. They are distinct in any number of ways, including what Casey has called their relative corrigibility and familiarity, their modes of operation, experiential senses, and outcomes. As he asserts,

> They co-operate precisely by being directed to the possible and to the actual respectively; by the crossing-over of one into the domain of the other (as when imagining fills in the gaps in imperfectly remembered material or when remembering offers an explicit basis for the projection of the future); and, more generally, by the fact that each effects what the other cannot--and yet needs as complementary to its own activity. The representation of a stably situated past and the pro-jection of an unsituated future call for each other as equally requisite epicenters of a time-consciousness whose moving center is the living present.[34]

We might even go so far as to suggest, as Casey himself does, that imagination and memory are co-constituents of perception itself. Kant, for example, virtually identifies perception and time-consciousness when he says that "it is a necessary law of our sensibility, and therefore a formal condition of all perceptions, that the preceding time necessarily determines the succeeding."[35] For his part, Casey adumbrates several characteristics of perception which argue for the engagement of memory and imagination in the perceptual act itself. Without going into a detailed analysis of them here, we can mention the following: (1) recognizability (To perceive this typewriter, I must be able to recognize it as this individual typewriter or at least as a typewriter.); (2) repeatability (It must possess the formal capability of being reencountered in recollection. If I could never remember what I now perceive, it could not count as a perception.); and (3) projectability (To be perceived, it must be capable of being envisioned in a future state.). The first two of these characteristics entail activities of remembering; the third, imagining.[36]

If it really is the case that remembering and imagining are involved in perceiving itself, then it cannot be that they are mere forms of "decaying sense." If they are ingredient in sense itself, they must be seen as co-essential to the very fabric of human experience in all its richness and variety. Even without making this claim of their engagement in the perceptual act, a more conservative analysis would still grant that, far from being mere offshoots to some more primordial act, memory and imagination are distinct modes of consciousness itself. As indispensable components of time-consciousness, they reveal themselves to be pervasive features of our experience.

Kant's Transcendental Imagination

Now this way of talking about memory and imagination roots back to Kant's critical philosophy. We can do no better than to turn to Kant for support and summary, not only of the contentions in the previous paragraph, but of the argument we have been advancing in the whole course of our inquiry. To do so, we shall be questioning how Kant grounds the activities of remembering and imagining. This notion of grounding is, of course, central to Kant's thought, for his philosophical project aims at discovering the basis upon which we can be said to know anything.

Both the classical and the empiricist traditions, as we have seen, ground memory and imagination in sense perception. Hobbes' notion of "decaying sense" and Hume's criterion of "vivacity" follow directly from this. In both cases, memory and imagination are distinguished from perception on the basis of the relative freshness or age, if you will, of the images of sense data. To use an analogy, the empiricist model of mind is like a truck full of goods which arrives at the unloading dock. The goods are sense data. After they are deposited, the imagination works on them, separating, arranging, and combining them for use by the mind in thought or for storage in memory. The sense data themselves, in other words, arrive intact into the mind; and only after they are unloaded are they worked over by the mind.

For Kant, however, memory and imagination cannot be grounded in sense perception because perceptions themselves are functions of a transcendental activity, i.e., they are made possible by the subject. This is Kant's celebrated "transcendental turn," the result of his famous "second Copernican revolution."

According to Kant, it was Hume who awakened him from his dogmatic slumbers.[37] Hume had concluded, as we have seen, that the grounds of knowledge lie "merely in ourselves" and that philosophy had nothing to oppose his consequent skepticism about the certainty and extent of our knowledge of the real world. For him, any belief we entertain in our reason can be nothing more than that: a mere belief, a natural instinct. Hume's conclusion is Kant's point of departure.

He takes his lead from the natural sciences which, while describing the nature of the empirical world, have already "learned that reason has insight only into that which it produces after a plan of its own . . . constraining nature to give answers of reason's own determining."[38] Kant suggests "a similar experiment":

> Hitherto it has been assumed that all our knowledge must conform to objects. But all attempts to extend our knowledge of objects by establishing something in regard to them a priori, by means of concepts, have, on this assumption, ended in failure. We must therefore make trial whether we may not have more success in the tasks of metaphysics, if we suppose that objects must conform to our knowledge.[39]

Such an hypothesis, Kant notes, is analogous to that proposed by Copernicus. Copernicus saw that the sun's appearing to move across the earth from east to west was no justification for concluding that the sun moves around a stationary earth. The observed movement would be the same if it were the earth which moved around the sun, and we with it. The question is whether the heliocentric or the geocentric hypothesis can more adequately explain astronomical phenomena. Subsequent investigations showed the heliocentric hypothesis to be the correct one. Analogously, he suggests, empirical reality would remain the same on the hypothesis that for objects to be known (i.e., to be objects of knowledge), they must conform to the mind and not vice versa.

Kant characterizes this as "our new method of thought, namely, that we can know a priori of things only what we ourselves put into them."[40] Let it be noted here, however, that his "second Copernican revolution" does not imply the view, identified with later German idealism, that reality can be reduced to the mind and its ideas. Rather than suggesting that the mind creates reality by thinking it, he is suggesting that we cannot know things except as they are subjected to certain conditions of knowledge on the part of the knowing subject. To return to our previous analogy, German idealism, following Kant, will claim that the loaded truck has no reality except as a construct of the subject. Kant does not deny the truck's existence, the "things-in-themselves"; he simply claims that we cannot know them in themselves, apart from the always already active synthesizing of our minds.

According to Richard Zaner, the consequence of this transcendental turn is that the "inquiry into the conditions of the possibility of experience and knowledge of phenomena purports to yield an entire 'geography' of consciousness."[41] Kant himself understands by this inquiry "the hitherto rarely attempted dissection of the faculty of the understanding itself."[42]

What emerges in such a "geography of consciousness," first of all, is that consciousness is fundamentally active in every act of knowing and never the merely passive recipient of sense data. Sense data come into the focus of thought already conditioned by the receptivity of our mind--"conditions," according to Kant, "under which alone it can receive representations of objects and which therefore must also affect the concepts of these objects."[43] Moreover, in order to know what is thus presented in sense perception, consciousness must synthesize it. Kant describes such synthesizing as "the act of putting different representations together, and of grasping what is manifold in them in one cognitive act."[44] Now both the conditioning of sensations (what Kant calls the transcendental schemata) and the synthesizing of thought (the categories) are, according to Kant, "the mere result of the power of imagination."[45] Thus at the very center of any cognitive act, he posits what he calls "transcendental imagination."

Transcendental imagination not only "sets the stage," as it were, on which entities may appear as objects of cognition; it also allows their appearance by establishing the horizon (spatio-temporal) within which they can come into view. Thus imagination is not a third faculty alongside perception and thought, but these activities' functioning structural unity. Despite some tendency to treat the two components of knowledge (perception and thought) independently, it can be argued that Kant's essential insight is that cognition is one unified activity.[46] Charles Sherover makes this point:

> If sensibility and thought are intrinsically and mutually implicatory, they are not two separate "things" but merely functionally distinguishable aspects of a common originating act. The synthesis of intuition and thought, then, is primal, not derivative; their necessary mutual reference to each other is presupposed from the outset in the unity of any cognitive act.[47]

Imagination itself is this common originating act of the mind; it fuses conceptually discernible sensibility and thought into one cognitive process. It is thus both "the productive source of possible experience and of limitations on possible objectivity in that experience."[48] As such, the activity of transcendental imagination is logically prior to all experience and presupposed in any experience. Heidegger will argue that it is imagination, "independent of experience, which first renders experience possible."[49] If Heidegger's interpretation of him is correct, imagination is less a faculty for Kant (although he speaks of it in this way) than a dynamic process, of which perception and thought are themselves stages.

By placing the activity of transcendental imagination at the center of all cognition, as its enabler and producer, Kant overturns in one sweep the whole history of philosophy from Plato and Aristotle onward, which understands perception as the primordial act of mind and imagination and memory as its poor relations. The great twentieth century philosophers of time and memory whose contributions we have acknowledged in the course of our inquiry--Bergson, William James, Whitehead, Husserl, and Heidegger--and, indeed, the whole phenomenological project itself, build on the foundation of Kant's transcendental turn. In his inquiry into the grounding of cognition, Kant identifies transcendental imagination as the fundamental unifying activity of mind of which all other activities, including perception itself, are the results. And he grounds imagination in the activity of the subject, which is indispensable to any knowledge of reality.

Now this transcendental turn, which places the imagining activity of the subject at the center of all acts of cognition, must have radical consequences for a theory of memory. It rules out, for example, certain common ways of conceiving of that activity: (1) Memory cannot simply be the result of the objective fact that some perceptions are weaker or older than others. (2) Nor can it be a strictly reproductive activity which reiterates previously perceived objective sense data. Rather, since it is given in the very synthesizing activity of the subject, memory must be a creative and constitutive activity. This is not to say that Kant himself focused on these characteristics of remembering, but he does make it possible to think about memory in these terms. Prior to Kant, for example, to attribute subjectivity or creativity to memory was equivalent to undermining its very nature. For memory to be true to itself must mean that it is free of such qualities, which would count as distortion and error. For Aristotle, let us recall, memory is "the having of an image regarded as a copy of that of which it is an image."[50] The test of memory's validity was how faithfully it matched the original perception which was itself the faithful image of empirical reality. Kant's turn can be seen to imply that memory is inherently self-constitutive and imaginative in the sense that it results from the synthesizing activity of the subject. At the same time, it does not commit us to an image theory of memory, since the imagination Kant details is more inclusive and more fundamental than the production of images. We might say that, by taking seriously the ultimate grounding of all our knowledge of empirical reality in the activity of consciousness, Kant allows memory to be memory, a distinct activity of consciousness itself which shapes empirical reality according to its own categories and schemata. It is a short step from Kant to Freud, who sees remembering activities as creative indeed.

To appreciate how radically Kant's point is taken, let us focus on its implications for the concept of time. Common sense seems to dictate our excepting space and time from the transcendental turn; and science likewise would argue that space and time are quantitative features of objects, and, as such, are real and objectively contained within them. Kant's revolution, however, extends even to time and space themselves. He holds that even such quantitative features are functions of the way we perceive and thus of the synthesizing activity of the subject. As he states at the outset of the _Critique of Pure Reason_,

All of our knowledge is thus finally subject to time, and the formal condition of inner sense. . . . This is a general observation which, throughout what follows, must be borne in mind as being quite fundamental.[51]

We have seen that, while agreeing with the empiricists that objects are given to us in sense experience, Kant disagrees that all human knowledge is derived from experience.[52] In other words, while thought can get to work only when objects are given to sense, what is thus given is already a synthesis performed by the activity of the subject. Things-in-themselves are never given to us as objects; what understanding finds before it is already a synthesis. This synthesis is the result of the imagination. The a priori element in all sense experience is precisely time and space as necessary conditions for perceiving.

This is not to say that time and space are unreal for Kant. Since there can never be an object which is not in time, and empirical reality is spatio-temporal, then we can say that space and time themselves must possess empirical reality. But since space and time are a priori forms of human sensibility, they can only apply to objects of our consciousness. In Kant's formulation, space and time are empirically real but transcendentally ideal.[53] The first, in the sense that what is given in experience is in space (if it is the object of the senses) and in time. Thus space and time are not illusions. But they are transcendentally ideal in the sense that they do not apply to things-in-themselves apart from our knowing of such things, i.e., apart from their being objects of our consciousness.

If such a formulation seems passing strange to our own commonsense attitude, we need only remind ourselves of Heidegger's phenomenology of human temporality, which we might see as an existential and ontological elaboration of Kant's insight about time.[54] In Heideggerian terms, not only is time a human form of experience, but it is that in which we find ourselves as human and the world as world. As Eva Schaper comments in "Kant's Schematism Reconsidered." it is "not that man imposes what he is himself (to a certain extent he obviously does) but that he discovers, via the schemata as underlying the possibility of things for him, his own nature and the nature of that in which he is, his being-in-the-world."[55] Dasein, says Heidegger, is inherently temporal.

If we read Kant in the light of Heidegger, we are led to conclude that it is because the transcendental imagination creates the temporal structuring of all representations that it establishes the experiential horizon, "the boundaries of that area within which human cognition must be contained to be operative."[56] Time cannot be understood as an enclosure within which imaginative synthesis operates. We are creating time by our various specific conscious acts. As the grounding of these activities, transcendental imagination must be the ground or source of time itself. The temporal horizon within which experience happens is formed by the transcendental imagination which is itself inherently temporal.

It is the transcendental synthesis which creates the possibility of discerning past, present, and future. It creates the horizon of the possible past by constituting the area of being-as-having-been. As such, it must be the a priori ground for recollection. We are speaking here not of what we might call "empirical imagination," understood as the source of an image-copy of a once perceived object now stored in memory; but of transcendental imagination, understood as the capacity for all conscious activities and thus for all rememberings.[57] In this sense, we can understand memory as "the imaginative maintenance of continuity."[58]

It is not surprising that we should have discovered remembering to be a rich and variegated and creative human activity, intricately connected with narrative forms, temporality, personal identity, and various imaginative activities. Nor is it surprising that it should emerge as intimately bound up with those two fundamental life questions, "Who am (are) I (we)?" and "What is the nature of reality?" Once Kant's transcendental turn is taken in the history of philosophy, remembering is freed to enter into its own as an act of consciousness, grounded in the active synthesizing of the subject. Co-constitutive with other activities of the very fabric of human experience, memory emerges--not as a lesser act of mind which can do no more than passively reproduce what has been given to it--but as that activity of the self which gives it its being as having-been, its continuity, and therefore intimately participates in its unity, coherence, and vitality.

[1]In the course of this essay, I have noted several scholars who are engaged in these tasks. See especially the work of Edward Casey, John Brough, Norman Malcolm, R. S. Benjamin, and Stuart Hampshire.

[2]Aristotle De Memoria 449^b 30.

[3]See chapter I, pp. 25-27.

[4]Aristotle De Memoria 449^b 30.

[5]Ibid., 450^a 22.

[6]Casey, "Imagining and Remembering," p. 188.

[7]Hobbes, Leviathan, ed. C. B. Macpherson (Gretna, LA: Pelican, 1968), p. 89.

[8]Hume, A Treatise of Human Nature, ed. Selby-Bigge (Oxford: Oxford U. Press, 1955), p. 85.

[9]Hume, An Inquiry Concerning Human Understanding, ed. C. W. Hendel (Indianapolis: Bobbs-Merrill, 1955), p. 27.

[10]Hume, A Treatise, I, 1, 1, cited by Malcolm, p. 18.

[11]Casey, "Imagining and Remembering," p. 188.

[12]Locke, An Essay Concerning Human Understanding, in The English Philosophers from Bacon to Mill, pp. 278-279.

[13]My own exposition closely follows his argument in "Imagining and Remembering."

[14]Ibid., p. 190.

[15]Ibid., pp. 192-193.

[16]Ibid., p. 189.

[17]Ibid., pp. 195-205.

[18]Ibid., p. 195.

[19]Collingwood, The Idea of History, p. 244.

[20]Freud, Studies in Hysteria, cited by Ricoeur, "The Question of Proof," p. 190.

[21]Freud, "From the History of an Infantile Neurosis," pp. 281-283.

[22]Cited by Casey, "Imagining and Remembering," p. 196.

[23]Freud, S.E. 3:318, cited by Casey, p. 197.

[24]Freud, S.E. 3:322, cited by Casey, ibid.

[25]Freud, "Infantile Neurosis," p. 239.

[26]Freud, S.E. 15:130, cited by Casey, p. 199.

[27]Richard Appignanesi, Freud for Beginners (N.Y.: Pantheon Books, 1979), p. 170. His definition of "dream work" is based on Charles Rycroft's A Critical Dictionary of Psychoanalysis.

[28]Casey, "Imagining and Remembering," p. 199.

[29]Husserl, The Phenomenology of Internal Time-Consciousness trans. James S. Churchill (Bloomington: Indiana U. Press, 1964), p. 70, translation modified by Casey, p. 200.

[30]Casey, "Imagining and Remembering," p. 200.

[31]Ibid., p. 201.

[32]Husserl, Analysen zur Passiven Synthesis (The Hague: Hijnoff, 1966), p. 326, cited by Casey, p. 201.

[33]Casey, "Imagining and Remembering," p. 203.

[34]Ibid., p. 205.

[35]Cited by Casey, p. 206.

[36]Casey, "Imagining and Remembering," pp. 207-208.

[37]Kant, Prolegomena to Any Future Metaphysic, Foreward, cited by Frederick Copleston, A History of Philosophy: Wolff to Kant (Westminster: The Newman Press, 1964), p. 218.

[38]Kant, Critique of Pure Reason, trans. Norman Kemp Smith (N.Y.: Macmillan & Co., 1929), p. 20, cited by Richard M. Zaner, The Way of Phenomenology: Criticism as a Philosophical Discipline (N.Y.: Pegasus, 1970), p. 102.

[39] Kant, _Critique_, p. 22, cited by Zaner, ibid., my italics.

[40] Kant, _Critique_, p. 23, cited by Zaner, ibid.

[41] Zaner, p. 104.

[42] Kant, _Critique_, p. 103, cited by Zaner, ibid.

[43] Kant, _Critique of Pure Reason_, p. 111, cited by Charles M. Sherover, _Heidegger, Kant and Time_ (Bloomington: Indiana U. Press, 1971), p. 61, Sherover's italics.

[44] Kant, _Kritik der reinen Vernunft_, p. 116, cited by Sherover, ibid.

[45] Kant, _Critique of Pure Reason_, p. 112, cited by Sherover, ibid.

[46] Thus argues Sherover, p. 62, following Heidegger.

[47] Ibid.

[48] Sherover, p. 134.

[49] Heidegger, _Kant and the Problem of Metaphysics_, p. 140, cited by Sherover, p. 136.

[50] Aristotle _De Memoria_ 451^a 14.

[51] Kant, _Critique of Pure Reason_, p. 131.

[52] Copleston, p. 217.

[53] Copleston, p. 241.

[54] This is the thesis of Sherover's _Heidegger, Kant and Time_. In _Kant and the Problem of Metaphysics_, Heidegger takes Kant to task for "failing to develop fully the spectacular truths that he glimpsed in his doctrine of the imagination" (Gelven, p. 182).

[55] Eva Schaper, "Kant's Schematism Reconsidered," _Review of Metaphysics_ 18 (1964):281.

[56] Sherover, p. 134.

[57] This is Sherover's distinction, p. 135.

[58] Sherover, p. 135.

PART III

REMEMBERING IN NARRATIVE FICTION

"The entire inner action of the novel is <u>nothing but</u> a struggle against the power of time."[1] Thus did Georg Lukacs first articulate what has since become a literary critical commonplace in this century. Since it can be argued that the whole panoply of modern dilemmas is time-bound and time-related, it is not surprising that one of the modern novel's predominant preoccupations is the problem of time. In modern fiction, however, that problem is not the Aristotelian question of "What is time?" It is more closely aligned with Heidegger's query: "What does it mean to be in time?" Indeed, the question at the heart of much of our modern fiction is whether the movement of time <u>is</u> meaningful--and if so, how discoverable such meaning is.

In fiction, of course, the question is not predominantly a philosophical one. It arises from the human anguish of the character who, if he wants life to continue, must find a new way to live. Typically, for such a character the future is blocked (for any number of reasons); and he is thus immured in an empty and hostile present. Invariably, this means that his relationship with his past is askew. Thus the narrative movement toward meaning--or often just the possibility of meaning or the conditions for such possibility--involves his finding a new relationship with his past. Such narratives thus entail a structure of remembering. This is especially the case in first person narratives, where the anguish over human time is the life-question of the narrator, and the story which unfolds is an exploration-- often painful--of it.

It would be hard to exaggerate the number of modern novels to which this very generalized description applies. For the purposes of our discussion, I have selected for interpretation just two: Margaret Atwood's <u>Surfacing</u> (1972) and Saul Bellow's <u>Henderson the Rain King</u> (1959).

Both are first person narratives in which the narrator has the role of main character. This establishes a peculiar cognitive position between narrative and reader. It forgoes the fiction of "objective" reality found in third person narratives where the reader is, as it were, commanded to accept narrative statements as unquestionable knowledge about the fictive world. The reader of a first person narrative does not have the advantage of such a privileged position vis-à-vis the narrative. We are always aware that we associate with the narrator, whose knowledge is of necessity limited. This is the case even when the narrator does not mention any lapses in memory. Since the narrator is equal to any other character, she is fallible. As readers, we are doomed to uncertainty; the narrator's knowledge must be corroborated if it is to be accepted.[2]

What is more, the narrator's statements not only report information and events; they are performative and emotive as well. Assumptions, fantasies, lies, and delusions can appear intermingled with reliable reportage. The narrative can misinform as well as inform. For this reason, first person narratives have what Gowinski calls a "multivalent narrative logic."[3] The narrator's possession of knowledge and lack of it, her reliability and unreliability, play equally important roles.

Besides this, since the narrator is not absent from the fictive world but a concrete speaking person in the story, what she says always depends, to a greater or lesser degree, on the situation in which her speakings occur. Sometimes such speakings emphasize the personality and perspective of the narrator; sometimes the situation or conditions in which they occur. This interdependence of speaker, speakings, and situation creates something close to a dialogue in the presence of the reader.[4] The narrative makes peculiar claims on us precisely as addressed. As readers, we are in possession of a text and yet involved, as it were, in the very act of creating and transmitting the story.

Not all first person narratives exploit this cognitive position fully, of course. The two novels we are considering do so, in different ways and to different degrees. What is significant for our purposes, however, is the implication of this narrative point of view for the texture of anamneses we identified as complicit, to varying extents, in all narrative fictions. Because of its peculiar cognitive position, the first person narrative can exploit narrative's multifarious rememberings more fully than other forms.

From a negative vantage, there is a problem with the first person point of view as a structural device for a novel which follows the thematic pattern outlined above, i.e., the forgetfulness of being which is inauthenticity. In each of our novels, the narrator is the only fully rounded character. One of the implications of this structure is that the world it creates does tend toward privacy, if not solipsism. In each case, however, solipsism is precisely the character's original situation. Neither of the two narrators is capable of authentic being with other persons in society. Thus a key critical question becomes: how convincing is the avowal (or suggestion) that this condition has been transcended if the proof itself occurs within the framework of a first person narrative and within a fictive world peopled largely by types? Can such a narrative deliver a transformation that goes deeper than the linguistic surfaces and theoretical and rhetorical levels, a transformation which is believable within the action and world of the fiction? I shall be claiming that the credibility of such transformative possibilities is grounded precisely in the anamnetic circle of text-interpretation/self-interpretation peculiar to first person narratives. More explicitly, my argument will be that in these two particular novels, though to differing degrees, the narrative itself partakes of the features of a ritualized anamnesis in which the reader constitutes the community to whom the remembering is addressed. Thus we shall expect to see in them certain analogies with liturgical anamnesis. Such a claim certainly cannot be made of every first person narrative. It can only be justified if the text itself has a ritual structure.

This brings us to certain other similarities and dissimilarities between our two texts which are worth mentioning before attending to each of them. Although both trade on mythic structures and are heavily ritualized, their attitudes toward such structures are quite divergent. Whereas Atwood exploits them with consummate seriousness, using them at the service of a deeply felt psychological realism, Bellow's work has more of the quality of fabulation and spoof. Both create fictions according to the pattern of a rite of passage; but Bellow is, at the same time, satirizing literary uses of myth and ritual. Unlike Surfacing, Henderson is a comic novel. Bellow is "fooling around," but he means his fooling to be "fairly serious."[5] This comic distance toward his use of myth-ritual materials must be taken into account in any responsible reading of the text.

Both novels tell the story of a physical journey. In each case, that journey becomes a mythic ordeal in which outward travel is prelude to an inward journey, and what purports to be a movement toward the future becomes a retrieval of the past or vice versa. Neither character, however, has the makings of a mythic hero. Their proportions are distinctively life-size: Atwood's, a young Canadian woman who is at best a mediocre commercial artist; Bellow's, a middle-aged American whose last gainful employment was pig-farming. In each case, though to varying degrees, the dis-ease of the character reflects a more pervasive dis-ease in the society.

<u>Surfacing</u>, however, intends a sharper cultural criticism than does <u>Henderson</u>. Both novels conclude this side of re-integration; neither carries its character across the threshold of the sought-for transformation of personal identity back into the social world. Finally, both characters interpret their life-problems in linguistic terms: re-membering oneself entails radical linguistic shifts and syntactical transformations. To recognize one's true self, to cognize oneself into a new story, thus necessitates a remembering beyond and before time and language. Such archetypal rememberings, however, are never extra-linguistic; as narratized, they are always this side of silence.

NOTES TO PART III, INTRODUCTION

[1]Lukacs, p. 122, my italics.

[2]Micha Gowinski, "On the First-Person Novel," New Literary History 9 (Autumn 1977):104. The essay is a translation of pp. 59 through 75 of Gry powiesciowe (Novelistic Games).

[3]Ibid.

[4]Ibid., p. 110.

[5]Saul Bellow, "The Art of Fiction 37: Saul Bellow," The Paris Review 36 (1965):49-73.

CHAPTER VII

ATWOOD'S SURFACING: REMEMBERING IN THE

RECONSTRUCTION OF IDENTITY

Since its publication in 1972, Surfacing has
received greater critical attention than perhaps any
other contemporary Canadian novel. The predominant
literary critical readings which have been offered can be
categorized as myth-ritual, psychoanalytic, and cultural
criticism, including sociological feminist. Such
criticism gives no more than passing recognition to the
crucial role remembering activities play in the text, yet
we have seen that such activities are central in each of
these modes of discourse. Ritual activity invariably
includes remembering in the form of an anamnesis in which
the performer re-presents the past in such a way as to
belie its very pastness. Psychoanalysis has shown how
remembering and forgetting are involved both in
psychopathologies and in the narrative process of healing
them. In its critique of culture, Critical Theory sees
remembering as a primary tool for countering both the
timelessness of repressive societies and their notions of
evolutionary progress.

Thus while the novel lends itself to each of these
literary critical methods, I suggest that a focus on how
remembering shapes the narrative and articulates its
thematic concerns can produce a fuller interpretation,
precisely because it accommodates the others and mediates
between them. At the same time, such attention to
remembering takes into account the formalistic concerns
which must be included in any reading. For the sake of
ordering and limiting our discussion, we shall approach
the text schematically, addressing the following issues:
(1) the character's life-problem and its cause(s); (2)
the movement and resolution of the narrative; and (3) the
primary motif and structure for engaging the reader in
this movement.

The Character's Life-Problem

"I can't believe I'm on this road again," muses the
narrator in the opening words of the novel.[1] At the
manifest level of the plot, the problem facing her is the
disappearance of her father from his primitive island
home. As his only living relative nearby, she has the
responsibility of investigating his disappearance. The

story opens in via, with her and her three traveling companions heading toward the northern Canada of her upbringing in search of him.

What begins as a fairly straightforward journey to find her missing father, however, soon becomes a journey in search of her lost and forgotten self ["It was no longer his death but my own that concerned me" (p. 127)], a ritual passage which will take her beyond civilization and society, beyond the limits of logic and language, beyond even the personal and historical past, back to some primordial source-time from which to begin living all over again.[2]

From the very start, the trip is presented in temporal and not simply spatial terms. It is, first of all, a return, a movement back to parents, childhood, biographical past. Naturally enough, then, it is generously punctuated throughout by the narrator's reminiscences, prompted at the start by the sights she sees along the way. The early pages of the novel are a point/counterpoint between these rememberings from her past and the narrative present: "In the car that time we sat with our feet wrapped in blankets . . . Now I'm in another car" (p. 9). "'That's where the rockets are,' I say. Were. I don't correct it" (p. 12). "The sign has bullet holes in it, rusting red around the edges. It always did" (p. 14). She is continually measuring her present perceptions against her memories, marking the way things have changed and remained the same. Her conclusion from the outset is that "Nothing is the same, I don't know the way anymore" (p.15); "We're on my home ground, foreign territory" (p. 14); and "It doesn't seem right, either the three of them are in the wrong place or I am" (p. 10).

As they approach her home territory, she sees a sign proclaiming "GATEWAY TO THE NORTH," remembers a political slogan from her childhood--"The future is in the North"--and her father's ironic retort that there was nothing in the North but the past and not much of that either. This memory in its turn recalls her to the purpose of the present journey, and she comments, "Wherever he is now, dead or alive and nobody knows which, he's no longer making epigrams" (p. 11). This narrative movement of her consciousness from present perception to memory and back again to present awareness illustrates the intermingling of temporal modes which is a pervasive feature of the story from its start.

Even before their arrival at her childhood cabin home, the narrative represents the journey as a movement into the past. Simply to travel north is to enter the past--as if the past were a place--and for her to return there is also to attend to her past. This journey interrupts her present, forces her inward, downward, and backward into her past dwelling in its own depths.

That the journey in search of her missing father so readily becomes a journey in search of her missing self, however, testifies to the problematic character of her present being. Indeed, we are not long into the narrative before we discover how pervasive her self-alienation is. While on first appearances she is an ordinary, relatively contented and discontented young professional woman, it soon becomes clear that she is without a future, immured in a vacuous present which involves no authentic presence. She does not live-toward anything at all; she anticipates nothing. Her self-alienation is so profound that it encompasses every aspect of her life.

First of all, she is at odds with the urban environment in which she lives. The city is "the present tense . . . where there is electricity and distraction. I'm used to it now, filling the time without it is an effort" (p. 59). Indeed, her urban life is itself a distraction in the Augustinian sense, a temporal distension, a soul-destructive stretching along in an unending succession of presents. It is as if by living in the city she has capitulated to her perennial enemy. It is as alien to her now as it was during the winter months of her childhood spent in towns where she was "shut off from the villagers" because she couldn't understand their language, in a succession of anonymous apartments, and in schools where she "didn't know the local customs, like a person from another culture: on me they could try out the tricks and minor tortures they'd already used up on each other" (p. 83). She contrasts the comfortable familiarity of the island's primitive naturalness with the mechanized, technological city.

> Flush toilets and vacuum cleaners, they roared and made things vanish, at that time I was afraid there was a machine that could make people vanish like that too, go nowhere, like a camera that could steal not only your soul but your body also. Levers and buttons, triggers, the machines sent them up as roots sent up flowers; tiny circles and oblongs, logic become visible, you couldn't tell in advance what would happen when you pressed them (p. 83).

Her childhood terror of machines taps into a more brooding, pervasive sense of the horror of technology, which she identifies with the imperialistic tendency of "the Americans." In their technological predilection for an unending present tense, cities corrupt by turning living things into objects.

Through her work, she herself is complicit in this corruption. Her career pigeonholes her: "I'm what they call a commercial artist" (p. 60). The classification "feels strapped" to her, "like an aqualung or an extra, artificial limb" (p. 60, my italics). She draws "young people with lobotomized grins, rapturous in their padded slots" for Department of Manpower manuals, and peoples children's storybooks with princesses with "emaciated fashion-model torso(s) and infantile face(s)" (p. 62). Her illustrations are "elegant and stylized, decoratively colored, like patisserie cakes . . . fake Walt Disney, Victorian etchings in sepia, Bavarian cookies, ersatz Eskimo for the home market" (p. 61). She learned early on how to compromise her artistic standards: "Now I compromise before I take the work in, it saves time" (p. 61).

The temporal disjunction, alienation, and inauthenticity of the city accompany her on her journey in the persons of her three companions. Joe, with whom she shares a basement apartment in the city (she calls it a "cellar"), is the new version of the underground man.

> From the side he's like the buffalo on the U.S. nickel, shaggy and blunt-snouted, with small clenched eyes and the defiant but insane look of a species once dominant, now threatened with extinction. That's how he thinks of himself, too: deposed, unjustly (p. 10).

Everything she values about him, she tells us, is physical: "The rest is either unknown, disagreeable, or ridiculous" (p. 66). She dislikes his temperament, which alternates between surliness and gloom, and despises the overgrown pots he mangles and mutilates, cutting "holes in them, strangling them, slashing them open" (p. 66). With their disagreeable mutant quality, they "accumulate in our already cluttered basement apartment like fragmentary memories or murder victims (p. 66, my italics).

Anna, the narrator's best friend, whom she has known for all of two months, personifies another version of the technological mask with its idolatry of the present, one closer to the narrator's fashion model princesses. She

wards off human meaning with a constant conversational
patter, an endless string of pop tunes, cigarette
smoking, sun-bathing, and murder mysteries. She refuses
to wear jeans because "she looks fat in them" (p. 13), is
afraid to be seen without her make-up, even by her
husband ("He doesn't like to see me without it,' and
then, contradicting herself, 'He doesn't know I wear it'"
p. 51). Her very soul is "closed in the gold compact"
(p. 205). At one point, when the narrator comments that
something they see along the way was not there before,
Anna asks blankly, "Before what?" (p. 17). For her there
is no before or after, just a series of instantaneous
present moments, like the filmic images of her:
"hundreds of tiny naked Annas . . . bottled and shelved"
(p. 195).

Anna's husband, David, fears any form of human
contact which is not genital. In contrast to Joe's
taciturnity, he uses language as a weapon to turn the
world into an object. For him, the wilderness beaver is
not an animal in nature but a vulgar term for a woman's
pudendum. He separates both the animal and female
sexuality from their proper life-worlds, subjecting them
to his own solipsistic imperialism.[3] He, more than the
others, rails against "the bloody fascist pig Yanks"
whose perverted values he personifies. He views their
seseless destruction of the heron as good film footage
for his Random Samples. A communications teacher (there
is a biting ironic wit in Atwood), David is "directing"
the film with Joe as cameraman. As the narrator reports
their description of the process, "When they've used up
their supply of film . . . they're going to look at what
they've collected and rearrange it."

> "How can you tell what to put in if you don't
> already know what it's about?" I asked David
> when he was describing it. He gave me one of
> his initiate-to-novice stares. "If you close
> your mind in advance like that you wreck it.
> What you need is flow." (pp. 12-13).

The Random Samples film beautifully expresses
David's attitude toward the world as collectible object.
In film-making and in life, there are no temporal
relationships of significance. Time is merely a
manipulative fiction; you construct and arrange it
according to your own uses. It is not surprising that
none of these characters has a past. "My friends' pasts
are vague to me and to each other also, anyone of us
could have amnesia for years and the others wouldn't
notice" (p. 35, my italics). They are thus embarrassed
by the narrator's movement into her past: "They all

disowned their parents long ago, the way you are supposed to: Joe never mentions his mother and father, Anna says hers were nothing people and David calls his "The Pigs" (pp. 19-20).

While it is certainly the case, as most critics point out, that these characters are little more than distasteful stereotypes, what is significant about them is the extent to which, precisely as types, they typify aspects of the narrator herself. For example, she responds to Joe's love-making "crisp as a typewriter" (p. 78). It's best, she admits, when you don't even know them. She sums him up, reifying him, dividing him into categories:

> He's good in bed, better than the one before; he's moody but he's not much bother, we split the rent and he doesn't talk much, that's an advantage. When he suggested that we should live together I didn't hesitate. It wasn't even a real decision, it was more like buying a goldfish or a potted cactus plant, not because you want one in advance but because you happen to be in the store and you see them lined up on the counter (pp. 43-49).

No decisions, no responsibilities. No past, no future. Likewise, Anna's vacuous and willingly exploited sexuality is mirrored in both the narrator's professional illustrations and her childhood drawings, derivatives of Rita Hayworth, Jane Powell, and Esther Williams. David's far-ranging exploitations, his conversion of everything into objects of his pleasure or derision, and his incapacity for any genuine human emotion match the narrator's own self-destructive and self-despising emotional deadness.

All four of them typify inauthentic being. They are, in most important senses, atemporal, self-regarding and self-mutilating caricatures of Care for their being. Joe, Anna, and David represent everything the narrator despises about what she calls "the present tense," everything she despises in her social, professional, and personal worlds. She is no less a manipulator, for all that, than they are. She uses them all the while she offers us a critique of their imperialistic attitudes. She wishes they weren't here, she tells us, but they had the car, and they are useful to ward off "the loss, the vacancy" (p. 46). The vacancy is a description of her present being; its roots are in the loss, not simply of her father, but of her past, her being as having-been. If we as readers care more about her than about the others, it is because <u>as narrator</u> she, alone among them, has the capacity to tell a story, a capacity, that is, to confront the past even in its facticity, to learn to understand out of her past, to remember.

Her companions increasingly become transformed into the kind of technological objects they use to manipulate their world: "Canned laughter, they carry it with them, the midget reels of tape and the On switch concealed somewhere in their chests, instant playback" (p. 92). As they evolve into humanoid machines, the narrator's own narratized remembering leads her to become more and more separated from them in her movement into the archeological past.

> I can smell them and the scent brings nausea, it's stale air, bus stations and nicotine smoke, mouths lined with soiled plush, acid taste of copper wiring or money. Their skins are red, green in squares, blue in lines, and it's a minute before I remember that these are fake skins, flags. Their real skins above the collars are white and plucked, with tufts of hair on top . . . They are evolving, they are halfway to machine, the left-over flesh atrophied and diseased, porous like an appendix (p. 215).

Before examining this narrative movement, however, it will be helpful to address the cause of the narrator's moribund present. Her version of the characters' self/world dichotomy and their concomitant distortion of temporality is the bifurcation between mind and body, thinking and feeling. "The problem is all in the knob at the top of our heads," she decides, or, more accurately still, in the neck, which creates the illusion that head and body are separate.

> If the head extended directly into the shoulders like a worm's or a frog's without that constriction, that lie, they wouldn't be able to look down at their bodies and move them around as if they were robots or puppets; they would have to realize that if the head is detached from the body both of them will die (p. 91).

Throughout the first two-thirds of the story, she repeatedly and consistently suggests that her present emotional incapacity is rooted in her past marriage, divorce, and abandonment of her child. "He said he loved me, the magic word, it was supposed to make everything

231

light up, I'll never trust that word again" (p. 55). Thus when Joe asks if she loves him, she hunts through her brain for any emotion. "It was the language again, I couldn't use it because it wasn't mine" (p. 127). Emotion words are inauthentic because they do not coincide with her experience.

> I didn't feel awful; I realized I didn't feel much of anything. I hadn't for a long time. Perhaps I'd been like that all my life . . . but if that was true I wouldn't have noticed the absence. At some point my neck must have closed over, pond freezing or a <u>wound</u>, shutting me into my head; since then everything had been glancing off me (p. 126).

That she notices the absence is precisely what distinguishes her from her companions and sets her looking for clues to the wound and to what she later calls her own death in her past experience. The narrative offers a clue in its first pages, when she remembers Anna's reading of her palm: "You had a good childhood but then there's this funny break" (p. 10). She searches through old photo albums in the cabin, trying to locate the break "by the differences in my former faces, alive up to a year, a day, then frozen" (p. 128). But the photos, mere mementoes of the past, are like "small gray and white windows opening to a place I could no longer reach" (p. 128).

> No hints or facts, I didn't know when it happened. I must have been all right then; but after that I'd allowed myself to be cut in two . . . The other half, the one locked away, was the only one that could live; I was the wrong half, detached, terminal (p. 129).

It is not surprising that these mementoes, old photos and scrapbooks, cannot give her the past she has lost or name the "funny break," for mementoes are simply signs that keep the past present <u>in its pastness</u>. A memento refers to the past by signifying that an element of that past has not disappeared. It only has value for someone who already and still recalls the past. When that past loses its significance or is "closed over," unallowed by consciousness, the memento loses its value. The past in its pastness does not contain the clue to her split; it is the constitutive reverberations of the past in her present being, which she refuses to remember, that must be the source of any possible healing. Such remembering must be a deliberate, painstaking, and painful task in the face of a profound propensity for forgetting. As Herbert Marcuse puts it, "To forget is also to forgive what should not be forgiven . . . to forget past suffering is to forgive the forces that caused it--without defeating these forces. The wounds that heal in time are also the wounds that contain the poison."[4]

For the narrator, the way to present healing cannot be found leafing through old photographs. A deeply personal, even visceral, re-membering, which takes the form of a narrative reconstruction and a ritual re-enactment, a remembering which must be regressive if it is to be progressive, a remembering imaginative enough to open the past to change--these are the only routes to re-integration. She must learn how to become once again a remembering self as the condition to becoming a self who anticipates and makes present in decision and responsibility. This very process of remembering, then, shapes the movement of the narrative.

The Movement of the Narrative

Atwood herself gives us a lead for interpreting the movement of Surfacing.

> There's a passage in Virgil's Aeneid which I found very useful, where Aeneas goes to the underworld to learn about his future. He's guided by the Sybil and he learns what he has to from his dead father, and then he returns home. It's a very ambiguous passage. . . .[5]

I am not sure the passage is all that ambiguous, but it certainly is intriguing. That Aeneas, a paradigm of anticipatory resoluteness, should interrupt his being-toward and travel backward and downward, into the depths of the past--and this for the very sake of his future being--surely gives the lie to any commonsense notion which would separate and objectify past and future. Aeneas' inspiration corresponds to both Freud's and Heidegger's insights. We live out of the future, understand out of the past.

The narrator in Surfacing does not enjoy Aeneas' anticipatory resoluteness. Indeed, she is closer to certain psychopathological personalities, for whom it is a conflictual and unresolved past which underlies the loss of future-directed being. Such psychopathologies, as Minkowski has brilliantly shown in Lived Time, result precisely in the empty present which characterizes her.[6]

From the start, then, as we have seen, the therapeutic movement is a narrative retrieval in order to learn the future, a return to the lost father, to the underworld, in search of the missing self. The movement is a spiral, for as Atwood goes on to say, "the heroine . . . does not end where she began."[7] It comes in well-defined stages, marked off by the novel's formal division into three parts.

The initial stage, in which she leaves the present tense of the city and returns to her island home, is a modest beginning in her effort to re-establish contact with her being as having-been and thus to find a way of living in the present. In fact, its first result is to intensify her self-alienation. Granted that it is "better here than in the city, with the exhaust-pipe fumes and damp heat, the burnt-rubber smell of the subway, the brown grease that congeals on your skin if you walk outside" (p. 84), still one carries one's present within. It is a lie to identify the city with insecurity and the island with safety. "I think hard about it, considering it, and it is a lie: sometimes I was terrified" even on the island (p. 84). Her dis-ease is not so neatly locatable "out there." The lie is to romanticize her past. She measures it against her present perceptions.

> I look around at the walls, the window; it's the same, it hasn't changed, but the shapes are inaccurate as though everything has warped slightly. I have to be more careful about my memories, I have to be sure they're my own and not the memories of other people telling me what I felt, how I acted, what I said: if the events are wrong the feelings I remember about them will be wrong too, I'll start inventing them and there will be no way of correcting it . . . To have the past but not the present, that means you're going senile (pp. 84-85).

This is the first explicit link between her emotional incapacities and her mis-rememberings. The rub, of course, is that she does not truly "have the past," indeed, can never have it again as past, and has actually distorted those aspects of her past she most needs contact with.

She recalls her brother's return from the dead, the drowning which "never affected him as much as I thought it should, he couldn't even remember it" (p. 85). She, in contrast, would have felt it was something special: "To be raised from the dead like that; I would have returned with secrets" (p. 86). This comes at the end of part I. In the concluding moment, she discovers she has lost her childhood spontaneity, the unity of self and world: "At that time I would dive and coast along the lake floor . . . my own body blurred and eroding" (p. 86). She thinks she must be growing old, incapable now of such unselfconscious diving under. "Can that be possible?", she stands there wondering, until finally "being in the air is more painful than being in the water" (p. 87). Being in the present is more painful than returning to the past; repressing the contents of her past, more painful than facing them. Part I ends with her pushing herself "reluctantly into the lake" (p. 87).

Part II opens with the description of her mind/body split quoted above, the metaphorical equivalent of her just-achieved insight and action. It is the first explicit articulation of her life-problem. Having once pushed herself into the lake, however reluctantly, she is now ready to "search through the past" (p. 101) in the form of such documents as she can find in the cabin (photo albums, scrapbooks, her father's apparently hallucinatory drawings). She has already learned that the search for clues to her empty present must lead her into her past. The photos and scrapbooks, however, prove useless. They merely record a dead past, the camera stealing body and soul, extracting images from lived experience.

Even though she is convinced that history falsifies past experience, she rummages through the cabin in search of messages. Attending once again to her father's unintelligible drawings, she learns their true significance. They are copies of prehistoric Indian rock paintings left in the area by the "original ones, the first explorers, leaving behind them their sign, word, but not its meaning" (p. 150). Earlier she had viewed her missing father as "an archeological problem" (p. 54); now she realizes that her father is probably dead and it is her own death that must concern her. The task at hand is nothing less than the archeology of the self. The source of her own dying must somehow be contained in these documents, she decides, these mediations from pre-history left her by her father. They are "like a puzzle he'd left for me to solve," a "game I would play . . . with him," a "treasure map" to offer clues to her heart's frozen lake (pp. 124-125). The excavation takes her diving once again.

She knows it is "hazardous" to dive by oneself, but she thinks she remembers how. She faces her own shape in the water: "not my _reflection_ but my _shadow_" (p. 165, my italics). Repeatedly she plunges in and surfaces, this time not reluctantly but urgently, elatedly, recklessly. Now with her father's "messages" as guide, she is able to go deeper, feeling "it was wonderful I was down so far" (p. 167). At last she discovers the gift from the past, the gift from the dead who have gone before.

> It was there but it wasn't a painting, it wasn't on the rock. It was below me, drifting towards me from the furthest level where there was no life, a dark oval trailing limbs. It was blurred but it had eyes, they were open, it was something I knew about, a dead thing, it was dead (p. 167).

Her immediate response to the discovery is to _feel_: "I turned, fear gushing out of my mouth in silver, panic closing my throat, the scream kept in and choking me" (p. 167). "It" is neither the image of her drowned brother nor her lost father. "I _recognize_ it: it wasn't ever my brother I'd been remembering, that had been a disguise" (p. 168, my italics). Whatever it is, she admits, "part of myself or a separate creature, I killed it. It wasn't a child but it could have been one, I didn't allow it" (p. 168). The moment of recognition is a moment of freedom. Whatever the terminology we use, Freudian or phenomenological, it is apparent that this quite visceral and deeply felt act of remembering and recognizing is enabling; it enables her to begin to recast her fraudulent memories so as to discover a pattern in her intolerable story and thus to find a new plot which will allow her to live. As an act of repentant remembering, it actually alters the past, opening it up to change.

Now she can admit that the story of her marriage, divorce, and separation from her child was really a "covering over the bad things," an "embroidery" (p. 157), a strategic fiction to deny the truth of her past: her affair with a married man, pregnancy, abortion, and loss of self. The narrative's recurrent rememberings of her "husband" were not real memories at all but screens and fantasies. She rehearses the whole wedding scene, correcting her recollection of it point by point. It is worth comparing the two versions.

> At my wedding we filled out forms, name, age, birthplace, blood type. We had it in a post office, a J. P. did it, oil portraits of former postmasters presided from the beige walls. I could recall the exact smells . . . and, from another doorway, the chill of

antiseptic. It was a hot day, when we stepped out into the sun we couldn't see for an instant; then there was a flock of draggled pigeons pecking at the scuffed post-office lawn beside the fountain. The fountain had dolphins and a cherub with part of the face missing. "It's over," he said, "feel better?" (p. 105).

He hadn't gone with me to the place where they did it; his own children, the real ones, were having a birthday party. But he came afterward to collect me. It was a hot day, when we stepped out into the sun we couldn't see for an instant. It wasn't a wedding, there were no pigeons, the post office and the lawn were in another part of the city where I went for stamps; the fountain with the dolphins and the cherub with half a face was from the company town, I'd put it in so there would be something of mine.
"It's over," he said, "feel better?" (p.169).

The fraudulent memory had been real enough, she says,

it was enough reality for ever, I couldn't accept it, that mutilation, ruin I'd made, I needed a different version. I placed it together the best way I could, flattening it, scrapbook, collage, pasting over the wrong parts. A faked album, the memories fraudulent as passports; but a paper house was better than none and I could almost live in it, I'd lived in it until now (p. 169).

As a strategy for survival, her fantasized remembering had remade the painful past into a tolerable fiction, but in losing the past she had lost her capacities for remembering and thus herself. The embroidered rememberings turned out to be as useless as the mementoes in picture albums and scrapbooks--abstracted from temporal experience, destructive of Care, amputations, anesthesias, dismemberments (these last, her words for them). As she expresses her strategy early on: "Anesthesia, that's one technique: if it hurts invent a different pain" (p. 15).

The problem with her fabrications is that they are too successful. In destroying the memory of the painful past, they destroyed as well her emotional capacities, her trust in language and experience, her connections with the world, her very identity. As she realized prior to her first plunge into the lake, as she was running over her "version" of her life, checking it like an alibi:

It fits, it's all there till the time I left. Then static, like a jumped track, for a moment I've lost it, wiped clean; my exact age even, I shut my eyes, what is it? (p. 85)

Even that first dive into her unconscious depths convinces her that "time is compressed like the fist I close on my knee in the darkening bedroom, I hold inside it the clues and solutions and the power for what I must do now" (p. 91). If, when she rose up through the anesthetic, she "could remember nothing" (p. 133), it was because she had underestimated the correspondence between her being and her time. It is only when she loses all sense of the first that she embarks on her search for clues in her childhood past and her rememberings. Until she **allows** her rememberings, she can do no more than rehearse emotions, "naming them: joy, peace, guilt, release, love and hate, react, relate; what to feel was like what to wear, you watched the others and memorized it. But the only thing there was the fear that I wasn't alive" (p. 132). The effort is as futile as her bizarre sense-making gesture as a child when she stuck pen nibs and compass points into her arm in an effort to understand (p. 133).

Now that she has uncovered "true vision," (whether through remembering or imagining is immaterial: Freud would say it is both, or rather, beyond the distinction), she can no longer assume her old role among her amnesiac and anesthetized companions. Afraid she would come apart again, "the lies would recapture" (p. 177), it is time now "to choose sides" (p. 181), to league herself against the human beings and with the gods.   "I wanted there to be a machine that could make them vanish, a button I could press that would evaporate them without disturbing anything else" (p. 181).   She is almost ready for the movement into a past beyond the past, a remembering before remembering; but first she seeks a "gift" from her mother which will complete her father's legacy.

She finds it in the old scrapbooks, which now offer meanings from the past, unlocked by her remembering.   The gift is a picture she had made as a child: "on the left was a woman with a round moon stomach: the baby was sitting up inside her gazing out . . . The baby was myself before I was born" (p. 185).   Together with the rock paintings, this must be her guide; she has to read new meanings into old pictures. She has to interpret her past, that is, out of her present. She uncloses her fist, freeing time's clues, as it were, and for the first time discovers "a network of trails, lifeline, past present and future, the break in it closing together as I purse my fingers" (p. 186). Part II ends with her realization that "nothing has died, everything is alive, everything is waiting to become alive" (p. 186). She is temporal once again.

Once having retrieved the gifts of the ancestors and having leagued herself with these "gods" over against "the Americans," the human beings, the narrator is ready in part III for a remembering before and beyond time. She engages in an archetypal anamnesis no longer restricted to her own personal experience. The past she now seeks is beyond collective as well as personal history, the pre-historical roots of being. Such remembering is mythic in status; its contents impersonal or pre-personal. As such, it must be ritually enacted. In her ritual anamnesis, she recollects the archaic immemorial past from the imagining of archetypal presences.[8]

After confronting the archetypal presence in the lake which acts as a reminder, offering her the agonizing power to reconnect her present with her past for a new meaning, she gives thanks to the gods for the gift of emotion and new life in a ritualized offering of her clothing. "I didn't know the names of the ones I was making the offering to; but they were there, they had power . . . Clothing was better [than candles, crutches, flowers], it was closer and more essential; and the gift had been greater, more than a hand or an eye, feeling was beginning to seep back into me" (p. 171). This marks the first stage of her rite of passage from the strategic fiction of powerlessness to the recognition of power and thus of responsibility. The gifts from her parents and the archetypal anamnesis from the depths occur on "the sixth day" (p. 157). That night, she guides Joe into her in a ritualized mating scene near the lake. "I can feel my lost child surfacing within me, forgiving me, rising from the lake where it has been prisoned for so long" (p. 191). She discovers within herself a new power for self-forgiveness and reconciliation with her past. By freeing her to recover her own repressed having-been, her remorse frees her to imagine a possible future being as well. Remembering is the womb of freedom. The fetus growing within her will be the new being, the first human being, "covered with shining fur, a god," and she "will never teach it any words" (p. 191).

After destroying the Random Samples film, "the invisible captured images . . . swimming away into the lake like tadpoles" (p. 195), she studies Anna to see if her release from its version of technological atemporality has made any difference, "but the green eyes regard me unaltered from the enamel face" (p. 195). She escapes into the bush when her companions leave the island on the seventh day at the pre-arranged time ("To go with them would be running away," she says), musing that for them she will be nothing more than a dead, objectified memory, "a half-remembered face in a year book . . . memorabilia, or possibly not even that" (p. 198).

Alone now on the island, on the eighth day of creation, she enters a liminal state, divested of her human being and awaiting the reappearance of the gods. In order to "make them come out" (p. 203), she ritualistically rids herself and the island of all its human trappings. Clothing is partial, a mere token, "but the gods are demanding, absolute, they want all" (p. 209). As the instruments of civilization's collective amnesia, all human-made things become taboo and must be destroyed. Before she can construct her identity all over again, she must deconstruct the historical fictions contained in the notions of imperialism and selfsufficiency. She must remember her way back before the self/world dichotomy which is so anesthetizing, even before the language which is its instrument.

In a radically de-historicizing rampage, she destroys all history's artifacts in the cabin. "The pages bunch in my hands; I add them one by one so the fire will not be smothered, then the paint tubes and brushes, this is no longer my future" (p. 206, my italics). She systematically "cancels" the samsonite case, the bogus wedding ring, the photo albums, the scrapbooks, her father's books. Even the rock paintings, maps, and her mother's pictograph offering "must be translated" (p. 207). Next the non-linguistic things must go; she "abolishes them," burning, breaking, slashing, and throwing pots and pans, mattresses, clothing, furniture. "Everything from history must be eliminated" (p. 207). The point of her devastating frenzy is to "clear a space" and create a new time for the gods' reappearance. She clears away the detritus of false pasts in order to reclaim an authentic past from which to begin the re-making and re-membering of herself. Realizing that she "must stop being in the mirror" (p. 205), she reverses it so that it will no longer trap her. "Not to see myself but to see" (p. 205) is the requirement of the new creation; for its sake she will even "gnaw off [her] arms and legs to get free" (p. 217).

She continues perforating the border between self and world until, finally, her de-historicizing works, the transformation comes.

The forest leaps upward, enormous, the way it was before they cut it, columns of sunlight frozen; the boulders float, melt, everything is made of water, even the rocks. In one of the languages there are no nouns, only verbs held for a longer moment.

The animals have no need for speech, why talk when you are a word
I lean against a tree, I am a tree leaning
I break out again into the bright sun and crumple, head against the ground
I am not an animal or a tree, I am the thing in which the trees and animals move and grow, I am a place (pp. 212-213).

"No nouns, only verbs"; earlier she had realized that "a language is everything you do" (p. 153); nouns substantize, turn human beings into things, deny that being human is verbal, is an activity, is temporalizing. In remembering her way back before time (now the island is freed of watches and clocks), she is cancelling the lineality that does not work, that reduces the activity that is human be-ing into a machine. To do so, she thinks she must enter her parents' time, before and beyond birth and death. She presses beyond history toward an archeological and teleological directedness, a first and last time before the beginning and after the end. Civilization's inauthentic temporality has destroyed her; her response is to destroy it by escaping from it. "It is time that separates us," she says. Once time itself is vanquished and she has worked her way back down the evolutionary scale, she is prepared for her parents' reappearance as ancestral gods.

The image of her mother comes to her in an appearance borrowed from her most vivid memories of her. Earlier, when she tried to think of her mother, all she could recall was a story her mother once told about how, "when she was little, she and her sister had made wings for themselves" in an effort to fly (p. 146). In recounting the story, her mother laughed about breaking both her ankles; the narrator had found the failure "unbearable" (p. 146). Now she sees her mother standing in front of the cabin feeding the birds. When she approaches the visionary presence, the jays fly away; she squints up at them, "trying to see her, trying to see

which one she is" (p. 213-214). Dream-like, the vision
borrows its content from her narrative rememberings,
transmogrifying her mother into the bird she could not
become. In a parallel scene, she sees a "father-thing"
which gazes at her "with its yellow eyes, wolf's eyes"
which neither approve nor disapprove of her (p. 218).
The wolf-image rehearses another childhood story told her
by her brother. Catholics believe, the story goes, that
you will turn into a wolf if you don't go to Mass.
Perhaps her father had "turned into a wolf," she thinks,
"he'd be a prime candidate" (p. 65).

In each instance, her temporal-being reasserts
itself in the form of narratized and memorial imaginings.
The visions of her parents, with their combination of
attention and detachment, unlock her last resistances.
For the first time, she cries. "But I'm not mourning,
I'm accusing them, Why did you? They chose it, they had
control over their death . . . Who would take care of me"
(p. 202). Once accepting her loss of them as
"irrecoverable," she is able to bid them goodbye in a
dream (earlier we learned she can't remember how to
dream, p. 148). "They were alive and becoming older;
they are in a boat . . . heading out of the bay"
(p. 219). In her dream, then, she lets them leave her,
allows them their death, their mortality, their finitude.
She gives them back their humanity, their temporality,
thereby accepting once again her own.

When she awakens, "the rules are over," her parents
are out of touch now; she reenters her own time (pp. 291,
222, 223). The gods recede, "back to the past, inside
the skull, is it the same place," she wonders (p. 221).
From now on, she will have to define them by their
absence, "love by its failures, power by its loss, its
renunciation."

No total salvation, resurrection. Our father,
our mother, I pray, Reach down for me, but it
won't work: they dwindle, grow, become what
they were, human. Something I never gave them
credit for (p. 221).

Once she allows her parents their humanity and their
death, she remembers her "fake husband, more clearly
though." He is no longer in "framed memories" (p. 54),
no longer re-playing in her head like "dial-the-weather"
(p. 162). "now I feel nothing for him but sorrow. He
was neither of the things I believed, he was only a
normal man, middle-aged, second-rate, selfish and kind in
the average proportions" (p. 220). In forgiving him, she

is at last accepting responsibility for her own past. The final chapter begins:

> This above all, to refuse to be a victim. Unless I can do that I can do nothing. I have to recant, give up the old belief that I am powerless and because of it nothing I can do will ever hurt anyone. A lie which was always more disastrous than the truth would have been. The word games, the winning and losing games are finished; at the moment there are no others but they will have to be invented, withdrawing is no longer possible and the alternative is death (pp. 222-223).

Reentering her own time, she brings with her from the "distant past" the "time-traveler, the primeval one" (p. 223), the promise of a human being capable of her past. What she is taking back with her is her new-found capacity to be a remembering self and the fledgling identity formed out of that capacity. She ends by reaffirming history, language, communication, even her love for Joe "useless as a third eye or possibility" (p. 224). If she goes with him back into the present tense, she realizes, "we will have to talk . . . we will have to begin" (p. 224). The novel concludes with his waiting and with her moment of decision. We never see her re-integrated into the human community, but we end with the hope of it. Now that she can remember, perhaps she can also anticipate and make present. Her therapeutic psychopathologizing is both a hoping backward and a remembering forward. As Atwood comments about the novel's conclusion, "She can't enter the world of the dead, and she realizes, OK, I've learned something. Now I have to make my own life."[9]

The novel seems to suggest, finally, that ritualized disintegration can be a mode of healing and that "private rituals" can capacitate mutuality. The narrator's compulsions transform, her regressions free, her dehumanization humanizes, her remembering re-members. We cannot dismiss her as a case-study in pathology without at the same time dismissing the novel's conclusion as flawed, inconclusive, and incredible. Nor can the pathological ritualization be seen simply as a moment of disorder which she somehow moves beyond. Anamnesis' archeological and teleological dimensions are in tensive balance. As Paul Ricoeur suggests in his analysis of symbolic meanings,

> Perhaps we ought even to refuse to choose between the interpretation that makes these

symbols the disguised expression of the
infantile and instinctual past of the psychism
and the interpretation that finds in them the
anticipation of our possibilities of evolution
and maturation. We shall have to explore an
interpretation according to which "regression"
is a roundabout way of "progression". . . Re-
immersion in our archaism is no doubt the
roundabout way by which we immerse ourselves in
the archaism of humanity, and this double
"regression" is possibly, in its turn, the way
to a discovery, a prospection, and a prophecy
concerning ourselves.[10]

Surfacing suggests that such re-immersion is an intricate
interplay of rememberings at the service of nothing less
than the re-construction of identity. If the narrative
displays how that process engages the narrator, its very
structure elicits the reader's own hermeneutical
retrieval in dialogue with the text. It remains for us
to comment on how this aspect of the text's anamnetic
character makes its claims on us.

The Hermeneutics of Retrieval

What does it mean to be in time? Our discussion
thus far has already made clear that this issue--and the
anguishing search for an authentic temporality--is the
central life-question of the narrator. Each of the
narrative's major themes and motifs ties into it.
Disease and mutilation, the city vs. nature, technology,
commercialization, exploitation, imperialism, instinct
vs. reason and logic, language, the gods vs. the
Americans, the humans: all are explicitly related to the
question of how it is possible to live authentically in
the face of the amnesia of civilization, society, and the
very self. Each represents how human beings are made
into objects when they are deprived and deprive
themselves of their distinctively human mode of being
temporal which involves living in a threshholding matrix
of being-toward, being as having-been, and making
present. Each represents, that is, the forgetfulness of
being.

By frequent citations from the novel, we have shown
that such an interpretation is not a reading of preconceptions into the text but a recognition in front of the
world of the text itself. In particular, the narrator's
preoccupation with her past discloses how it is that the
kind of life possible for her in the present is keyed
into her capacities for remembering. Twice she tries to

find a _modus vivendi_, a way of getting hold of herself, by escaping from her temporal being. In the first instance, her situation at the novel's start, she does this by recasting her past in false memories. This re-writing of her personal history to contain an acceptable version of reality achieves nothing less than the sterilization of her capacity to experience. We meet the result of this strategy in the first part of the novel: personality disease and disorder, depression, frigidity, a split that borders on autism at times.

For example, she catches herself speaking about herself in the third person. "That won't work, I can't call them 'they' as if they were somebody else's family: I have to keep myself from telling that story" (p. 18). Well before she _tells_ us about being "cut in two," she _shows_ us the evidences of her split in her ways of speaking and acting. Before she tells us that she is the wrong half, detached and terminal, we see its results in her incapacities for feeling and remembering. Not, of course, that she is literally an amnesia victim. But the only kinds of remembering she is capable of are factual (she recalls an abundant store of useless information and cliches) or distorted. She still has the mental faculty of remembering--she would do well in the tests of experimental psychologists!--but she has lost her capacities for the human activity of remembering we have been describing in the course of this essay. Without that capacity, her life is less than human, as mechanized and futile as her companions'. In Freud's terms, she can neither love nor work.

Her first effort at "working through" the split, prompted by her return to the scenes of her childhood, is still an escape from time. She tries to recapture the past in its pastness. It soon becomes a mythic solution, an effort to get back beyond her past to the primordial past of the ancestors and to the atemporal beginnings. This stage involves, as we have seen, other disorders of her time-sense. Now she gives full play to her schizoid, obsessive/compulsive, and paranoid tendencies. If this archetypal remembering is a healing madness, as the novel seems to suggest, a regression for the sake of progression, still the mythic solution with its radically ahistorical rhetoric is only a stage on the way. At the conclusion, she rejects it, recognizing the need to reenter her own time.

What the ritualization teaches her, however, is that the past, both archetypal and personal, must fund the present and the future through rememberings. It is precisely the gift of creative remembering that she brings back with her from the underworld of death, nightmare, and madness. At each stage, it is a symbolic remembering which unlocks her. In the first, her feelings are unlocked when she faces the truth of the abortion. In the second, her responsibility for her own life is unlocked when she faces the mortality of her parents. They--and thus she--are only human, she finally admits. She can become neither god nor animal; the only time available to her is temporality.

At the start of her journey into the past, when she loses her way and seeks directions, a woman tells her, "You must mean the old road. It's been closed for years, what you need is the new one" (p. 15). "But they've cheated," she soon realizes, "I can't really get here unless I've suffered . . . the first view of the lake . . . should be through tears and vomit" (p. 18). In the last line of the novel, the other side of tears and vomit, "the lake [like the visions of her parents] is quiet, asking and giving nothing" (p. 224). In the meantime, the suffering has come in the form of working through, of learning how to tell an acceptable story which allows her to be temporal once again, of learning to remember herself through recovering her repressed past in all its pain. The power she discovers in herself at the conclusion is precisely this power of a storied and imaginative remembering, revealed as both a psychological and moral task.

Remembering is not simply the controlling motif of the novel which interlaces all the others; it is as well a pervasive feature of the narrative structure. It is what the experience means precisely because it is what, structurally, the experience is. It remains for us to take note of these narrative strategies which unify the novel's theme and structure and to reflect on how they mold our response to the fiction's meaning. Without doing a full-scale structural analysis, we shall content ourselves with brief comments on: (1) the use of the present tense, (2) flashbacks, (3) repetitions and reformulations, and (4) the narrator's unreliability.

(1) The use of the present tense grants the narrative a ritual quality from the start. Its atemporal character prepares us for the regression from history at the novel's center. The narrator's recitation of her actions in a constant simple present tense gives the story an eerie sense by depersonalizing the action even as it is being narrated in the first person, and is consonant with her proclivity, noted above, to slip from first to third person in her speakings about herself and her past. I have chosen a few examples from random pages

in the text: "He comes to the gas station . . . Anna and I follow . . . I go up to David . . . We slur down the last hill . . . We head towards the door . . . I walk down the hill" (pp. 16-19). "I turn over and shove Joe . . . I surface again . . . I throw back the covers . . . I get dressed . . . I go outside . . . I reach for the eggs . . . I carry the food inside . . . I crouch down in front of the stove" (pp. 50-52). As we read this strangely static and impersonal catalogue of activities on page after page, we imbibe an overwhelming sense of the claustrophobia of the narrator's immured present.

(2) In contrast with the static quality of the narrator's present tense is the fluid movement back and forth between the narration of events from the past and present. She shifts temporal location constantly, as her present perceptions prompt reminiscences and recollections, but these temporal shifts still occur within the narrative present. In other words, we as readers are frequently unsure about what she is telling us. Did it happen years ago? Does it refer to her father, brother, husband, Joe? While most of these ambiguities are resolved, they require the reader's constant attention and re-interpretation. The peculiar effect of this is not simply to unsettle the reader as to the temporal location of events and therefore of their meaning, but to bring the past _in its pastness_, as it were, into the narrative present. The result is simply a variation on the stasis achieved by the constant present tense. As the narrator herself comments, she "replays" the past for a specious solace (p. 30), her husband making "the brief appearances, framed memories he specializes in" (p. 54). Such "memories" are not her own. It's as if they happen _to_ her; they are "framed" like the photo mementoes; she is as much a recording tape as her companions are. The point here is not simply that she _tells_ us this, but that the narrative's rhetorical strategies _show_ us it as well, involving us in her own brand of static present and unassimilable past.

(3) This melding of static past and present gets further narrative articulation in the multiple repetitions of key words, images, and scenes. Sometimes such reiterations eventuate in reformulations and revelations, as we saw in the narrator's rehearsal of the wedding scene. At other times, however, they are exact repetitions, lifted out of one temporal context and plopped into another. A minor but powerful example occurs with David's recitation late in the story of a jingle which first appears much earlier as a memory from her childhood initiation into churchgoing. After the Sunday School service, she would return with her

companion's family for a lunch of pork and beans. After the father said grace, he would invariably add his own version of a little impropriety: "Pork and beans and musical fruit; the more you eat the more you toot" (p. 164). When David's reiteration of the jingle occurs, uncommented upon, its effect borders on the horrifying. Nothing, it seems, has changed. Memory serves only to reveal how essentially static experience is. Past and present are indistinguishable; the exploitations of religion and sex speak the same inane language. The narrator was and remains fundamentally alienated from her companions and her surroundings. In this instance, it is not her memory but ours which serves to underline the point.

(4) The most significant of these narrative strategies is the unreliability of the narrator herself, her propensity to embroider and falsify her memories. We have already referred to this aspect of the narrative structure at some length in our discussion of the novel's overriding theme and movement. What is worth commenting upon here, however, is the effect of this deception on us as readers. We are increasingly thrust out of the role of sympathetic listener and into the role of skeptical investigator. The narrative structure positively requires of us a hermeneutic of suspicion. By the time the narrator admits her memory-lies, we have already learned to mistrust her veracity. This manipulation of reader-response is accomplished by elaborate patterns of enigmas, deceptions, and revelations.[11]

It is not too long into the narrative before the attentive reader becomes confused by apparent contradictions in the narrator's recounting of events. We begin to suspect that we are ourselves the victims of her strategic fictions; she is manipulating our tendency to sympathize with the first person point of view in a story. Increasingly we realize that she is not simply inconsistent and self-contradictory; she is downright clever in her deceptions. She tells us outright lies that initially hook us into belief, only to discover later that we have been thoroughly duped. For example, she presumably takes us into her confidence regarding her divorce and abandonment of her child. Neither her parents' friends nor her own companions know the "true" story. She lets us know that she is prepared to lie to them about it; they will not be capable of accepting the truth. We are flattered by the role of confidante, teased by her deception and our own gullibility into thinking we have inside knowledge.

248

This position of superiority soon gets dashed, of course, when the truth of the past is revealed after her plunge into the lake to confront the memorial symbol. Even here, however, the narrator is deceptive, first telling us she actually saw the aborted fetus, then confessing immediately "That was wrong, I never saw it" (p. 168). The first description, like all her previous confidences, was pretense.

If we grant that such manipulations are other than the sadistic toying of the author with her readers, it seems that their point must be to make us, like the narrator herself, into archaeologists. We are required not only to engage in her process, but also to experience the deleterious effects of her particular brand of amnesia and memory-distortion. If she is alienated from her companions, it is not simply because of their own vacuity, but more importantly because of fundamental incapacities in herself. These incapacities, now directed against us, modulate our own response from sympathetic therapist-confessor to skeptical investigator and, finally, to participant observer. What is more, they make her radical de-historicizing a conceivable and acceptable alternative in the face of the deceptive games her memory plays. Having been through those games with her, we are perhaps ready to try her mythic solution and ready, finally, to welcome her back into her own time, now purged from "the lies, the word games, the winning and losing games" (p. 223). As participant-observers, we are in the position to appreciate the extent to which her life-patterns have been destructive, the extent to which, becoming a question and problem to herself, she also became incapable of being-with others.

While her re-integration into the human community is promised rather than achieved at the novel's conclusion, in another sense it is already achieved because we (and we alone) have been present throughout the whole ordeal. As narrated to us, her experience has never been completely solipsistic; and insofar as we stay with her through it all, despite her lies and falsifications of memory, we have been invited to engage in our own anamnesis, our own confusing working-through to a new story and a healing identity. According to Walker Percy,

> The modern literature of alienation is in reality the triumphant reversal through its re-presenting. It is not an existential solution . . . but is an aesthetic victory of comradeliness, a recognition of plight in common.[12]

I want to refrain, however, from making exaggerated claims for the novel's achievement. A cogent and demurring critical opinion finds this very combination of the narrator's unreliability with the narrative present tense a serious structural flaw.[13] It certainly raises critical questions about the reader's relation to the temporality of the telling. According to this critical opinion, the present tense usage is inadequate to the task of aligning us to the changing consciousness of the narrator.

The power of the present tense, as we have noted, is its immediacy, its ritualistic quality, and its capacity to engage us in the narrator's psychopathologies. Supposedly we are meant to be accompanying her as she undergoes her transforming ordeal. No matter what the authorial tricks, however, the nature of narrative itself would seem to require the past tense. What is more, the peculiar cognitive position generated by a first person narrative presupposes the narrator's complex and sustained remembering activities in the very act of story-telling.

Atwood opens herself to the charge of straining the multivalent logic of all first person narratives in her combination of unreliable narrator with present narration. In doing so, she risks undermining the very meaning she evidently intends to convey. If, as she has claimed, the narrative movement is a spiral in that the heroine does not end where she began, we would expect her new capacities to be displayed syntactically. Our expectation finds support in the novel's very preoccupation with language and with remembering. If, however, the narrator never develops the capacity for speaking in the past tense, can we find her supposed re-entry into human time convincing? Her movement from strategic fictions to right rememberings is crucial to the credibility of the claim for a reconstructed identity. Within the framework of the telling, however, she never learns to use the tensed language which would be the objective correlative to her temporal re-integration. At the rhetorical level of the text, the narrator never displays the full narrative capacities which give free play to one's rememberings in the search to understand what it means to be human.

The progressive teleology of her regressions would be more convincing if it were displayed as the narrator's capacity to tell a story about her being as having-been. What Surfacing gains in psychological immediacy through its sustained present tense comes at the cost of a portrayal of authentic temporal identity which is structurally unconvincing. For a more structurally satisfying fiction, let us turn to Bellow's Henderson the Rain King. This novel exploits other aspects of the multifarious rememberings ingredient in a hermeneutic of narrative fiction. In Surfacing, we have seen remembering's role in the reconstruction of identity; in Henderson, we shall explore how narrative itself becomes an anamnesis.

[1]Margaret Atwood, Surfacing (N.Y.: Popular Library, 1972), p. 9. All other references cited in the text are to this edition.

[2]Donna Gerstenberger, "Conceptions Literary and Otherwise: Women Writers and the Modern Imagination," Novel 9 (Winter 1976):145.

[3]Ibid., p. 146.

[4]Marcuse, Eros and Civilization, p. 212.

[5]Margaret Atwood, cited by Linda Sandler, "Interview with Margaret Atwood," The Malahat Review 41 (Jan. 1977):16.

[6]Eugene Minkowski, Lived Time: Phenomenological and Psychopathological Studies, trans. Nancy Metzel (Evanston: Northwestern U. Press, 1970).

[7]Atwood, "Interview," The Malahat Review, p. 11.

[8]Casey, "Imagining and Remembering: In Time and Beyond Time," p. 8.

[9]Atwood, "Interview," The Malahat Review, p. 11.

[10]Paul Ricoeur, The Symbolism of Evil, pp. 12-13.

[11]See Barbara Lefcowitz's unpublished essay, "Margaret Atwood's Surfacing: An Analysis of Reader Response" for a detailed analysis of this issue. My exposition here draws on her argument.

[12]Walker Percy, "The Man on the Train," The Message in the Bottle (N.Y.: Farrar, Straus and Giroux, 1975), p. 39, cited by Lefcowitz, p. 22.

[13]I am indebted to Prof. Robert Detweiler, of Emory University's Institute of the Liberal Arts, for this insight.

CHAPTER VIII

BELLOW'S HENDERSON THE RAIN KING:

NARRATIVE AS ANAMNESIS

Like Surfacing, Henderson the Rain King tells the story of a physical journey which has the mythic character of a quest and an ordeal. Unlike the narrator's journey in Surfacing, however, Henderson's is not a painful return but a rollicking adventure, not a reluctant movement into the past but a deliberate effort to escape the present in search of a new future. Nevertheless, in each case the journey becomes the search for a new mode of being which requires a fresh relationship with one's past.

While the narrator in Surfacing has lost access to her past being through her use of strategic memory-fictions, Henderson's past is all too present to him in its stark reality. As he tells us on the novel's first page, his memories pile into him from all sides, turning into chaos.

> A disorderly rush begins--my parents, my wives, my girls, my children, my farm, my animals, my habits, my money, my music lessons, my drunkenness, my prejudices, my brutality, my teeth, my face, my soul! I have to cry, "No, no, get back, curse you, let me alone!" But how can they let me alone? They belong to me. They are mine.[1]

He considers himself an expert on memory and the suffering it entails: "The repetition of a man's bad self, that's the worst suffering that's ever been known" (p. 276); "It's the memory of past defeats--past defeats, you can ask me about this problem of past defeats. Brother, I could really tell you" (p. 157). "Curse my memory," he wails, "for being so complete!" (p. 237).

Both characters anguish over their skewed temporality, though for different reasons. The narrator in Surfacing is immured in a vacuous and sterile present because she has systematically denied her having-been; Henderson finds his present being intolerable because his having-been is too much with him. If he curses his memory, it is because he views the past under the dimension of fate. For him, memory is indeed a storehouse, a collection of refuse, a "pawn shop . . . filled with unredeemed pleasures, old clarinets and cameras, and moth-eaten furs" (p. 71). To find a new relationship to his past will require undermining the mechanistic model of memory he holds. As long as his rememberings merely reiterate the past in its pastness, he is doomed to repetition and incapable of change. His transformation requires his discovering the force of certain neglected features of remembering: its imaginative and narrative capacities. This discovery is made explicit in the narrative. He begins by cursing his memory; he concludes by acknowledging that "my memory did me a great favor," and "something of benefit can be found in the past" (p. 282).

While their versions of disordered temporality differ, the result is the same in each novel, i.e., the incapacity to be-with others. In Henderson's way of putting it, "Society is what beats me" (p. 45). In an effort to escape a final defeat, he buys a one-way ticket to Africa. His object, he tells us, "was to leave certain things behind" (p. 41). What he is not able to leave behind, he soon discovers to his chagrin, are himself and his rememberings. His change of venue is simply propaedeutic to an instruction which will entail a personal conversion, a thoroughgoing re-membering of his being as having-been.

The clue to this comes early in the narrative in his paradoxical realization that entering Africa is like "entering the past--the real past" (p. 42). "The antiquity of the place had struck me so, I was sure I had got into someplace new" (p. 48). He tells his guide that he has a "funny feeling" about it. "Hell, it looks like the original place. It must be older than the city of Ur . . . I have a hunch this spot is going to be very good for me" (pp. 43-44). That hunch is testimony to his comic ongoingness of character--a trait in stark contrast with the narrator's self-seriousness and fatalism in our previous novel. But it signals as well that in certain important ways his experience will not be unlike hers. He, too, will enter a "pre-human past" (p. 42), will recollect a past beyond memory, in order to learn how to re-enter his own time. His African adventure will become a rite of passage; and, like hers, at its heart it will be an imaginative anamnesis. "Travel," he comes to understand, "is advisable. And believe me, the world is a mind. Travel is mental travel" (p. 142).

This insight, as we shall see, is the fruit of a series of symbolic activities which free his rememberings from facticity and open them up to novelty. "The world of facts is real, all right, and not to be altered. The physical is all there, and it belongs to science. But then there is the noumenal department, and there we create and create" (p. 142). Rememberings must be wrested from science and returned to their proper home in the noumenal. His rememberings, that is, must develop imaginative dimensions.

> All human accomplishment has this same origin, identically. Imagination is a force of nature. Is this not enough to make a person full of ecstasy? Imagination, imagination, imagination! It converts to actual. It sustains, it alters, it redeems! (pp. 228-229).

Henderson already knows "what it is to lie buried in yourself" (p. 233); what he learns through his ritualizing is the rebirth and remembering of the self which is a power of the imagination. As long as his memory is limited to storing the past in its pastness, "the dead are (his) boarders" (p. 242) and he is doomed to repetition, to living in the past. His task, "to redeem the present and discover the future" (p. 233), requires a conversion in his way of picturing memory. Not memory but remembering, not time but temporalizing.

As symbolic activity, ritual is well suited to this task. Enacted in the present, it takes the past into itself; by re-presenting the past, it actually changes it. Ritual anamnesis functions as a hermeneutic for the re-interpretation of one's past being. The "great favor" Henderson's memory does him is enabled by this ritual activity; and it, in its turn, is the enabler of his being-toward. For him, the guarantee of his new-found capacities for remembering is the new story he learns to tell. In Surfacing, the young narrator needs to accept her mortality if she is "to refuse to be a victim." The middle-aged Henderson needs to become like a child again if the world is to remove its wrath from him. To see how this conversion is achieved, let us trace through certain key threads in the text. Our reading will focus on (1) the narrative's structure and (2) the metaphors which are central to Henderson's rite of passage.

Narrative Structure

The narrative begins with a question, a question which Eugene Henderson, millionaire, twice-married, one time pig farmer, poses to himself and to his readers.

> What made me take this trip to Africa? There is no quick explanation. Things got

worse and worse and worse and pretty soon they
were too complicated (p. 7).

The point of view is first person confessional. The
situation is that Henderson is a changed man: "The world
which I thought so mighty an oppressor has removed its
wrath from me" (p. 7). The narrative is both response to
and actualization of that transformation. Telling the
story, recollecting the past, becomes the only mode
available to him to live the transformed present. He
must present the present to us by means of the past, for
he has a need to "make sense to you people and explain,"
a need which requires that he "face up to the facts" (p.
7). But he finds that it is not possible simply to tell
the _facts_ of the past. The Henderson who is telling this
story has already been educated out of such a de-
humanized attitude toward his past being. After several
abortive starts, he remains dissatisfied by his
narration, while recognizing that an explanation is
necessary, "for living proof of something of the highest
importance has been presented to me so I am obliged to
communicate it" (p. 22).

Telling the story is a requirement somehow placed
upon him by the experience itself, the guarantee that
living proof of something of the highest importance has
been presented to him. The narrative is thus the making
present of the significance of the experience; it makes
the experience live. He knows, however, that there is no
other way into the living present except through the
past, or better, through his having-been. His access to
the past is already a process of creative remembering.
Such a process is beyond the recitation of facts, not so
much tidy and logical as associative and storied. It
requires imaginings. It is not simply _the_ past he
recounts, but his past being as it has been taken up by
and transformed into his being-present, modified by his
anticipatory being. This process of narratized
remembering affects the telling in several key ways.

First of all, it discards a mere chronological
sequence. Chronology is at the service of vision; the
past is deconstructed of strict sequentiality, its facts
reshaped according to the new pattern. Events from a
remoter past often follow rather than precede the more
proximate past. What we learn about Frances, his first
wife, is woven in and out of what we learn about Lily,
his second. Details of his childhood are prompted by
memories of his adulthood; events from his life with Lily
are told before events from their courtship. In this, of
course, _Henderson's_ narrative structure parallels
Surfacing's.

And as in Surfacing, past events are constantly repeated. Significant experiences and insights reappear over and over again in the narrative; but in Henderson's case, each time with a deepened, expanded, or changed significance. In the gyre-like narrative, he keeps spiraling around and back, constantly re-collecting experiences into new syntheses, combinations, and revisions. Let me cite one small example from the hundreds in the text. When Henderson first recounts overhearing Lily say he is unkillable, it makes him very bitter, though he recognizes even in his first telling that he "put an antagonistic interpretation on it even though I knew better" (pp. 9-10). Much later he interprets her positive response to his desire to study medicine at the age of fifty-five as a "corollary to her belief I was unkillable" (p. 69). The comment's significance--because his interpretation of it--has been changed. When he says at the end of the story, "listen to me, Romilayu, I'm unkillable" (p. 177), the transformation of its meaning has been completed because internalized.

This narrative repetition to enhance and enlarge meaning gives us a clue, it seems to me, that the storytelling is itself subsumed into a rite of transformation. The narrative is not only taken up into the transformation of the character; it is its embodiment. The narrative is itself an anamnesis; Henderson's remembering collects past into present and presents it within ritual activity. In and through the narrative structure, Henderson engages in a kind of ritual action which reconstructs his biography. His new story is at once continuous and discontinuous with his former self. It is on the narrative itself that the convincingness of his transformation must rest. The novel's first person confessional form becomes crucial to the viability of its vision. Anamnesis is both structure and meaning in the text, for in the mode of narration itself Bellow has presented the formal objective correlative to the vision. In doing so, he has offered a structural solution to the flaw we identified in Surfacing.

I think this anamnetic character is a key to a proper reading of the text--borne out, in my judgment, by a major theme in the novel which is introduced on its first page. Henderson himself offers us this clue:

I thought myself a bum and had my reasons, the main reason being that I behaved like a bum. But privately when things got very bad I often

looked into books to see whether I could find
some helpful words, and one day I read, "The
forgiveness of sins is perpetual and righteousness first is not required." This impressed me
so deeply that I went around saying it to
myself. But then I forgot which book it was
(p. 7).

Try as he might to locate it, he tells us, he "never
found that statement about forgiveness" (p. 7).
Henderson's life-problem is precisely a forgetfulness,
and his rite of passage is a training in right remembering. The truth which he seeks has already been given to
him from the start (a very Platonic theory of
knowledge!), but he has lost its reference and blocked it
from his memory. The symptoms of that forgetfulness show
up in his life pattern, and the quest he undertakes
becomes the enabler of recovery. At each stage of his
passage, obstacles are removed through ritual actions
until he has at last arrived at the position of unity
which precedes his dis-ease and split. As T. S. Eliot
would have it,

> We had the experience but missed the meaning,
> And approach to the meaning restores the experience
> In a different form, beyond any meaning
> We can assign to happiness.[2]

The restoration of experience in a different form is
a work of remembering, imaged in the deconstructed
chronology and repetitiousness of the narrative.
Henderson engages the reader in the very recovery,
thereby inviting us to participate in the process of
self-forgetfulness and self-continuity. The statement
about forgiveness comes to Henderson's mind at key points
in the story, as the events he undergoes free him to
recover more of its meaning. So, for example, when
Willatale asks him who he is and where he comes from, he
wants to explain that he had ruined the original piece of
goods issued to him and is in search of a remedy, that he
"had read somewhere that the forgiveness of sin was
perpetual but with typical carelessness had lost the
book" (p. 67). From the Arnewi Henderson begins to learn
acceptance, but to do so he must face his own lack of
self-acceptance, his misguided pre-occupation with self,
and his frantic need for self-justification. His insight
here that he had lost the book through carelessness
prepares him for the deeper insight into a carelessness
that goes to the heart of his own identity and is the
source of the world's wrath toward him. He lost far more
than the book in which he first read the statement; he

lost, as he will come to see, the capacity to remember the statement's meaning.

At a later stage in his passage, when he confronts the unavoidable lion, Henderson the avoider recalls:

> All I can truly say is that when I read in one of my father's books, "The forgiveness of sin is perpetual," it was just the same as being hit in the head with a rock (p. 205).

This, of course, connects with his early realization that truth comes in blows, but full recovery of the statement's significance does not come until the final pages of the text. In order to understand it there, we must begin to look in some detail at Henderson's ritual of passage.

Henderson's Rite of Passage

Henderson's process of recovery and reconstruction is bound up with two kinds of metaphors which are central to the transformation he undergoes: (1) animal imagery and (2) ritual actions of penitence and forgiveness. Both function at two levels in the text, that of action and of narrative. Henderson is a pig farmer; the Arnewi raise cattle; Dahfu does, indeed, keep a lion named Atti--and Henderson has experiences with each of these. Likewise, Mrs. Lenox dies of his ragings; he destroys the Arnewi cistern, participates in the Wariri rain dance, and allows himself to be moved by Dahfu's death. At the level of action, that is, he undergoes certain events which are narrated chronologically within the text. Yet each of these experiences is, in addition, a source of significant revelation and a stage in his transformation. It is only by the process of anamnesis, a reflection which grows deeper with each new event, and through the activity of narration itself, that Henderson comprehends the union of meaning and event.

The text constantly plays with these literal and metaphorical dimensions, letting the storytelling process itself lead him and us gradually into full realization of their inherency. So, for example, toward the end of the story, Henderson recognizes the full import of his literal involvement early on with the pigs.

> The hogs were my defiance. I was telling the world that it was a pig. I must begin to think how to live (p. 242).

261

He had the experience but missed the meaning. So, too, with the actions. He undergoes certain ritualistic actions which are metaphorical in that they are comprised of a physical and spiritual dimension. The body dimension is given at a point in time contained within the chronology of the narrative; it is anamnesis which opens up the deeper significance of the event. Successive rituals inform and enlarge Henderson's capacities to internalize previous actions he has undergone, just as the storytelling itself does. The implication of this, as it is worked out within the novel's narrative structure, is that the reader is taken up into the action in a way analogous to Henderson's own transformation. We participate in the growth of the revelation. We, too, are given the experience before we recover its full import; in recognition we enter into communion with Henderson and his text by "texting" ourselves.

(1) "I was a pig man," Henderson tells us at the start of his story. He recalls the words of the prophet Daniel: "They shall drive thee from among men, and thy dwelling shall be with the beasts of the field" (p. 22). Daniel's prophecy functions as a leitmotif through the narrative, both as statement of Henderson's animal involvement and condition and as the hint or promise of repentance. He conveys the literal dimension of himself as pig man with comic vigor:

> I took all the handsome old farm buildings, the carriage house with paneled stalls--in the old days a rich man's horses were handled like opera singers--and the fine old barn with the belvedere above the hayloft, a beautiful piece of architecture, and I filled them up with pigs, a pig kingdom, with pig houses on the lawn and in the flower garden. The greenhouse, too--I let them root out the old bulbs. Statues from Florence and Salzburg were turned over. The place stank of swill and pigs and the mashes cooking, and dung (p. 21).

He has taken what is old and fine, beautiful and handsome, and turned it all over to the pigs. We get a picture of the disorder, chaos, and filth of his surroundings. But that is not all, for, as he says, "Those animals have become a part of me" (p. 22). Henderson himself is a pig: violent, mad, raging, grieving, drunken, and clever like his pigs. The qualities of a pig characterize not only his own inner dispositions but his relationships with his family and neighbors as well. Becoming a pig farmer, he sees, "maybe illustrates what I thought of life in general" (p. 21). From the start, this metaphorical identification between Henderson and pigs is given in the text, though not reflected upon:

> I came, a great weight, a huge shadow on those stairs, with my face full of country color and booze, and yellow pigskin gloves on my hands, and a ceaseless voice in my heart that said, I want, I want, oh, I want--yes, go on, I said to myself, Strike, strike, strike! And I kept going on the staircase in my thick padded coat, in pigskin gloves and pigskin shoes, a pigskin wallet in my pocket, seething with lust and seething with trouble . . . (p. 14).

Henderson has transformed himself, the world, and life in general into a pig. In his encounter with Atti and his efforts to "act lion," he emits grunts rather than roars. It is only than that he begins to sense that "I've ruined myself with pigs" (p. 262) and that he has "had a little too much business with a certain type of creature" (pp. 252-253) for his own good. "If I had it to do over again, it would be different." The realization that it could be different, that change is possible, is one of the lessons he learns from the lion.

> I must change. I must not live in the past, it will ruin me. The dead are boarders, eating me out of house and home. The hogs were my defience. I was telling the world that it was a pig. I must begin to think how to live (p. 242).

As he shifts from a static to a dynamic mode of remembering, Henderson is freed from his bondage to the past and opened to the future. His constant moving forward with expectation into the future is engendered by a fresh and ever-deepening re-appropriation of his past being. But full realization of his possibilities comes only at the narrative's completion, a lesson he learns beyond what Dahfu can teach him, through his own recollection. Actually, he realizes, pigs don't have a monopoly on grunting, either; and through the memory of his earlier involvement with a bear, he understands something of himself:

> I didn't come to the pigs as a tabula rasa. It only stands to reason. Something deep already was inscribed on me (p. 284).

Like the fine, old house of beautiful dimensions, Henderson is a work of art which has been spoiled by the pigs. He must find his way back to the original beauty, the something deep already inscribed. In his organic process of recovery, he gets from pigs to the bear and the lamb only by way of cattle and lions. Let us trace that movement.

By the time Henderson leaves home for Africa, he has got rid of the literal pigs--for he has assumed their identity. By a kind of rite of incorporation, he has become a pig. His first encounter in Africa is with the Arnewi, who are, both literally and figuratively, cattle folk.

> Romilayu explained to me that the Arnewi were very sensitive to the condition of their cattle, who they regarded as their relatives, more or less, and not as domestic animals (p. 44).

To be cattle people is a step up from pigs, as Henderson himself realizes.

> You have to understand that these people love their cattle like brothers and sisters, like children; they have more than fifty terms just to describe the various shapes of the horns, and Itelo explained to me that there were hundreds of words for the facial expressions of cattle and a whole language of cow behavior. To a limited extent I could appreciate this. I have had great affection for certain pigs myself. But a pig is basically a career animal; he responds very sensitively to human ambitions or drives and therefore doesn't require a separate vocabulary (p. 51).

From their involvement with cattle, the Arnewi have imbibed certain cow-like attitudes toward life--attitudes which it becomes important for Henderson to learn in his growth up the animal scale from pigs. They are mild, placid, nurturing, accepting people. In his association with them, Henderson begins to modify his own attitudes. He becomes less aggressive and violent, less self-oriented, more accepting of life. He learns contrition.

He sees, as well, however, the limitations and liabilities of being cow-like. The Arnewi allow their beloved cattle to die of thirst rather than let them drink from the frog-infested cistern.

The Jews had Jehovah, but wouldn't defend themselves on the Sabbath. And the Eskimos would perish of hunger with plenty of caribou around because it was forbidden to eat caribou in fish season, or fish in caribou season. Everything depends on the values--the values. And where's reality? I ask you, where is it? I myself, dying of misery and boredom, had happiness, and objective happiness, too, all around me, as abundant as the water in that cistern where cattle were forbidden to drink (p. 76, my italics).

What may look like acceptance of the real, he begins to sense in a Kantian insight, may indeed be nothing more than acceptance of our own projections and preconceptions. This, then, is his first hint of the significance of the imagination and of its power to transform a static memory into a creative activity. The Arnewi experience is thus crucial for Henderson in two ways: it opens him up to novelty and to his first insight into the power of the imagination; and through it he imbibes something of the cow-like qualities of acceptance which enable him to encounter the lion.

It is in and through his lionizing at the hands of Dahfu that Henderson begins to comprehend the significance of his animal association. His involvement with pigs and cattle was unreflective, whereas his engagement with Atti is a project of instruction. Experience and meaning are beginning to come together. Dahfu has the insight to match the experience. He leads Henderson first into the lion's presence and eventually into lion behavior. And he explains why:

"What a Christian might feel in Saint Sophia's church, which I visited in Turkey as a student, I absorb from lion. When she gives her tail a flex, it strikes against my heart. You ask, what can she do for you? Many things. First she is unavoidable. And this is what you need, as you are an avoider. Oh, you have accomplished momentous avoidances. But she will change that. She will make consciousness to shine. She will burnish you. She will force the present moment upon you. Second, lions are experiencers. . . Moreover, observe Atti. Contemplate her . . . the vital continuity between her parts" (p. 219, my italics).

Chief among these "momentous avoidances" has been his living in the past, which not only sentences him to futile repetitions but frees him from decision and responsibility for his present being. It begins to come clear that Henderson, in accepting the fatedness of his past, has manipulated his rememberings for his own version of victimhood. He wallows in his guilt as a defense against repentance. If lion can teach him, he comes to see, then it follows as a corollary that he can change. Dahfu, he marvels, "really appeared to see a future for me" (p. 201); "he believed that it was never too late for any man to change, no matter how fully formed. And he took me for an instance" (p. 213). This very imagining of a future--even on the part of another for him--prompts the loosening of the grip of a fated past. For the first time, Henderson prays with remorse:

> Oh, you . . . Something, I said, you Something because of whom there is not Nothing. Help me to do Thy will. Take off my stupid sins. Untrammel me. Heavenly Father, open up my dumb heart and for Christ's sake preserve me from unreal things. Oh, Thou who tookest me from pigs, let me not be killed over lions. And forgive my crimes and nonsense and let me return to Lily and the kids (p. 213).

Dahfu, in fact, believes that he can be noble like the lion; and, though Henderson cannot go this far (one index of his comic character), he figures he "might pick up a small gain here and there in the attempt" (p. 250). The lessons he learns from the lion are basically three: first, the very possibility of change; second, to experience rather than avoid life (which will be the way out of the imprisonment of the "I want"); and, finally, the union of mind and body (the escape from ego-emphasis).

Throughout the narrative, Henderson has had a lively relationship with his own body. From the start, he has a Bergsonian comic distance on it.

> Just then I deeply felt my physical discrepancies. My face is like some sort of terminal; it's like Grand Central, I mean--the big horse nose and the wide mouth that opens into the nostrils, and the eyes like tunnels (p. 47).

But it is a humor of disgust, a comedy which itself needs transformation. His face is no common face, but "like an unfinished church" (p. 67), "a regular bargain basement of deformities" (p. 73).

> Oh, my body, my body! Why have we never really
> got together as friends? (p. 155).
> . . . .
> If I was the painter of my own nose and fore-
> head and of such a burly stoop and such arms
> and fingers, why, it was an out and out felony
> against myself. What had I done! A bungled
> lump of humanity. Oh, ho, ho, ho, ho! Would
> death please wash me away and dissolve this
> giant collection of errors (p. 226).

Through his association with Dahfu and the lion, he comes
to see the body not as something at war with the spirit
but as its incarnation.

> Briefly, he had a full scientific
> explanation of the way in which people were
> shaped. For him it was not enough that there
> might be disorders of the body that originated
> in the brain. Everything originated there.
> . . . .
> In the course of further discussions I
> told him, "I admit that this idea of yours
> really hits me where I live--am I so respon-
> sible for my own appearance? I admit I have
> had one hell of a time over my external man.
> Physically, I am a puzzle to myself."
> He said, "The spirit of the person in a
> sense is the author of his body" (p. 200).

Henderson learns that he is indeed animal, but a very
special animal whose mystery is not exhausted or
encompassed by his engagement with pigs, cattle, or even
lions. If, as the Daniel prophecy suggests, his dwelling
shall be with the beasts of the field, this does not
simply imply that he "was not entirely fit for human
companionship" (p. 194). It suggests as well that
through his association with them, he undergoes a peni-
tential transformation. As Dahfu instructs him, "Be the
beast! You will recover humanity later, but for the
moment, be it utterly'" (p. 225).

> And so I was the beast. I gave myself to
> it, and all my sorrow came out in the roaring.
> My lungs supplied the air but the note came
> from my soul. The roaring scalded my throat
> and hurt the corners of my mouth and presently
> I filled the den like a bass pipe organ. This
> was where my heart had sent me, with its
> clamor. This is where I ended up. Oh,
> Nebuchadnezzar! How well I understand that

267

prophecy of Daniel. For I had claws, and hair,
and some teeth, and I was bursting with hot
noise, but when all this had come forth, there
was still a remainder. The last thing of all
was my human longing (p. 225).

Henderson comes to understand that Dahfu and Atti have
instructed him in the first blessing, but now he must go
beyond.

But then what could an animal do for me? In
the last analysis? Really? A beast of prey?
Even supposing that an animal enjoys a natural
blessing? We had our share of this creature-
blessing until infancy indeed. But now aren't
we required to complete something else--project
number two--the second blessing? (p. 242).

But to talk about this second blessing we must now
retrace our steps in the narrative and examine the other
metaphorical pattern which is key to Henderson's transformation, the ritual actions and their relationship to
his spiritual disease and his spirit's sleep.

(2) If the physical and external correlative of
Henderson's unredeemed state is the pigs, its interior
and spiritual correlative is the voice within him which
repeats, "I want, I want."

Now I have already mentioned that there
was a disturbance in my heart, a voice that
spoke there and said, _I want, I want, I want!_
It happened every afternoon, and when I tried
to suppress it it got even stronger. It only
said one thing, _I want, I want!_
And I would ask, "What do you want?"
But this was all it would ever tell me.
It never said a thing except _I want, I want, I
want!_ (p. 24).

We have already seen how this is intermingled metaphorically from the start with his pig-like qualities.

Two incidents in his pig phase prompt him to set out
in search of an answer to the voice within him. Both are
physical actions--incarnations of spiritual states--whose
givenness precedes his understanding of them. The first
is his sudden intuition about the truth:

Beside my cellar door last winter I was
chopping wood for the fire. . . Owing to the
extreme cold I didn't realize what had happened

until I saw the blood on my mackinaw. Lily cried out, "You broke your nose." No, it wasn't broken. I have a lot of protective flesh over it but I carried a bruise there for some time. However as I felt the blow my only thought was truth. Does truth come in blows? (p. 23).

The insight functions as challenge and promise to the Henderson who, at this stage, thinks he is on "damned good terms with reality."

The second is the death of Mrs. Lenox on the "actual day of tears and madness." Henderson is fighting with his wife and during his rage, the old woman's heart stops. In one sense, it is the final blow; in another, the first.

And I thought, "Oh, shame, shame! Oh, crying shame! How can we? Why do we allow ourselves? What are we doing? The last little room of dirt is waiting. Without windows. So for God's sake make a move, Henderson, put forth effort. You, too, will die of this pestilence. Death will annihilate you and nothing will remain, and there will be nothing left but junk. Because nothing will have been and so nothing will be left. While something still is--now! For the sake of all, get out" (p. 37).

Get out he does--to Africa and the Arnewi.

Fresh from these experiences of violence (within and without the self), Henderson approaches the wrestling ritual of acquaintance apprehensively. He fears he is incapable of non-violent physicality. He tries to avoid the contest, but for the Arnewi the ritual is essential. So his desire for their friendship as well as his comic ongoingness of character triumph. Through the bodily encounter, not only is he known to Itelo ["I know you now. Oh, sir. I know you now" (p. 62)], but he receives new insight into the truth through the blows.

Since that day of zero weather when I was chopping wood and was struck by the flying log and thought, "Truth comes with blows," I had evidently discovered how to take advantage of such experiences, and this was useful to me now, only it took a different form; not "Truth comes with blows," but other words, and these words could not easily have been stranger.

They went like this: "I do remember well the hour which burst my spirit's sleep" (p. 60).

Thus is he enabled to receive Willatale's truth, the grun-tu-molani: that man, Henderson, does indeed want to live. This life force, "the thing, the source, the germ . . . the mystery, you know" (p. 69) is both a hope and a memory. But he still feels the inner compulsion to self-justification as the way to gain an acceptance which has already been given him.

Meanwhile my heart was all stirred and I swore to myself every other minute that I would do something. I would make a contribution here. "I hope I may die," I said to myself, "if I don't drive out, exterminate, and crush those frogs" (p. 64).

Having forgotten that "righteousness first is not required," he is determined to prove "that I was deserving" (p. 86).

Once again, however, experience precedes understanding, and it is only in and through the cistern disaster that the spirit's sleep is burst. What this failure teaches Henderson is the beginning of repentance.

"Oh, God, what's happened?" I said to them. "This is ruination. I have made a disaster... Itelo, kill me! All I've got to offer is my life. So take it. Go ahead, I'm waiting" (p.94).

Henderson's perceptions of reality have moved from "During my rage, her heart had stopped" to "I have made a disaster." He is beginning to own his actions; and though he leaves the Arnewi with "the unbearable complications at heart," having demolished both their water and his hopes, he realizes he cannot now turn back. He accepts the blows of truth and sets out into the desert once again. But he now no longer speaks of going out of the world but rather of going into the world on a quest. Such comic ongoingness in the face of contradictions, now coupled with accountability, is the prologue to forgiveness.

Remembering the frogs and many things besides I sat beside the fire and glowered at the coals, thinking of my shame and ruin, but a man goes on living and, living, things are either better or worse to a fellow. This will never stop, and all survivors know it. And when you

don't die of a trouble somehow you begin to
convert it--make use of it, I mean (p. 98).

To convert a trouble, to make use of it, requires a
particular kind of remembering. Henderson's way of
understanding out of the past must change. He must begin
to see the past as a fund, and not exclusively a
limitation, of possibility. In Dahfu's formulation, he
still suffers from a "blockaded imagination" (p. 228).

The novel's central ritual action is the Wariri
festival of the rain dance. It is, as the title
suggests, the crucial turning point for Henderson, the
point at which he makes use of all of his experience up
to this time. He gets caught up into the festive
atmosphere immediately. He who earlier had "the
conviction that I filled a place in existence which
should be filled properly by someone else" (p. 68), now
realizes "that chaos doesn't run the whole show. That
this is not a sick and hasty ride, helpless, through a
dream into oblivion. No, sir!" (p. 149). The metaphor,
with its suggestion of an amusement park ride, is a
foreshadowing of the final moment of recollection when he
recovers the lost statement about forgiveness.

In his action of confronting the unavoidable and
moving the immovable (the later insight is put: "I
should move from the states that I myself make [e.g., the
cistern disaster] into the states which are of
themselves" (p. 239), Henderson undergoes purgation. The
rain falls; he is baptized in the muddy pool into a new
relationship with the earth, the world, and his own body;
he receives a new name. If the rain dance festival is
his rite of initiation in which he dies to the old
constricted self and is born again, his encounter with
the lion, as we have seen, is his rite of incorporation.
What has already happened to him in the event of the
festival becomes cognized, internalized, and fulfilled,
once again, by the process of creative remembering.

It is in the letter he writes to Lily (a letter
never delivered) that we see most clearly this process of
anamnesis at work. The letter is, in fact, the model for
the narrative as a whole. It is in and through the
telling--and the telling as addressed in dialogue to
another--that the transformation is achieved.

"I had a voice that said, I want! _I_ want? It
should have told me she wants, he wants, they
want. And moreover, it's love that makes
reality reality. The opposite makes the
opposite" (p. 241).

271

The syntactical change signals Henderson's conversion of heart. As with Augustine, out of repentance issues the rebirth of his essential self. At last Henderson is ready for the final revelation, ready to recover the lost reference about the forgiveness of sin. To receive it he must move beyond what pigs, cattle, and lions can teach him and move back into relationship with his past world, its surroundings, responsibilities, and people. Dahfu's death functions, as did Mrs. Lenox's and the cistern disaster, as the impetus to take the next step.

That death marks the conclusion of Henderson's African experience and he sets out for home with the Dahfu-lion in tow, an enigmatic form of a dear friend and an embodied form of remembering. The lion serves as the final memento of a past which awaits one last anamnesis for full recovery.

> And during this leg of the flight, my memory did me a great favor. Yes, I was granted certain recollections and they have made a sizable difference to me (p. 282).

Henderson remembers his encounter with a certain old brown bear at an amusement park where he worked in his youth. This "poor broken ruined creature" and he rode the ferris wheel together twice a day to entertain the crowds. Both were outcasts--Smolak, because of his old age; Henderson, because of his brother's death and his own realization that his father would rather it were he who had died. So before pigs ever came on his horizon, he realizes, he received a deep impression from a bear.

> Whatever gains I ever made were always due to love and nothing else. And as Smolak...and I rode together, and as he cried out at the top, beginning the bottomless rush over those skimpy yellow supports, and up once again against eternity's blue (oh, the stuff that has been done within this envelope of color, this subtle bag of life-giving gases!), ...we hugged each other, the bear and I, with something greater than terror and flew in those gilded cars. I shut my eyes in his wretched, time-abused fur. He held me in his arms and gave me comfort. <u>And the great thing is he didn't blame me</u>. He had seen too much of life, and somewhere in his huge head he had worked it out that for creatures there is nothing that ever runs unmingled (p. 284, my italics).

"And the great thing is he didn't blame me." Henderson has remembered his way back to a time before pigs, to an experience with a bear, an experience he now has the capacity to understand. Surely what he recovers through this anamnesis is that love is not only primary but prior. The forgiveness of sin is perpetual and righteousness first is not required. He had, indeed, had the experience but missed the meaning. The meaning is given now, both to him and to us, in and through the whole experience of his passage and its narration.

Now Henderson is eager to see Lily and the children. "I love them very much--I think" (p. 281). That "I think" is but one comic indication at the close of the narrative that we are offered no guarantees, only possibilities. The possibilities are perhaps enlarged to probabilities through the final scene of his caring for the Persian-American child who, like him, has black curly hair. The suggestion is, of course, that Henderson who left home as a pig returns as a lamb. The landing in Newfoundland and the exuberant pair's running around the plane are the text's final promises. Should we need to construct the novel's affirmative vision on such slight metaphorical scaffolding, we might indeed question whether Henderson or Bellow deliver what they promise.

Our real guarantee, however, is in the telling itself. Isn't this precisely the power of the first person narrative? If ritual action requires community, then we are the community of believers to whom Henderson's transformation is addressed. As he says on the novel's first page, he needs to make sense of his experience to us. The narrative "I" makes a call on us to engage in the very process of anamnesis and thus to be, ourselves, transformed. This is the task of art, self-representation intended as recognition. "There may be some truths which are, after all," says Bellow, "our friends in the universe."[3]

Henderson the Rain King has peculiar merit for our discussion precisely because it opens out to a whole range of anamnetic contexts or levels. There is, first of all, the anamnesis (recognition) in the reading itself. Secondly, we can speak of the anamnesis in the narrative of a fictive world, a universe of present and presence which gathers one's being as having-been up into itself, focuses it, and reveals its future directedness. Thirdly, Henderson's own construction of a new identity is a process of anamnesis; the narrative he tells is subsumed into his remembering. His anamnesis, what is more, is embedded in ritual activities. Henderson's remembering is played off the temporality ingredient in narration. And finally, because the process is addressed to us by a first person narrator, we find ourselves drawn into the very activity; our own anamnetic construction of biography is elicited. We, too, are implicated in the search for the forgotten words. The text offers us the invitation to allow the world to remove its wrath from us by rediscovering that the forgiveness of sin is perpetual and righteousness first is not required.

[1]Saul Bellow, <u>Henderson the Rain King</u> (Greenwich, Ct.: Fawcett Publications, Inc., 1958), p. 7. All other references cited in the text are to this edition.

[2]T. S. Eliot, "Four Quartets," in <u>The Complete Poems and Plays 1909-1950</u> (N. Y.: Harcourt, Brace & World, 1952), p. 133.

[3]Saul Bellow, "The Writer as Moralist," <u>Atlantic</u> (March 1963), p. 62.

CONCLUSION

In part III, we have been exploring some concrete instances of remembering's complicity in narrative fictions. While the reader of Surfacing need look no deeper than the novel's linguistic surfaces to confirm remembering's centrality, Henderson's anamnetic structure is not so immediately evident. In each case, however, we demonstrated how attention to remembering can offer fresh insights into the text's meanings and bring together various apparently divergent strands of critical analysis. But an adequate account of the intricate interplays between fiction and remembering requires a more robust understanding of the human activity of remembering than is readily available to the literary critic. As long as we persist in seeing memory as a faculty of mind which merely repeats the past in its pastness, we miss how essential it is to the interiority and ecology of human being.[1]

The narrator in Surfacing engages in programmatic misrememberings at the cost of her very self; Henderson lies buried in himself because of his inability to re-member his past creatively. Although their strategies differ, both characters view the past under the category of fate. For them, memory is the agent of facticity. "Curse my memory," exclaims Henderson, "for being so complete." Unable to revise a guilty past, both characters are deprived of freedom and responsibility for their present being.

In each case, the movement of the narrative is a retrieval which belies the very pastness of the past by opening it up to novelty. Such new interpretations reveal remembering's imaginative dimensions. Through an intricate process of creative remembering, each character undergoes a transformation of identity which involves re-cognizing oneself into a new life-story. It is the narrative quality of experience--a dimension of being temporal--which makes such transformation possible.

In Henderson especially we see how the fictive text itself becomes the guarantor of such re-membering. Narrative is at the service of anamnesis--a deeply embodied, symbolic, and self-constitutive remembering. In both Henderson and Surfacing, remembering displays certain normative capabilities. On the one hand, the characters' various false rememberings signal the pervasive dis-ease of the person whose story has become intolerable; on the other, finding a new story to tell requires new attitudes toward and uses of remembering.

277

Both witness that the past is neither "dead and gone" nor impervious to change. Each reveals how being human means being a remembering self and how the quality of one's life is therefore not unrelated to the right exercise of one's rememberings. In each novel, the narrative resolution is a recognition that, precisely because of our remembering capacities, the past--better understood as a fundamental mode of being, our being as having-been--is not comprised only by facticity. By revealing our past as a fundament of possibilities as well, remembering brings liberation.

Eliciting a way of picturing remembering rich enough to be a hermeneutical tool for such narrative fictions comprised parts I and II of this essay. Since we have frequently punctuated our reflection with summaries of our conclusions, we shall not now recapitulate the argument in detail. Suffice it to recall here that we elicited certain interrelated features of our multifarious rememberings in our reflection on remembering as both a way of knowing and a fundamental way of being human. These features--remembering's temporal density, its narrative and imaginative qualities, and its self-constituting character--have been either underplayed or totally ignored by the philosophical tradition on memory. We wagered that, rather than being mere accompaniments to the mental faculty or act of memory, they were central enough to serve as paradigms for what remembering is in our lives. This is the case because they contribute to our under-standing of the inherent relationship between our remembering capacities and our identity. In keeping with our literary critical aim, our reflection on these features took the form of describing remembering as a human activity in fictions and in life and as a hermeneutical instrument. We expected that these neglected aspects of what remembering is in our life, if attended to, would give us hermeneutical tools.

Our readings of Surfacing and Henderson have borne this out, thus confirming the viability of a "remembering hermeneutic." It is precisely because of the hermeneutical nature of the project that the result is less a seamless web of reflection than a generative inquiry. We have preferred juxtapositions and conflicts of interpretation to a tightly ordered unity of perspective. The reader must judge whether it is the case that what the essay lacks in coherence it gains in suggestiveness.

I am not unaware of certain unresolved issues in what has already been said and of further questions to be addressed. Among the first of these, we can name the following. A remembering hermeneutic must: (1) mediate between a Freudian "archeological" directedness toward the past and a Heideggerian "teleological" preference for the future;[2] (2) confront the apparent contradiction between an Augustinian tendency toward the isolated self and its rememberings and a phenomenological denial of "the inner man;[3] (3) probe more deeply the shift in emphases between the early and the later Heidegger on remembering and the implications of Kant's transcendental imagination; (4) take account of post-Freudian psychoanalytic refinements and reformulations of remembering's role in therapy; (5) be educated by other psychologies, most notably Piaget's, on remembering's constitutive function in human development; and (6) explore further the implications raised by ritual forms of remembering, in which persons are linked to memories not of their own devising. Here an attention to Alfred Schutz's provocative work on the phenomenology of the social world can prove useful. Remembering is not simply personal; it is an intersubjective and relational activity as well.

Among further issues to be addressed, I shall highlight two of special significance. The first arises from the suppressed assumption of the correlation between remembering and identity which we find in the philosophical tradition and which runs like a leitmotif throughout our reflection. Beyond the dialectic of text-interpretation/self-interpretation, we need to tease out the concept of personhood implicit in our way of picturing remembering. What would be the form of a philosophy of personal identity alive to fundamental remembering capacities?

Secondly, a whole range of literary critical issues suggest themselves for further inquiry. (1) We have been focusing exclusively on fiction. Does a remembering hermeneutic have value for other literary forms, most notably poetry? What would be the peculiar features of such a hermeneutic? (2) Our attention has been on modern fiction. Could it be that modern fiction is the privileged artistic expression of recent revisions in memory theory? Can we use our hermeneutic to draw out some conclusions about "the modern"? Does our hermeneutic apply as well to pre- and post-modern fictions? (3) The literary texts we chose are both first person narratives. Can a remembering hermeneutic lend itself equally well to the interpretation of novels with a different cognitive position? (4) Can fictions show us something about the logic of remembering not yet articulated in other fields of inquiry? It could be, for example, that our readings will uncover other features of remembering not included here. (5) Can a remembering hermeneutic serve as a tool for the discernment of the artistic success or failure of particular fictions? If part of what we recognize in fictions is that "that's the way it is," then this recognition suggests just such a normative usefulness.

I look on these questions--and others which will suggest themselves to the reader--as invitations. If our project has merit, the remembering hermeneutic it proposes will lead us back to literature. We can expect that it will organize our responses to the world of the text differently. In our re-readings as well as our new readings, parts will recombine into new wholes and fresh movements will emerge. How, for example, might a remembering hermeneutic revise and enliven our reading of Proust, Joyce, or Faulkner? If we let our attention to the human activity of remembering cleanse the doors of our perception, we may discover, in Rilke's image, "materials which it is a festival to unfold." Such a discovery can only be possible, however, when we have learned how our remembering capacities are woven into the very fabric of our human life. "Great is the power of memory," marvels Augustine, "a deep and boundless manifoldness . . . and this am I myself . . . a life various and manifold, and exceedingly immense."

NOTES TO CONCLUSION

[1]I have borrowed this phrasing from H. Ganse Little, _Decision and Responsibility: A Wrinkle in Time._

[2]This useful distinction between an archeological and a teleological directedness is borrowed from Paul Ricoeur. See his _Freud and Philosophy_.

[3]Merleau-Ponty's formulation.

SELECTED BIBLIOGRAPHY

I. Books

Arendt, Hannah. Between Past and Future. New York: The
    Viking Press, 1961.

_____. The Human Condition. Chicago: Chicago
    University Press, 1958.

Atwood, Margaret. Surfacing. New York: Popular
    Library, 1972.

Augustine, Saint. The Confessions. Translated by
    Edward B. Pusey. London: Collier-Macmillan, Ltd.,
    1969.

Bellow, Saul. Henderson the Rain King. Greenwich,
    Conn.: Fawcett Publications, Inc. 1959.

Bergson, Henri. Matter and Memory. London: George
    Allen and Unwin Ltd., 1950.

Bruss, Elizabeth W. Autobiographical Acts: The
    Changing Situation of a Literary Genre. Baltimore:
    The Johns Hopkins Press, 1976.

Casey, Edward S. Imagining: A Phenomenological Study.
    Studies in Phenomenology and Existential Philosophy.
    General editor, James M. Edie. Bloomington:
    Indiana University Press, 1976.

Childs, Brevard. Memory and Tradition in Israel.
    London: SCM Press, Ltd., 1962.

Collingwood, R. G. The Idea of History. New York:
    Oxford University Press, 1956.

Copleston, Frederick, S. J. A History of Philosophy.
    Vol. 5: Hobbes to Hume. Westminister, Md.: The
    Newman Press, 1964.

_____. A History of Philosophy. Vol. 6: Wolff to
Kant. Westminister, Md.: The Newman Press, 1964.

Cuming, G. J., and Jasper, R. C. D., eds. Prayers of the
    Eucharist: Early and Reformed. London: Collins,
    1975.

Dahl, Nils. Jesus in the Memory of the Early Church.
    Minneapolis: Augsburg Publishing House, 1976.

283

Dix, Dom Gregory. The Shape of the Liturgy. London: Dacre Press, 1970.

Douglas, Mary. Natural Symbols: Explorations in Cosmology. New York: Vintage Books, 1973.

Eliade, Mircea. Patterns in Comparative Religion. Translated by Rosemary Sheed. New York: World Publishing Company, 1958.

Ey, Henri. Consciousness: A Phenomenological Study of Being Conscious and Becoming Conscious. Translated by John H. Flodstrom. Bloomington: Indiana University Press, 1978.

Forster, E. M. Aspects of the Novel. New York: Harcourt, Brace & Co., 1927.

Frazer, J. T. The Voices of Time: A Cooperative Survey of Man's Views of Time as Expressed by the Sciences and by the Humanities. New York: George Braziller, 1966.

Freud, Sigmund. The Standard Edition of the Complete Psychological Works. Ed. James Strachey, 24 vols. London: Hogarth Press, 1953-1974.

_____. Three Case Histories. The Collected Papers of Sigmund Freud. General editor, Philip Rieff. New York: Collier Books, 1977.

Gadamer, Hans-Georg. Truth and Method. New York: Seabury Press, 1975.

Gallie, W. B. Philosophy and Historical Understanding. New York: Schocken Press, 1964.

Gelven, Michael. A Commentary on Heidegger's "Being and Time." New York: Harper and Row, 1970.

Habermas, Jürgen. Knowledge and Human Interests. Translated by Jeremy Shapiro. Boston: Beacon Press, 1971.

Hart, Ray. Unfinished Man and the Imagination. New York: Herder & Herder, 1968.

Heidegger, Martin. Being and Time. Translated by John Macquarrie and Edward Robinson. London: SCM Press, Ltd. 1962.

_____. _The End of Philosophy_. Translated by Joan Stanbaugh. New York: Harper and Row, 1973.

_____. _What Is Called Thinking?_ Translated by J. Glenn Gray and F. Wieck. Vol. 21 of Religious Perspectives. General editor Ruth N. Anshen. New York: Harper and Row, 1968.

Hillman, James. _The Myth of Analysis_. Evanston: Northwestern University Press, 1972.

Hobbes, Thomas. _Leviathan_. Edited by C. B. Macpherson. Gretna, La.: Pelican, 1968.

Hume, David. _An Inquiry Concerning Human Understanding_. Edited by C. W. Hendel. Indianapolis: Bobbs-Merrill, 1955.

_____. _A Treatise of Human Nature_. Edited by Selby-Bigge. Oxford: Oxford University Press, 1955.

Husserl, Edmund. _The Phenomenology of Internal Time-Consciousness_. Translated by James S. Churchill. Bloomington: Indiana University Press, 1964.

James, William. _Principles of Psychology_. New York: Dover, 1950.

The Jerusalem Bible. Alexander Jones, general editor. Garden City, N.Y.: Doubleday and Company, Inc., 1966.

Jones, Cheslyn; Wainwright, Geoffrey; and Yarnold, Edward, S.J., eds. _The Study of Liturgy_. New York: Oxford University Press, 1978.

Jungmann, J. A. _The Eucharistic Prayer_. London: Challoner Books, 1956.

Kermode, Frank. _The Sense of an Ending_. New York: Oxford University Press, 1967.

Kierkegaard, Søren. _Repetition: An Essay in Experimental Psychology_. Translated by Walter Lowrie. New York: Harper Torchbooks, 1941.

Kohler, Wolfgang. _The Place of Value in a World of Facts_. New York: Liveright, 1938.

Leydon, Wolfgang von. Remembering: A Philosophical Problem. London: Gerald Duckworth & Co., Ltd., 1961.

Little, H. Ganse. Decision and Responsibility: A Wrinkle in Time. American Academy of Religion Studies in Religion, no. 8. Tallahassee, Fla.: American Academy of Religion, 1974.

Locke, John. An Essay Concerning Human Understanding. In The English Philosophers from Bacon to Mill, pp. 238-402. Edited by Edwin Burtt. New York: Modern Library, 1939.

Lukacs, Georg. The Theory of the Novel. Translated by Anna Bostock. Cambridge, Mass.: The M.I.T. Press, 1971.

Malcolm, Norman. Knowledge and Certainty. Englewood Cliffs: Prentice Hall, Inc., 1963.

_____. Memory and Mind. Ithaca, N.Y.: Cornell University Press, 1977.

Marcuse, Herbert. Eros and Civilization: A Philosophical Inquiry into Freud. New York: Vintage Books, 1962.

Mendilow, A. A. Time and the Novel. London: Peter Nevell, 1952.

Merleau-Ponty, Maurice. The Primacy of Perception. Edited by James Edie. Evanston, Ill.: Northwestern University Press, 1964.

Meyerhoff, Hans. Time in Literature. Berkeley: University of California Press, 1955.

Minkowski, Eugene. Lived Time: Phenomenological and Psychopathological Studies. Translated by Nancy Metzel. Evanston, Ill.: Northwestern University Press, 1970.

Misch, Georg. A History of Autobiography in Antiquity. 2 vols. Translated by E. W. Dickes. 3rd edition. Cambridge, Mass.: Harvard University Press, 1951.

Murdoch, Iris. The Sovereignty of Good. Studies in Ethics and the Philosophy of Religion. General editor, D. Z. Phillips. New York: Schocken Books, 1971.

Murray, Michael. _Modern Critical Theory: A Phenomenological Introduction_. The Hague: Martinus Nijhoff, 1975.

O'Connell, Robert J. _St. Augustine's Confessions: The Odyssey of Soul_. Cambridge, Mass.: The Belknap Press of Harvard University Press, 1969.

Olney, James. _Metaphors of Self: The Meaning of Autobiography_. Princeton, N.J.: Princeton University Press, 1972.

Pascal, Roy. _Design and Truth in Autobiography_. London: Routledge & Kegan Paul, 1960.

Perry, John, ed. _Personal Identity_. Topics in Philosophy Series. Berkeley: University of California Press, 1975.

Plato. _The Dialogues_. Translated by B. Jowett. 2 vols. New York: Random House, 1937.

Poulet, Georges. _Studies in Human Time_. Baltimore: Johns Hopkins Press, 1956.

Pritchett, V. S. _Autobiography_. London: The English Association, 1977.

Ricoeur, Paul. _Freud and Philosophy: An Essay on Interpretation_. Translated by Denis Savage. New Haven: Yale University Press, 1970.

_____. _Interpretation Theory: Discourse and the Surplus of Meaning_. Fort Worth: Texas Christian University Press, 1976.

_____. _The Symbolism of Evil_. Translated by Emerson Buchanan. Boston: Beacon Press, 1967.

Rorty, Amélie Oksenberg, ed. _The Identities of Persons_. Topics in Philosophy Series. Berkeley: University of California Press, 1976.

Russell, Bertrand. _Analysis of Mind_. London: Allen & Unwin, 1921.

Sayre, Robert. _The Examined Self_. Princeton: Princeton University Press, 1964.

Scheler, Max. _On the Eternal in Man_. London: SCM Press, 1960.

Schmemann, Alexander. Introduction to Liturgical
    Theology. Translated by Asheleigh E. Moorhouse.
    New York: St. Vladimir's Seminary Press, 1966.

Scholes, Robert, and Kellogg, Robert. The Nature of
    Narrative. New York: Oxford University Press,
    1971.

Sherover, Charles M. Heidegger, Kant and Time.
    Bloomington: Indiana University Press, 1971.

Sherwood, Michael. The Logic of Explanation in
    Psychoanalysis. New York: The Academic Press,
    1969.

Smith, Brian. Memory. New York: Humanities Press,
    Inc., 1966.

Sorabji, Richard. Aristotle on Memory. Providence,
    R.I.: Brown University Press, 1972.

Spacks, Patricia. Imagining a Self. Cambridge, Mass.:
    Harvard University Press, 1976.

Spencer, Sharon. Space, Time and Structure in the
    Modern Novel. New York: New York University Press,
    1971.

Spiegelbert, Herbert. The Phenomenological Movement: A
    Historical Introduction. 2 vols. The Hague:
    Martinus Nijhoff, 1960.

Stevick, Philip, ed. The Theory of the Novel. New
    York: The Free Press, 1967.

Taylor, A. E. Plato: The Man and His Work. London:
    Methuen, 1892.

Thurian, Max. The Eucharistic Memorial. Part 2, The
    New Testament. Translated by J. G. Davies.
    Ecumenical Studies in Worship, no. 8. General
    editors, J. G. Davies and Raymond George. Richmond,
    Va.: John Knox Press, n.d.

White, Hayden. Metahistory: The Historical Imagination
    in Nineteenth-Century Europe. Baltimore: Johns
    Hopkins University Press, 1973.

Wittgenstein, Ludwig. Philosophical Investigations.
    3rd ed. Translated by G. E. M. Anscombe. New York:
    The Macmillan Company, 1958.

Yates, Frances A. _The Art of Memory_. Chicago: University of Chicago Press, 1966.

Zaner, Richard M. _The Way of Phenomenology: Criticism as a Philosophical Discipline_. New York: Pegasus, 1970.

II. Articles

Audet, J. P. "Literary Forms and Contents of a Normal _Eucharistia_ in the First Century." _Texte and Utersuchungen_ 73 (1959):643-662.

Bellow, Saul. "The Art of Fiction 37: Saul Bellow." _The Paris Review_ 36(1965):49-73.

_____. "The Writer as Moralist." _Atlantic_, March 1963, pp. 52-62.

Benjamin, R. S. "Remembering." In _Essays in Philosophical Psychology_, pp. 171-194. Edited by D. F. Gustafson. Garden City, N.Y.: Anchor Press, Doubleday, 1964.

Brough, John B. "The Emergence of an Absolute Consciousness in Husserl's Early Writings on Time-Consciousness." _Man and World_ 5 (Aug. 1972):298-326.

_____. "Husserl on Memory." _The Monist_ 59 (1975-76):40-62.

Cairns, Dorion. "Perceiving, Remembering, Image-Awareness, Feigning Awareness." In _Phenomenology: Continuation and Criticism: Essays in Memory of Dorian Cairns_. The Hague: Martinus Nijhoff, 1973.

Casey, Edward S. "Comparative Phenomenology of Mental Activity: Memory, Hallucination, and Fantasy Contrasted with Imagination." _Research in Phenomenology_ 6 (1976):1-25.

_____. "Imagining and Remembering." _Review of Metaphysics_ 31 (Dec. 1977):187-209.

_____. "Toward an Archetypal Imagination." Spring (1974):1-32.

Crites, Stephen. "The Narrative Quality of Experience." _Journal of the American Academy of Religion_ 39 (Sept. 1971):291-311.

Dahl, Nils. "Anamnesis: Memory and Community in Early Christianity." Studia Theologica 1 (1947):75.

Dupré, Louis. "Alienation and Redemption through Time and Memory: An Essay on Religious Time-Consciousness." Journal of the American Academy of Religion 43 (Dec. 1975):671-679.

The Encyclopedia of Philosophy, 1972 ed. S.v. "David Hume," by D. G. C. MacNabb.

The Encyclopedia of Philosophy, 1972 ed. S.v. "Empiricism," by D. W. Hamlyn.

The Encyclopedia of Philosophy, 1972. ed. S.v. "Thomas Hobbes," by R. S. Peters.

Gerstenberger, Donna. "Conceptions Literary and Otherwise: Women Writers and the Modern Imagination." Novel 9 (Winter 1976): 14-150.

Glowinski, Michal. "On the First-Person Novel." New Literary History 9 (Autumn 1977):103-114.

Gray, J. Glenn. "Heidegger on Remembering and Remembering Heidegger." Man and World 10 (1977):62-78.

Gulley, Norman. "Plato's Theory of Recollection." Classical Quarterly 1 (1954):194-213.

Hampshire, Stuart. "Disposition and Memory." In Freud: A Collection of Critical Essays, pp. 113-131. Garden City, N.Y.: Anchor Books, 1974.

Hillman, James. "The Fiction of Case History: A Round." In Religion as Story, pp. 123-173. Edited by James B. Wiggins. New York: Harper & Row, Publishers, 1975.

Lawrence, Nathaniel. "The Illusion of Monolinear Time." In Patterns of the Life-World, pp. 298-314. Edited by James Edie. Evanston, Ill.: Northwestern University Press, 1970.

The New Catholic Encyclopedia, 1967 ed. S.v. "Anamnesis."

Noon, William T. "Modern Literature and the Sense of Time." In The Theory of the Novel, pp. 280-313. Edited by Philip Stevick. New York: The Free Press, 1967.

O'Neill, John. "Critique and Rememberance." In On Critical Theory, pp. 1-11. Edited by John O'Neill. New York: Seabury Press, 1976.

Ricoeur, Paul. "Explanation and Understanding: On Some Remarkable Connections among the Theory of the Text, Theory of Action and Theory of History." In The Philosophy of Paul Ricoeur: An Anthology of His Work, pp. 149-166. Edited by Charles E. Reagan and David Stewart. Boston: Beacon Press, 1978.

_____. "The Function of Fiction in Shaping Reality." Man and World 12 (1979):123-141.

_____. "The Hermeneutics of Symbols and Philosophical Reflection." In The Philosophy of Paul Ricoeur: An Anthology of His Work, pp. 36-58. Edited by Charles E. Reagan and David Stewart. Boston: Beacon Press, 1978.

_____. "The Narrative Function." Semeia 13 (1978):177-202.

_____. "A Philosophical Interpretation of Freud." In The Philosophy of Paul Ricoeur: An Anthology of His Work, pp. 169-183. Edited by Charles E. Reagan and David Stewart. Boston: Beacon Press, 1978.

_____. "The Question of Proof in Freud's Psychoanalytic Writings." In The Philosophy of Paul Ricoeur: An Anthology of His Work, pp. 184-210. Edited by Charles E. Reagan and David Stewart. Boston: Beacon Press, 1978.

Saliers, Don E. "Theology and Prayer: Some Conceptual Reminders." Worship 48 (1974):230-235.

Salzman, Leon, M.D. "Memory and Psychotherapy." In The Phenomenology of Memory, pp. 123-137. Edited by Erwin Straus. Pittsburgh: Duquesne University Press, 1970.

Sandler, Linda. "Interview with Margaret Atwood." The Malahat Review 41 (Jan. 1977):1-16.

Schaper, Eva. "Kant's Schematism Reconsidered." Review of Metaphysics 18 (1964):267-290.

Straus, Erwin. "The Phenomenology of Memory." In The Phenomenology of Memory, pp. 45-63. The Third Lexington Conference on Pure and Applied Phenomenology. Edited by Erwin Straus. Pittsburgh: Duquesne University Press, 1970.

Thomas, John E. "Anamnesis in New Dress." The New Scholasticism 51 (Summer 1977):328-349.

Vlastos, Gregory. "Anamnesis in the Meno." Dialogue (1965):143-167.

White, Hayden. "The Historical Text as Literary Object." Clio 3 (1974):277-303.

Wyatt, Frederick. "The Reconstruction of the Individual and of the Collective Past." In The Study of Lives: Essays in Honor of Henry A. Murray, pp. 304-320. Edited by Robert W. White. New York: Atherton Press, 1963.

Wyschogrod, Michael. "Memory in the History of Philosophy." In The Phenomenology of Memory, pp. 3-19. Edited by Erwin Straus. Pittsburgh: Duquesne University Press, 1970.

III. Other Sources

Casey, Edward S. "Imagining and Remembering: In Time and Beyond Time." Unpublished paper.

_____. "Piaget and Freud on Childhood Memory." Unpublished paper.

Lefcowitz, Barbara F. "Margaret Atwood's Surfacing: An Analysis of Reader Response." Unpublished paper.

Ricoeur, Paul. "Narrative and the Paradoxes of Time." Taped lecture. Yale University Taylor Lectures, February 1979.

_____. "The Paradox of Time in Augustine and Heidegger." Taped lecture. Yale University Taylor Lectures, February 1979.

Wardlaw, Ruth Pierson. "Recastings of the Self: Interaction of Metaphor and Personal History." M.A. thesis, Emory University, 1976.